"LET NO GUILTY MAN ESCAPE"

"Let No Guilty Man Escape"

A Judicial Biography of "Hanging Judge" Isaac C. Parker

Roger H. Tuller

UNIVERSITY OF OKLAHOMA : NORMAN

This book is published with the generous assistance of the Wallace C. Thompson Endowment Fund, University of Oklahoma Foundation.

Library of Congress Cataloging-in-Publication Data

Tuller, Roger H. (Roger Harold), 1959–
    Let no guilty man escape : a judicial biography of "Hanging Judge" Isaac C. Parker / by Roger H. Tuller.
        p.   cm. — (Legal history of North America ; v. 9)
    Includes bibliographical references and index.
    ISBN 978-0-8061-3306-5 (cloth)
    ISBN 978-0-8061-9196-6 (paper)
    1. Parker, Isaac Charles, 1838–1896.   2. Judges—Arkansas—Biography.   3. Judges—Oklahoma—Biography.   4. Criminal justice, Administration of—Oklahoma—History.   I. Title. II. Series.

KF368.P32 T85 2001
347.73'14'092—dc21
[B]
                                                    00–061558

For my Mother and my Father

CONTENTS

ILLUSTRATIONS

FIGURES

MAPS

ACKNOWLEDGMENTS

My initial impulse is to acknowledge everyone who contributed in any way to the completion of this work, from the elementary school teacher who first encouraged my interest in writing (Harriet Hallock, of Beloit, Wisconsin) to the copy shop where the I prepared the final draft of the manuscript for submission (Kathy's Copies, in Kingsville, Texas). Such total recognition is impossible, of course. But many people nevertheless deserve mention for their efforts; without their professional expertise and personal dedication, this book would not have been possible.

Archivists and librarians around the United States have aided me immeasurably. Kent Carter's staff at the National Archives, Southwest Region—especially Margaret Schmidt Hacker, Barbara Rust, and Beverly Moody—offered me their professional insights and good humor through five years of research. Cynthia Fox, Ann Cummings, and John Vanderveet provided essential guidance in navigating the daunting mass of documents in the National Archives, both in Washington, D.C. and in Archives II at College Park, Maryland. The staffs of the Office of the City Clerk and the Northwest Missouri Genealogical Society (both in Saint Joseph, Missouri) hospitably adjusted their schedules to provide me access to documents heretofore unseen by any Parker researcher. My thanks also to the research librarians at the University of Texas Collection Deposits Library, The University of Oklahoma Western History Collection, Southern Methodist University, Texas A&M University at Kingsville, and the University of Texas at Arlington libraries, as well as the Fort Smith (Arkansas) Public Library.

Several of my graduate colleagues at Texas Christian University also earned my gratitude by providing their assistance. Shannon Baker, Mark Barringer, Mark Beasley, Terry Cargill, Ty Cashion, Dallas Cothrum, Page Foshee, Aimee Harris-Johnson, Jorge Hernandez, Jeffrey Pilcher, William G. Tudor, and Bruce Winders all edited portions of the manuscript in its early stages of development. C. Edward Weller provided useful research contacts in his hometown of Fort Smith, Arkansas, while his mother, Mrs. Sarah Weller, proved a gracious hostess during my research there.

I wish to express my deepest gratitude to everyone connected with this project at the University of Oklahoma Press. I especially thank John Drayton, Jean Hurtado, and Jo Ann Reece for their support and patience. Special thanks are also due general editor Gordon Bakken of California State University, Fullerton, for the guidance he provided in turning my dissertation into a book.

My gratitude to my mentors, Ben Procter at Texas Christian University, Jack Filipiak at the University of Wisconsin, Whitewater, and Bill Beezley at the University of Arizona, extends beyond their sizeable contributions to this project. They have trained me for my chosen profession, providing examples that I shall draw upon for the rest of my career. My life is immeasurably better for having known these men.

And, finally, my thanks to my wife, Shannon, for her unflagging support. Throughout the research, writing, editing, and rewriting of this study she shared my victories, assuaged my frustrations, tolerated my anxieties, endured my "brainstorming," and sustained my efforts.

"Let No Guilty Man Escape"

"TO VINDICATE THE LAW"

A Report to the Attorney General

On February 17, 1896, United States Department of Justice Examiner Leigh Chalmers submitted a laudatory report to Attorney General Judson Harmon regarding the operations of the U.S. Court for the Western District of Arkansas. He marveled at the comparative frugality with which this "largest criminal court in the world" transacted an "enormous amount" of business. Despite a volume of over nine hundred cases in the past year, the officers worked "in perfect accord . . . to keep down expenses"; thus the court operated "as economically as possible." Chalmers, after attending trials, observing masses of witnesses and "desperate" defendants from the nearby Indian Territory, and viewing the "corageous efforts" of court officials "to vindicate the magesty of the law," concluded that the functionaries of the Western District deserved "the thanks of the country for their good work and should be encouraged and upheld in it."[1]

Chalmers appended to his report a peculiar document, a "history" of the court written by Judge Isaac Charles Parker, the notorious and contentious jurist who had established a formidable reputation while supervising the district for over twenty years. Newspaper accounts describing the executions of sixty-nine murderers and rapists in the Western District since 1875—often in

groups of four, five, or six, before thousands of morbid specta-
tors—had provided him national renown as the "Hanging Judge."
In recent years Parker had provoked controversy with his harsh
denunciations both of the United States Supreme Court and the
Department of Justice for their handling of appeals from his district.
On February 3, 1896, only nine days before composing his "history"
for Chalmers, he had published an open letter in the *Saint Louis
Globe-Democrat* attacking the high court, as well as Attorney General
Harmon and Solicitor General Lawrence Maxwell.[2]

Writing to vindicate himself in light of such discord with his
superiors, Parker opened his account of the court. Like the historians that he read for pleasure, the judge began with the background of his jurisdiction. For the first twenty years of its existence,
the Western District Court met at Van Buren, Arkansas. Since 1871,
proceedings had been held at Fort Smith, nine miles closer to the
Indian Territory. From 1851 to 1883, the Western District "had criminal jurisdiction over the whole of the Indian country . . . from its
eastern boundary to the Texas and Colorado lines." In 1883,
however, such authority was "divided" among Fort Smith and
United States district courts in eastern Texas and southern Kansas.
"More recently [1889]," Parker noted, Congress had established
federal district courts" in the Indian country."[3]

The significance of the Western District, not only as a source of
justice, but also as an agent of progress, stemmed from its criminal jurisdiction of the Indian Territory frontier, according to Parker.
The vast majority of offenses tried at Fort Smith were "crimes
committed in the Indian country by . . . refugee criminals from
every state in the Union" who fled to "the Nations" to avoid prosecution. As a consequence, more "cases of great magnitude" had
appeared on the docket—more "desperados, murderers, and outlaws" had been "brought to merited punishment" before Parker—
"than in any other courts in the world." The judge had labored for
over twenty years to "establish the supremacy of law in the Indian
country," he wrote, because "the law as upheld by the courts repre-
sents a state of order and tranquility," opposed to the "savageism

and brutality" of the lawless. "Courts are the greatest agencies of civilization . . . in any system of government," he asserted, "because . . . they overcome the great enemy of peace and order . . . the man of crime, the man of blood."[4]

Among the chief beneficiaries of such endeavors, Parker continued, were the American Indians who inhabited his jurisdiction. The courts of the Five Civilized Tribes—Cherokee, Chickasaw, Choctaw, Muskogee (or Creek), and Seminole—held no authority over crimes committed by United States citizens. "If they had," Parker explained, they would have lacked the power "to contend with and punish this vast horde of refugee criminals." American Indians were more often the victims, not the perpetrators, of crime in the Indian Territory, but the court at Fort Smith had "taught them to rely upon that great handmaiden of civilization . . . the law." Parker had thus "fearlessly declared and vindicated" Indian rights; and his court had done "more than all agencies . . . to make civilization a reality in the Indian country." "The greatest blessing the Indian people have had is this court," Parker concluded, "for it has aided them in their journey along the pathway of civilization."[5]

Despite the fact that in 1895 President Grover Cleveland had signed legislation that would completely extinguish Parker's jurisdiction over the Indian Territory on September 1, 1896, the aging jurist used his "history" to illuminate the many achievements of the Western District Court in a vain attempt to maintain his authority. "This court," he declared, "has done more than any court anywhere to uphold the laws of the land, to protect the innocent by the punishment of the guilty." Enforcement of the law under Parker had "rightfully, properly, and justly been vigorous, impartial, just, and most efficient." In addition to upholding Indian rights and promoting civilization in the Indian Territory, "the certainty of punishment" at Fort Smith had prevented the occurrence of mob violence in the region. The U.S. Court for the Western District of Arkansas had provided "an object lesson . . . for the whole country." "This strong judicial arm of the government should remain extended over the Indian country," Judge Parker concluded, until the region was "able to place its star on our flag, until its autonomy is changed . . . to statehood."[6]

Subsequent accounts by popular writers paralleled the version of events that Parker had outlined in his "history." In 1898, the publication of a remarkable account of his career, *Hell on the Border: He Hanged Eighty-Eight Men*, by Samuel W. Harman, a hotel proprietor and frequent juror in the Fort Smith court, sealed Parker's reputation as the "Hanging Judge." This 714-page tome was as ponderous as its subtitle, *A History of the Great United States Criminal Court at Fort Smith Arkansas, and of Crime and Criminals in the Indian Territory, and the Trial and Punishment Therof Before His Honor Judge Isaac C. Parker, "The Terror of Law-Breakers," and by the Courts of Said Territory, Embracing the Leading Sentences and Charges to Grand and Petit Juries Delivered by the World Famous Jurist—His Acknowledged Masterpieces, Besides Much other Legal Lore of Untold Value to Attorneys, And of Interest to Readers in Every Walk of Life—A Book for the Millions—Illustrated With Over Fifty Half-Tones.* It combined a curious admixture of lurid crime reportage, morally uplifting commentary, and wretched poetry to praise Parker. Its abundant brief accounts of infamous crimes and base criminals, transformed into modern morality plays by the intervention of intrepid U.S. deputy marshals and an implacable district judge, the brief biographies of court officers, with special attention given to executioner George Maledon ("The Prince of Hangmen"), and, of course, the detailed descriptions of mass executions viewed by thousands of onlookers—all set the pattern for twentieth-century writers to follow.[7]

Drawn by its colorful style, popular authors Homer Croy and J. Gladston Emery copied, to some extent, the mixture of anecdote and commentary contained in *Hell on the Border*; unfortunately, like Harman, they emphasized action over analysis. In 1952, *He Hanged Them High: An Authentic Account of the Fanatical Judge Who Hanged Eighty-Eight Men*, by retired Missouri newspaperman Homer Croy, although contributing some original research, essentially condensed the Harman book. Combining short pieces on brutal outlaws, courageous lawmen, and a zealous "Hanging Judge," *He Hanged Them High* became the most widely read Parker biography. In 1959, *Court of the Damned: Being A Factual Story of the Court of Judge Isaac C. Parker and the Life and Times of the Indian Territory and Old Fort Smith*, by J. Gladstone Emery, offered little more than a rehash of *Hell on the Border* and *He Hanged Them High*.[8]

The distorted, composite image of Isaac Parker that emerged from such works was that of a "Hanging Judge" driven relentlessly by a Biblical sense of justice to administer absolute authority over a lawless jurisdiction inhabited by bold outlaws. Duty compelled him to attend each public execution that he ordered for seventy-nine— or eighty-three or eighty-eight, depending on the author—deserving evildoers. For twenty-one years he carried on his remorseless battle against violent crime, gaining the respect of every law-abiding citizen in his sprawling bailiwick. As a consequence of such per-serverence, and despite the deceit of pettifogging defense lawyers and the interference of ill-advised Supreme Court justices, Parker retired from his labors satisfied that he had established law and order in the Indian Territory.[9]

Historical accounts of the "strong judicial arm" at Fort Smith, and of its judge, have belied such simplistic interpretations. For almost forty years, *Hanging Judge*, by Fred Harvey Harrington, remained the only published account of the Parker court by an academic historian. Harrington moved beyond the traditional emphasis on desperadoes and executions to include a balanced assessment of Parker's battle with the U.S. Supreme Court and his opinions on Indian affairs. But, despite excellent research and a highly readable style, *Hanging Judge* never attained the commer-cial success of the popular narratives; in fact, it remained out of print until reissued in 1996. In 1957, yet another account appeared. With *Law West of Fort Smith: A History of Frontier Justice in the Indian Territory, 1834–1896*, Glenn Shirley, a former Oklahoma police chief, hoped to "demystify the western outlaw" by emphasizing the brutality of frontier crime and by praising the efforts of Parker and his deputies to stem lawlessness. Like Croy, Shirley contributed some new research while accenting dramatic episodes culled from Harman, but included more historical analysis—much of it borrowed from Harrington—than other popular writers. In 1988, historian Mary M. Stolberg, a Fort Smith native, published two articles drawn from her master's thesis at the University of Virginia that emphasized Parker's political expertise and his role as a reformer.[10]

Such works have begun to reveal the historical reality underlying the Hanging Judge image. For example, although the Western District Court did not try more cases than "any other courts in the world," it docketed over 12,800 cases during Parker's tenure. And if the percentage of defendants punished failed to exceed that of "any court in the Union," the rate was impressive enough. Just over 73 percent—8,791 of the 12,031 criminal cases completed between July 1, 1875, and June 30, 1896—ended in conviction. Although executive clemency and, after 1889, Supreme Court reversals somewhat undermined the "terror of certain punishment" that Parker sought to inculcate in evildoers, his reputation for dispensing swift and severe justice spread far beyond the borders of his jurisdiction. Surely, Isaac Parker was not the "zealot" who condemned murderers to be hanged until "dead, dead, dead," and then retired to his chambers to weep over his Bible, as Homer Croy portrayed him. But just as certainly, he ordered 161 convicts to the gallows, and 79 of those sentences were carried out.[11]

To Parker, such duties constituted a distasteful but necessary part of the "civilizing" influence that his court exerted over the Indian Territory. Yet contemporary reproach and current research have raised serious questions regarding the efficacy of the Western District Court in establishing "public order" in the region. Despite a staggeringly successful conviction rate and widely publicized mass executions, crime continued as a major problem in the Territory during and after Parker's tenure. The robberies and murders described in area newspapers and government documents frequently exceeded the number of cases on the crowded docket in Fort Smith. In 1894, for example, a report by the Dawes Commission to the Five Civilized Tribes cited 128 reported murders in "the Nations"; Parker tried only 20 such cases that year, while critics decried a "reign of terror" by the lawless, branding his court "a farce." Notwithstanding a steadily shrinking jurisdiction, the number of cases before the court fluctuated annually. Certainly the size of the district and the number of peace officers available, as well as the political motives of Parker's supporters and detractors, merited attention in explaining the apparent disparity between the rates of crime and punishment. But the effectiveness of the Fort Smith criminal justice system has remained a critical question in the Parker saga.[12]

In his "history" Parker described a two-decade battle against "the man of blood," the violent "refugee criminal" of the Indian Territory; but careful examination of court documents and other sources has once again revealed a more complex picture and raised new questions about the nature of crime and violence in the Western District. Violent crime—murder, rape, assault—made up less than 25 percent of Parker's caseload. Although such serious felonies consumed more trial time in the courtroom than misdemeanors, the majority of his docket consisted of minor infractions. Introduction, sale, and production of liquor in violation of the Indian Intercourse Acts and Internal Revenue Code were far more common in Fort Smith than reckless shootouts between vicious outlaws and intrepid lawmen. And the character of many murders tried in the Parker court lacked the romanticized "Wild West" flavor of popular accounts. Abusive fathers and husbands, quarreling friends and neighbors, and besotted traveling companions armed with rocks, cudgels, axes, knives, or cheap pocket pistols have appeared more frequently in the records than desperadoes with "blazing" six-shooters.[13]

Parker, although portraying himself as an unflagging defender of Indian rights, may ultimately have done the Five Civilized Tribes more harm than good with his mixed record on American Indian issues. As a Missouri congressman for two terms (1871–75), he had sponsored unsuccessful legislation to extend the Homestead

Act of 1862 to American Indians and had supported the Indian "Peace Policy" of the Ulysses S. Grant administration. While on the Fort Smith bench, he ousted white interlopers from the Indian Territory and decried the illegal cutting of Indian timber by settlers. But his advocacy was decidedly paternalistic, typical of nineteenth-century humanitarians who believed their duty was to aid American Indians "in their journey along the pathway of civilization." Seldom given to self-doubt, Isaac Parker never appeared to question his belief in the inherent superiority of his own culture. Nor did he waver in his conviction of the ultimate dominion of the United States over the tribal governments of the Indian Territory. Time and again he ruled against the Five Civilized Tribes, declaring that they could not prevent the construction of railroads across their lands, denying their rights to extradite criminals or to try adopted citizens. In fact, Parker contributed to the diminution of tribal self-determination and hastened the territorial status that he stridently opposed by consistently undermining American Indian sovereignty.[14]

Parker asserted that his court had instructed Indians to "rely upon . . . the law"; such a statement belied his own inconsistencies regarding legal authority and personal power. Frequently criticized for his carelessness in courtroom procedure, the judge cared more for the spirit than the letter of the law. Despite a reputation for honesty and incorruptibility, he had attempted unsuccessfully, early in his career, to use his office to secure government employment for his brother-in-law and to remove a United States marshal he personally disliked. Even though Parker himself often sought presidential pardons or commutations for condemned criminals, attorneys who intiated similar proceedings became the subject of his vitriolic abuse; he characterized them as "corrupt" and charged that they filed pardon applications "just to get a fee." His response to Supreme Court reversals of his rulings likewise cast a shadow over his veneration for the law. Parker, after years of exercising virtually absolute judicial power, grew unaccustomed and sensitive to criticism. Clinging to outdated legal principles and procedures, he defied the high court by continuing the same practices that had prompted its adverse decisions. He attempted to direct government strategy regarding appeals from Fort Smith, and, when rebuffed, used the press to launch an unseemly attack on his superiors.[15]

Such contradictions defined Isaac Parker's character and his singular career. An Indian advocate who hastened the political demise of the Five Civilized Tribes, a crusader against violence who devoted most of his caseload to petty crime, a worshiper of the law who rebelled against judicial reproof, he defied easy categorization. For two-thirds of his tenure on the federal bench he wielded virtually absolute power over the largest criminal jurisdiction in the country; yet he remained unable to reduce lawlessness in the Indian Territory permanently. Vain enough to offer unsolicited advice to American presidents, he was considerate enough to write an apology to a young boy whose father was detained in Fort Smith for jury duty. Parker began his career as a political reformer, supporting suffrage for American Indians and women; he ended his life as a judicial anachronism, upholding legal principles long since discarded by most courts. An ambitious attorney who made a career of public office, he became the youngest federal district judge in America, only thirty-seven when appointed in 1875. He died in 1896 at fifty-eight, his health broken by twenty-one years of dedicated toil in the position that finally earned him national recognition. He was the "Hanging Judge" who sent seventy-nine felons to the gibbet, but who, in his last interview, claimed to support abolition of the death penalty.[16]

CHAPTER ONE

"DEAFENING SHOUTS AND HUZZAHS"

From Log Cabin to Congress

Born and raised in a rural region barely past its frontier stages, Isaac Parker followed his forebears into an early career of steady political advancement. He obtained a rudimentary primary education in a public school, then worked his way through a local secondary institution, or academy. Parker followed the example of influential relatives by choosing the law both as a profession and a means for advancement in public office. Westering to the Missouri-Kansas frontier, he progressed from fledgling attorney to national officeholder before his thirty-second birthday.

The migrations and careers of his forebears foreshadowed those of Parker. His paternal ancestors emigrated from England to the New World, the first arriving in colonial Massachusetts. By the early years of the nineteenth century, the family resided in western Maryland. On October 7, 1815, Joseph Parker, Isaac's father, purchased two full sections in Jefferson County, Ohio. He met and married strong-willed Jane Shannon, whose Irish progenitors first reached North America in 1700 and had lived in Ohio since 1794. The Shannons were an influential family; six of Jane's uncles pursued legal careers leading to local, state, and national public offices. Most important was the youngest, Wilson Shannon, the first native-born governor of Ohio. After rising from county prosecutor to two gubernatorial terms (1838–40 and 1842–44), he served as minister to Mexico until President James Polk recalled him in 1845. Following an unsuccessful expedition to the California gold fields, Shannon won a term in Congress, voted for the Kansas-Nebraska Act, then received an appointment as governor of the Kansas Territory from President Franklin Pierce in 1855. This nationally prominent relative would influence young Isaac Parker through the example of his career and by his direct support.[1]

Isaac Charles Parker, the youngest son of Joseph and Jane Shannon Parker, was born October 15, 1838, in a log cabin near Barnesville, Belmont County, Ohio. Incorporated from portions of Jefferson and Washington Counties, this area became the setting for Parker's youth and early manhood. Although no longer a frontier region, southeastern Ohio was nevertheless in an early stage of development. In 1840 the region was primarily agricultural, with over five thousand of the nearly thirty-one thousand inhabitants listing farming as their source of income. They raised a wide variety of crops, including wheat, oats, rye, and hay, the primary product of the Parker farm. A few small "manufactories"—several flour mills, three woolen mills, and fifteen distilleries—employed less than a thousand of the residents. Sixty-three primary schools served nearly sixteen hundred students, and three academies provided secondary education to fifty-six older pupils. Despite the availability of such educational opportunities, more than nine hundred white residents over the age of twenty could not read or write. Because the Ohio River flowed on its eastern border and the National Road passed through its seat at Saint Clairesville, Belmont County was able to connect with the commercial centers of the East and the expanding frontiers of the West.[2]

Although both parents—locally "respected for their industry, strong domestic discipline, [and] intellectual strength"—naturally influenced Parker as he grew, his mother's impact was greater. Joseph Parker never inculcated a love of farming in his son, who "wasn't no [sic] hand for . . . hard work." "It was hard to shame him," his nephew reported years later, "to where he would clasp a pitchfork handle." Jane Shannon Parker oversaw her son's moral and religious development, while encouraging his worldly ambitions. A "firm-believing Methodist," she fostered in young Parker a simple but strong belief in the Bible, emphasizing strict morality, "hell-fire and brimstone" emotionalism, and fear of a justly wrathful God. Raised in the "most important family" in southeastern Ohio (her uncle, Wilson Shannon, was elected governor just after Isaac was born), she could point to her kin and their successes as examples of how far her son could rise with the proper drive and schooling.[3]

"Always a hand to get an education," Parker made the most of the academic opportunities available to him in Belmont County. When not compelled to work on the family farm, he attended the Breeze Hill primary school. Even during haying season he carried books with him, exploring their contents whenever a break in his labors permitted. After completing the basic curriculum at Breeze Hill, he chose to continue his education at the Barnesville Classical Institute, a private secondary institution. To finance his attendance, he alternated terms of scholarship with teaching in a country primary school. His studies produced a lasting affinity for English literature and, especially, history; Washington Irving's *Life of Washington*, George Bancroft's *History of the United States*, and Thomas McCauley's *History of England* occupied favored spots on his bookshelf for the rest of his life. He also developed a strong facility for debate during his four years at the institute. As national controversy raged over the Kansas-Nebraska Bill, Parker threw himself into the discussion, earning a reputation as a speaker "not to be talked into submission."[4]

At the age of seventeen Parker decided to pursue law as his profession. It was a logical choice. Parker disdained manual labor, farming, and mechanical trades as sheer drudgery. His proclivity for learning and love of books certainly suited the study of law, and his debating skills would serve him well in the courtroom. But, most importantly, a legal career offered the promise of social and economic advancement. His great-uncle had parlayed his legal training into a prestigious career in public service. What was to prevent Isaac Parker from following that example?[5]

His legal training was typical of the period, a combination of apprenticeship and self-directed study in the legal classics that emphasized general practice over technical specialization. Parker "read law . . . as was the custom" with a Barnesville attorney. With only thirteen law schools then operating in the United States, most aspiring solicitors followed this course of study. They paid local lawyers to work as clerks in exchange for directing their studies of the law, while training themselves through immersion in the entire legal process. From the drawing up of contracts and wills in their proper form, to watching their mentors plead cases before juries, to long hours of contemplating tomes such as *Greenleaf on Evidence*, students remained enveloped in the culture of legal practice. Such a system produced generations of generalists, vague on the technicalities of the law but gifted in swaying juries and judges through a combination of spellbinding oratory and acute logic.[6]

During the first half of the nineteenth century, knowledge of only a few standard works—William Blackstone's *Commentaries on the English Law*, U.S. Supreme Court Justice Joseph Story's *Commentaries on Equity Jurisprudence*, James Kent's *Commentaries on American Law*—and a bit of practical experience often constituted sufficient preparation for the bar examinations. "Oh Hell!—that fellow can take care of himself. Let's go liquor," announced one Ohio jurist upon admitting a young attorney to the profession after a cursory, five-minute examination. Late in the 1850s, Charles Francis Adams received a more formal written test in Massachusetts. But "on several . . . subjects . . . I knew absolutely nothing," he recalled in his *Autobiography*. Despite such gaps in his training, Adams gained immediate admission to the bar. An examinee in California answered only two questions, both incorrectly, before State Supreme Court Justice Edward Norton replied, "Young man, that's not the law," then ordered: "Mr. Clerk, swear him in." Even a lawyer's planned destination could play a role in the results. Vermont examiner E. L. Chittenden passed two "ignorant" young men because they planned to migrate to the West. Such varied examination procedures reflected both the democratization of the legal profession and its emphasis on general practice; technical specialization and standardized professional criteria developed in the last half of the nineteenth century.[7]

In 1859 Isaac Parker passed his bar examination. Now twenty-one, with piercing blue eyes, carrying two hundred pounds on a six-foot-tall frame, he journeyed west by steamboat to Saint Joseph, Missouri, a town offering plentiful professional opportunities for an ambitious young attorney. A Missouri River port and stepping-off point for immigrants entering Kansas Territory, "St. Joe" was a growing trade center in northwest Missouri. For Parker, such expansion translated into work drafting and enforcing commercial contracts. A steady influx of settlers held the promise of further income, with land claims to file and business agreements to defend. The city also provided possibilities for the practice of criminal law, since the Ninth Missouri Circuit Court held two sessions at the Buchanan County seat each year. Most importantly, however, Saint Joseph offered Parker a chance of employment with an established law firm.[8]

Previous Parker biographers have not adequately explained why the young lawyer chose to abandon Ohio and settle in Missouri, ascribing his move to a national "fever to go West" or merely expressing bewilderment at the decision. But documentary evidence has suggested a plausible explanation: Parker journeyed to the edge of the frontier to join a relative's law firm. In 1859 his maternal uncle, D. E. Shannon, established a Saint Joseph legal practice in partnership with attorney H. B. Branch. They located their offices on Market Square, in the heart of the busy commercial district, offering services in all counties of the Ninth Missouri Judicial Circuit, the Kansas Territory, and the Missouri State Supreme Court. One of their advertisements included references from prominent local businessmen and from Wilson Shannon, Parker's great-uncle and former governor of Kansas Territory, now residing in nearby Lecompton. Parker joined the firm soon after his arrival in Saint Joseph, and early in 1860 the concern bore the name "Branch, Shannon, and Parker."[9]

Yet by the end of the year Branch, Shannon, and Parker dissolved; the frequent formation and dissolution of legal partnerships were common practices in the fluid environment of the frontier. In 1861 Parker occupied his own offices on Market Square, where he immediately began to establish an independent career, dealing with a variety of cases. In addition to customary legal duties—drawing up wills and contracts, filing land claims and lawsuits—Parker gained trial experience in the municipal and county criminal courts. In June, Circuit Judge Silas Woodson appointed him to defend one John Dick against a charge of "felonious wounding." The defendant pled "not guilty," but a jury found otherwise, and Judge Woodson sentenced him to four years at hard labor. Parker occasionally experienced trouble collecting his fees, twice in 1861 securing judgment against former clients to recover his remuneration. One, Servis Pratt, did not possess even ten dollars worth of property needed to satisfy the claim. In the second case, Michael Costelo forfeited "two horses, one wagon, and harness," all of which Justice of the Peace John Dolman awarded to Parker in satisfaction of an unpaid account.[10]

Parker gained community recognition as well as experience in the courts; therefore, early in 1861, he parlayed his growing stature and political allegiance into a successful bid for public office. After satisfying the local eligibility requirement with two years' residence in Saint Joseph, he declared for the position of city attorney as a Democrat, the dominant political party in "Saint Joe." Parker had organized a Stephen Douglas club during the presidential election of 1860, thereby increasing his popularity with voters. In addition, he was related to the influential Shannon family and enjoyed the support of many members of the local legal establishment. Consequently, he emerged victorious from the balloting on April 1, 1861.[11]

The city attorney, although serving in an ostensibly part-time position, performed many important functions for his pay during a one-year term. Local ordinances required Parker to prosecute all violations of municipal regulations before the justice of the peace or city recorder, as well as defend all actions against the town. His duties included litigating "in any court of record" suits to which Saint Joseph was party, and filing appeals on behalf of the community. Parker also served the City Council in an advisory capacity. He had to maintain financial accounts for his office and to record all legal actions pertaining to the municipality in Missouri circuit and supreme courts. In exchange for these services, Parker received $2.50 per conviction in the municipal courts, and $5.00 for successful appeals; in order to earn any money, he had to win cases.[12]

Parker, upon assuming his duties, almost immediately provided legal advice to the City Council on a series of tort claims that charged negligence by municipal construction workers. On April 23, 1861, he formed a committee with two councilmen to evaluate a suit by one John Corly—who had endorsed the legal work of Branch and Shannon in their 1859 advertisement—contending that digging by a city street crew had caused his house to collapse. The officials initially recommended against payment, but reconsidered their decision and finally authorized compensation of $125. One week later Parker joined a second consultation regarding a horse, owned by one Edward Gideon, that was killed upon falling into an unfenced excavation on Tenth Street. The city honored the claim. The following month businessman George Brand pled that *his* horse died in a fall from an embankment "left . . . in a dangerous condition"; once again the council referred the matter to the new city attorney, who counseled against settling, and the petition was tabled.[13]

Parker also served as an intermediary among private citizens, public employees, and the City Council, although such actions were not part of his official duties. On April 30, 1861, he appeared on behalf of the local police to request that the day-shift pay be raised to forty dollars per month, the same compensation received by the night tour. The council members had set the day salary at thirty-five dollars during the previous meeting; now they granted

the city attorney's request. Four weeks later Parker presented a
petition, "at [the] request of several citizens," to revoke an order
enforcing the municipal hog ordinance, which authorized the street
commissioner to destroy free-roaming swine. Once again the council voted to comply with the request.[14]

In addition to such advisory duties, Parker brought action
against violators of local ordinances in the City Recorder's Court.
On April 8, 1861, his first day in office, he successfully prosecuted
six defendants for minor infractions. Among the malefactors was
Saint Joseph founder Joseph Robideaux, convicted of public
drunkenness and sentenced to work off his standard $1.00 fine as
part of a street-repair crew. Three other individuals found guilty
of intoxication paid fines of $1.00, plus $6.25 in court costs; $2.50 of
each penalty went to the city attorney. Besides muletying imbibers,
Parker won fines in a "mutual assault" case. The first convict,
Francis Keren, worked off his penalty performing street improvements while his codefendant, one Bell, paid his forfeiture and was
discharged.[15]

The misdemeanors that Parker prosecuted as city attorney were
not serious offenses—the circuit court tried felonies—yet they
reflected the boisterous frontier conditions in and around Saint
Joseph during the 1860s. Public intoxication constituted the vast
majority of cases tried during his first weeks in office, representing 40 percent of the record. Rowdy behaviors were the next most
frequent violations, with 26 percent of the docket devoted to crimes
such as engaging in "obstreperous conduct," using "foul and offen-
sive" language, frequenting bawdy houses, or "fast riding" (the
nineteenth-century equivalent of reckless driving). Less frequent,
but still substantial in number, crimes of interpersonal violence,
"assaulting and striking" or simply "fighting," composed 23 percent of the total.[16]

More serious forms of mayhem soon predominated, however.
Just four days after Parker took office as city attorney, Confederate
forces fired on Fort Sumter and plunged the nation into civil war.
Sectional chaos had plagued the Missouri-Kansas border since

1854, but the commencement of hostilities in the East further raised the level of tension and violence in northwest Missouri for the duration of the war. "Jayhawkers" and "Red Legs," pro-Union guerrillas based in Kansas, frequently raided into Missouri to attack Confederate sympathizers both real and imagined. In turn, secessionists in and around "Saint Joe" provided support and manpower to irregular forces led by such brutal raiders as William Clark Quantrill and "Bloody Bill" Anderson. The conflict developed the aura of a blood feud as casualties mounted on both sides; personal revenge became as common a motivation for bloodshed as political allegiance. Consequently, Union troops occupied Saint Joseph and enforced martial law to restore order. On August 30, 1861, General John C. Frémont, commander of the Department of Missouri, decreed that anyone carrying arms inside Union lines be court-martialed, and, if found guilty of supporting the South, suffer the death penalty. His successors somewhat softened these provisions, but Confederate guerrillas remained subject to summary execution, and their supporters liable to trial by military commission and forfeiture of their property. Yet such harsh measures proved only marginally successful as hostile actions by Southern sympathizers continued, followed by more Union retribution. For example, in August 1863, Parker's great-uncle, Wilson Shannon, narrowly avoided Quantrill's bloody raid on Lawrence, Kansas; and in June 1864, twenty Lincoln supporters, living near Saint Joseph, received death threats from their "secesh" neighbors.[17]

Parker, although initially hoping that Americans would avert war by political negotiation, aligned himself firmly with the Union and took up arms when hostilities began. On February 8, 1861, he addressed a "Workingmen's Meeting" on the secession crisis and assured his listeners that compromise could still prevent the dismemberment of the nation. Once his prediction proved incorrect, Parker stood firmly against the Confederate insurrection. He enlisted in a local home-guard unit, the Sixty-first Missouri Emergency Regiment. His military career was hardly spectacular, though; the Sixty-first saw little action—merely a few minor skirmishes—

and Parker rose only to the rank of corporal. Yet this volunteer service clearly demonstrated his commitment to the Union.[18]

Amid the pressures of military duties and sectional factionalism, as well as the competing responsibilities of public office and private practice, Parker somehow found time for courtship and marriage. Precisely how he met the "laughing, dark-eyed" Mary O'Toole, a graduate of the Convent of the Sacred Heart in Saint Joseph, has remained obscure. But their growing devotion overcame any reservations the staunchly Catholic O'Tooles may have had about their daughter uniting with the "firm-believing" Methodist, Isaac Parker. The two were married on December 12, 1861.[19]

Soon after his wedding, wartime divisions affected Parker in his official capacity as well. Hoping to abate the violence over sectional allegiance, the City Council passed an ordinance prohibiting the erection of potentially inflammatory flags in Saint Joseph. Apparently no one attempted to enforce the new regulation until March 20, 1862, when City Constable Edward Byrnes removed an American flag displayed in front of a private residence. Unionists were outraged; thus Byrnes turned to the city attorney for a ruling on his actions. Parker, in turn, interpreted the ordinance as applying only to political party banners; therefore, the lawman had exceeded his authority. Notified of the decision, Byrnes announced that he had merely acted as a private citizen attempting to avert trouble, returned the banner, and avoided further confrontations.[20]

A majority of Saint Joseph voters apparently approved of Parker's interpretation and enforcement of city regulations; on April 1, 1862, they reelected him on the "Unconditional Union Ticket." During his second and third terms—he was again reelected in April 1863 by a margin of 539 to 192 over local attorney P. B. Locke—Parker added to his advisory and enforcement duties by successfully appealing to the circuit court a number of cases that the city had lost at the local level. On September 19, 1863, Circuit Judge Silas Woodson overturned two municipal court decisions, awarding to the town judgments of $1.00 and $3.00, plus costs, and further ordering that the "City Atty be allowed a fee of $5.00." In October,

Judge Woodson also dismissed two city appeals, but at the expense—including Parker's fee—of the defendants, Molly McNutt and Mary Dunster. The city attorney appeared again during the next session of the circuit court (March 1864), attempting to reverse five more local decisions. On March 31, 1864, he won three appeals; Judge William Herren continued the remaining cases to the fall term.[21]

While arguing such appeals early in 1864, Parker was already considering higher office as well as changing party allegiance; his decisions soon led to continued advancement, despite intense opposition. Now in his third term as city attorney, he sought greater prestige and responsibility than prosecuting drunkards and winning small cash judgments for the city. In the five years since his arrival, he had gained experience in his profession and stature in the community; ever ambitious, he pursued further elevation. Consequently, he ran for county prosecutor of the Ninth Judicial Circuit as a Republican. Saint Joseph Democrats opposed him fiercely, accusing him—quite accurately—of "bolting" the party. And such charges reflected genuine hostility, not mere partisan rhetoric. On April 2, 1864, while Parker addressed "a large gathering of citizens" during the mayoral election campaign, three angry Democrats menacingly approached the podium, brandishing horsewhips. "If you endeavor to do what is plainly in your minds," he warned them, "you will die considerably before your time." The would-be horsewhippers withdrew and Parker continued his speech, announcing that the Democratic mayor of Saint Joseph had previously threatened to kill him. In spite of such attempted intimidation, he won the November 1864 race, as well as a position as a presidential elector for Abraham Lincoln.[22]

Parker's transformation from Douglas Democrat to Lincoln Republican combined conviction and ambition with the political vicissitudes of wartime Missouri. Certainly the slavery issue played a role. Unlike many Buchanan County Democrats, Parker had never been a slaveholder. On the contrary, he had grown up surrounded by strong antislavery sentiments; during the 1850s, Belmont County, Ohio, was a frequent refuge for escaped bondsmen on the Underground Railroad. The outbreak of open warfare between North and South—and the turmoil it brought to northwest Missouri—further distanced him from local Democrats, most of whom were Southern in ancestry and allegiance. Like his political hero, Stephen Douglas, Parker had advanced the doctrine of "popular sovereignty" to preserve the Union, not to cause its dissolution. Furthermore, as historian Eric Foner has convincingly illustrated, advocates of Lincoln and Douglas in the 1860 election shared more ideological values than they disputed; thus Parker's party switch demanded no major philosophical conversion. By 1864, however, the future dominance of the Republicans, both in Missouri and the nation, was obvious to Parker. An ambitious politician hoping for continued advancement, he wisely cast his lot with the winners; within a year, a new state constitution would disfranchise former rebels and guarantee Republican supremacy. Yet his decision cannot be ascribed completely to opportunism. He endured threats of personal violence to gain office, and he remained loyal to the party for the rest of his life.[23]

On March 20, 1865, County Prosecutor Isaac Parker assumed new duties in a legal environment vastly different from the municipal Recorder's Court. The Ninth Circuit Court now met in Saint Joseph four times each year, with its sessions lasting from ten days to two weeks. Parker tried civil cases as well as more serious criminal offenses, and necessarily at a swifter pace. On his first day Parker prosecuted twenty-five perpetrators, compared to the six he had handled in his first outing as city attorney. During the March session he engaged in 161 actions related to 108 individual charges. Rather than dealing with drunken rowdies and reckless horsemen, he now labored to convict thieves, burglars, and, at times, murderers. In one early case he recused himself as prosecutor upon realizing that his own law firm represented an accused arsonist, Clark Cummings; Parker then obtained a dismissal on technical grounds.[24]

Although the cases prosecuted before the circuit court were more serious in nature than violations of city ordinances, an examination of available records has belied the popular image of rampant brutality on the frontier. The violent crimes tried during the March 1865 term comprised five murders, eight assaults with intent to kill, and two arsons. Those fifteen indictments represented less than 14 percent of the docket. Far more common was the charge of selling liquor without a license (thirty-two actions, or 29.6 percent of the total), an infraction that Parker would often confront from the federal bench in later years. Vice offenses appeared next in frequency, with fourteen counts of illegal gaming—including two against former Circuit Court Judge Silas Woodson—and thirteen charges of "keeping a bawdy house" against defendants like the improbably named madam, Maggie Butts. Property crimes—robbery and larceny—followed at 19 percent (twenty-one proceedings). Of course, such an analysis excluded incidents by wartime combatants, which were tried before courts-martial. But the civilian statistics, if representative, depicted a region considerably less violent than popular accounts of the frontier have portrayed.[25]

When his term expired late in 1867, Parker refocused his attention on private legal practice, but he did not abandon interest in advancement through elective office. In 1865 he had formed a new partnership with a Saint Joseph attorney named Strong, and his successor as county prosecutor, Jefferson Chandler. With the increased income from this combination, Parker was able to purchase a home at a "select" location on the corner of Thirteenth and Felix Streets. Despite such commercial success, however, his ambition and political aspirations continued unabated. Thus in 1868 he took the next logical step in his public career. Seasoned by nine years of legal practice, experienced with the workings of the courts, and eager for further success and recognition, Parker sought and won a six-year term as judge of the Twelfth Missouri Circuit by a vote of 1,301 to 922 over incumbent Democrat William Herren.[26]

Although familiar with circuit court procedures and cases, Parker assumed new responsibilities as judge. The accused and their offenses remained similar, but now they came from communities throughout northwestern Missouri, not only from Saint Joseph and Buchanan County. And, in addition to such criminal matters,

Parker also bore responsibility in all civil suits brought before the
court, further increasing his workload. For example, during the first
week of the May 1869 (May 10–June 3) term, he heard motions,
listened to testimony, or ruled on some aspect of 128 civil and 130
criminal actions.[27]

Because of a crowded docket, Judge Parker sought to expedite
his caseload, a process that served him well in the future. Like his
predecessors, he held court six days per week. In order to move
cases through the judicial system quickly, he encouraged guilty
pleas and dismissals whenever possible and continued ongoing
cases to hear the actions he could resolve immediately. He punished
witnesses who failed to appear by attaching their property and
issued warrants for defendants who jumped bail. Years later Parker,
while presiding over the U.S. District Court at Fort Smith, applied
the same techniques to clear an even greater backlog of cases.[28]

Although Parker employed expedient strategies foreshadowing
his future methods, his sentencing on the Twelfth Circuit bore little
resemblance to his later practice as the "Hanging Judge." His
surviving fragmentary records of penalties have suggested that
Parker was no more severe than any predecessor. His sentences
were as varied as the convicts and their offenses. One adultery case
resulted in a fine of fifty dollars plus costs, grand larceny produced
a seven-year prison term, and assault with intent to kill led to a
comparatively light one-hundred-dollar fine and three-month
incarceration. Furthermore, this jurist who later became notorious
for handing down 161 death sentences ordered no executions in
Missouri.[29]

Political ambition, however, shortened Parker's judicial career
for the next five years; on September 13, 1870, he became a nominee in the Seventh Congressional District for the U.S. House of
Representatives. Although the origins of his candidacy are unclear,
he secured it after supporters openly manipulated the nomination
process. The vociferous campaign that followed, featuring charges
of fraud and an unusually high level of disparaging rhetoric on
both sides, nevertheless resulted in a narrow Parker victory.

Missouri Republicans entered the 1870 political season deeply divided over state and national issues to the point that two complete tickets ran under the party banner. The tariff supplied one source of contention; the liberal wing favored a low import duty, while Radical Republicans advocated a high protection. Amendments to the state constitution of 1865—which disfranchised former Confederates who refused to sign a loyalty oath— provoked the most acrimonious debate, however. Liberals, led by St. Louis businessman Benjamin Gratz Brown, put forward two revisions to loosen the voting requirements. Radical incumbent Governor John McClurg and his followers opposed these measures. As a result, the state nominating convention dissolved into chaos when the two factions proposed separate platforms, each claiming the support of loyal Republicans.[30]

Under these disuniting conditions, the delegates of the Seventh Congressional District met to choose their candidate on September 13, 1870. And from the beginning Parker supporters outmaneuvered the opposition. The popular favorite, incumbent Representative Joel F. Asper, a lawyer from Chillicothe, Missouri, claimed the support of "five-sixths" of the district, according to the Liberal organ, the Saint Joseph Daily Herald. Yet, at the caucus, his support in critical counties wavered. The Committee on Credentials, chaired by Parker's law partner, Jefferson Chandler, validated the votes of sixteen delegates from three outlying townships, despite the fact that their communities had never held nominating canvasses for the convention. Next, the chairman, another Parker supporter, refused to seat the seven African-American representatives present, all of whom backed Asper. Then the Asper deputation from populous Buchanan County inexplicably changed its votes on the first ballot. When the final count was tallied, the Radical Republicans overtook the conclave and their aspirant, Isaac Parker, won by a "landslide" vote of eighty-four to eighty-three, whereupon the convention declared his nomination "unanimous."[31]

The nominee, "forcibly dragged from his seat . . . amid deafening shouts and huzzas," now addressed the convocation. Parker thanked the delegates for honoring him with their nomination, then denied rumors that "certain men would bolt" when they learned the results of the convention. He promised to carry the district "with fully 8,000 majority" and "to see to it that the State [Radical] ticket . . . [had] the same figures." After crediting "these mechanics, laborers and artisans" for establishing his political career in Saint Joseph, he reaffirmed his support for the McClurg ticket and his opposition to the suffrage amendments. He further vowed to resign his judgeship, to "drop the ermine which I have ever tried to wear worthily and never soil," and devote full efforts to campaigning for himself and McClurg. Explaining that his wife, confined to bed by illness, was "anxious to learn the results of your deliberations," he once more thanked the delegates, then left the podium, "followed by another terrific storm of applause."[32]

Unimpressed by such an enthusiastic response, the Liberal editors of the *Herald* charged that Parker had secured the nomination through chicanery, inaugurating an ugly campaign in the Seventh District. The convention had been "packed," they asserted, with the "most shameful frauds and tricks known to the lowest political scavengers." On September 14 an editorial recounted multiple irregularities in the acceptance of credentials, referring to Jefferson Chandler as "the wire-puller" who denied Buchanan County Republicans their rightful choice of Joel Asper. "On such frauds, perjuries and forgeries as these" voters had been "swindled," the *Herald* averred. Six days later, accusations of bribery joined the litany: "The enemies of Col. Asper openly boast of the free use of money in purchasing votes"; such practices "must be condemned and repudiated."[33]

This campaign of vilification continued for the next two months. On September 21, 1870, responding to an open letter from his supporters in the previous day's *Herald*, Asper announced his candidacy to retain his seat in the House of Representatives. He assured Republican voters that they were "absolved of any obligation" to support Parker, in view of the methods employed to secure the nomination. The *Herald* supported Asper unwaveringly, calling his honesty "proverbial," his congressional record "pure as the driven snow." As for Parker, the *Herald* attested, he remained a "chronic bolter . . . very 'regular' in supporting the nomination and election of himself." He would beseech voters "as the pettifogger appeals to . . . a jury to mislead and mystify them." The *Herald* even hinted that the Radical candidate's loyalty to the Union in the early days of the Civil War was suspect.[34]

Undeterred by his opponents, Parker fought back with equally reckless rhetoric while advancing the Radical agenda. Addressing a "small" audience at Marysville, Missouri, he condemned his adopted hometown of Saint Joseph as a "hell-hole" and described its politicians as "hopelessly depraved." Supporters of Asper were the real "bolters," he declared repeatedly, ignoring his own frequent shifts in party alignment. Then, upon turning his attention to more substantive issues, Parker reiterated his opposition to suffrage for former secessionists and his support for a high protective tariff and Governor McClurg.[35]

Unexpected developments, however, closed this choleric campaign, with Parker triumphant. On October 25, Joel Asper withdrew from the race in favor of another Liberal candidate, a Dr. Ellis, of Chillicothe. On November 8, 1870, Parker defeated the latecomer. But his margin of victory was not so wide as the 8,000 votes he had predicted when he accepted the nomination in September. On the contrary, Judge Parker became Congressman Parker, the *Herald* noted gleefully, "by the skin of his eyelids."[36]

In the eleven years since his arrival, Isaac Parker had gained and maintained the support of voters in the Saint Joseph area, despite widespread sectional and political divisions. He won every election in which he ran, first as a Douglas Democrat, then as an "Unconditional Unionist," a Lincoln Republican, and again as a Radical after his party divided in 1870. Parker proved himself in a succession of positions, each time garnering promotion from his constituents, culminating finally with his election to Congress.

Yet these attainments in public office have raised questions regarding Parker's professional abilities. Some legal scholars have concluded that the least successful attorneys were often the most likely to hold elective positions on the frontier. Although the fragmentary record has not provided sufficient evidence to judge securely his skills as a private litigator, Parker definitely devoted most of his energies to public service in Saint Joseph. In 1861 he lost his first criminal case, and later, as county prosecutor, he attempted to proceed against his own client until reminded of his relationship with the accused. Such incidents did not indicate superior legal ability on Parker's part, but other evidence, now lost, might have cast his skills in a better light. Regardless of his aptitude, he devoted himself exclusively to private practice for less than three of his first eleven years in "Saint Joe." As soon as he had satisfied the residency requirement, he ran for city attorney and continued to seek and hold offices based on his legal and political acumen (except for a brief period in 1867–68) for the remainder of his time in Missouri. Clearly, then, the law served Parker more as a means of official advancement than as a profession in and of itself.[37]

Parker's political skills have not entered into the popular "Hanging Judge" image, but they were at least as necessary to his advancement as the legal and judicial experience that he acquired in Saint Joseph. His docket-clearing techniques on the Twelfth Circuit, as well as an understanding of frontier conditions experienced over a decade in "Saint Joe," surely enhanced his future performance as a federal judge presiding over the lawless Indian Territory. But without the political discernment obtained through nine years of annual campaigning, he could not have won a congressional seat, become an effective legislator, achieved national recognition, or secured appointment to the federal bench. Isaac Parker left Missouri for Washington well prepared for future success.

CHAPTER TWO

"NO MORE TRUSTED . . . REPRESENTATIVE"

U.S. Congressman

At noon on Saturday, March 4, 1871, the House of Representatives convened for the first session of the Forty-second Congress, and Isaac C. Parker, freshman representative of the Seventh District of Missouri, took his seat in the chamber. The next four years would be eventful for him. He would gain in prominence and influence within the Congress and the Republican Party, although never rising to major leadership. His congressional career would be marked by dutiful attention to the concerns of constituents, staunch loyalty to an evolving party, and a growing advocacy of American Indian issues.[1]

His earliest activities in the lower house concentrated largely on legislation directly affecting his home district, an emphasis that would continue even as his political interests expanded. On March 13, 1871, Parker introduced his first private bill (H.R. 112) for the relief of one G. S. Baker of Marysville, Missouri—located in one of the Seventh District townships that had voted heavily in his favor the previous November. Although involved with larger issues during his two terms, Parker continued to serve the people who sent him to Washington. In every session he presented private legislation authorizing pensions for veterans or their heirs in his home district, offered petitions from groups as diverse as St. Joseph newspaper publishers and the Northwest Missouri Beekeepers Association, and championed public works projects for Buchanan County and its environs.[2]

During both of his terms, Parker doggedly promoted one such project, the construction of a new federal building in Saint Joseph. He first introduced legislation to fund the edifice on March 20, 1871 (H.R. 254). When the bill finally came to the House floor for discussion—over a year later, on April 6, 1872—Parker used all his rhetorical powers to sway his colleagues. The building would house a post office, that "mighty civilizer" of the nation through which voters received news and education, an agency that did "more to inculcate feelings of loyalty and patriotism . . . than any other branch of the Government." Simple patriotic duty required that Congress provide funding. And Saint Joseph, the "bright, prosperous and energetic . . . queen city of the Missouri Valley," clearly merited the expenditure because its phenomenal growth mirrored that of the expanding nation. In sharp contrast to his 1870 campaign speeches describing the community as a "hell-hole," Parker traced "Saint Joe's" history in glowing terms, from its founding by "grand old patriarch of the West" Joseph Robideaux (whose 1861 conviction for public drunkenness by City Attorney Isaac Parker was, of course, omitted) to its current prosperity. Similar progress could be expected in the future, not only in northwestern Missouri, but also throughout the West, if given proper support from Washington. But despite such arguments, the House voted a joint resolution instructing the secretary of the Treasury Department to "inform this House of the necessity" for the new building instead of passing the bill. And Parker, although reintroducing the measure again in the Forty-third Congress, was unable to realize its enactment before leaving Congress in March 1875.[3]

Parker also represented the Radical Republican constituency that elected him through his pronouncements and votes on Reconstruction issues. Recalling the horrific guerrilla war in northwestern Missouri from 1861 to 1864, he continued to support relief for Unionists and restrictions on former Confederates. In 1872, he introduced one bill to extend federal benefits to loyal Missouri militiamen and another to provide pensions for the survivors of Union soldiers massacred by "Bloody Bill" Anderson's Rebel partisans. When Missouri Democrat James G. Blair supported a general amnesty for all former Confederates, Parker denounced him with "bloody-shirt" bombast. A few Southern aristocrats who "sought to build up a slave empire[,] . . . who hated freedom and loved bondage[,]" had foisted war upon the United States, he declared. They had provoked an "extremely wicked" act that had "caused the destruction of hundreds of thousands of the bravest and best men in the land." Now, through the "charity" and "forgiveness" of the Republican Party, only those Confederates who had been Federal officials in 1861 remained disfranchised, and justly so, for their acts amounted to "treason." Parker remained equally steadfast on related legislation, supporting extension of the Enforcement Acts that authorized the president to use troops in the South to uphold the Thirteenth, Fourteenth, and Fifteenth amendments (which had ended slavery, established African-American citizenship, and enfranchised African-American men). He also favored passage in 1875 of an expanded Civil Rights Act guaranteeing equal treatment in public places regardless of color, and he voted against amendments to the Ku Klux Act of 1871 authorizing federal action against Klan activities.[4]

His positions on Reconstruction placed Parker firmly in the emerging Stalwart camp as the Republican Party realigned itself during his terms in Congress. The Radical coalition that had undertaken harsh measures against the fallen Confederacy and impeached President Andrew Johnson dissolved with the ascendancy of Ulysses S. Grant. Aging Radicals died or lost power to younger members of the party who were less concerned with idealism than with maintaining Republican dominance. Grant, although upholding Reconstruction measures and retaining troops in the South, tended to preserve the political status quo characterized by Republican supremacy, high tariffs, limited currency supply, and, all too frequently, the corruption of self-advancing officeholders.

Those who supported this "Grantism" were dubbed Stalwarts; their reformist opponents within the party, Liberals. Isaac Parker clearly identified with the presidential faction. He had been elected by opposing Missouri's Liberals two years before the reformers launched their national movement. Furthermore, he supported administration policies on Reconstruction and most other issues. He even voted against a resolution condemning Massachusetts Representative Samuel Hooper for his participation in the infamous Credit Mobilier scandal involving the Union Pacific Railroad.[5]

During the second session of the Forty-second Congress (December 4, 1871–June 10, 1872), Parker began carving out his own identity as a legislator. To be sure, he remained a Stalwart loyalist and he continued to introduce private bills and petitions on behalf of his constituents. But other legislation he initiated and supported showed a broader scope, a wider range of interests than his previous efforts. Parker proposed unsuccessfully a constitutional amendment forbidding members of Congress from seeking the presidency during, or for two years after, their terms. He also introduced a bill allowing women to vote and hold office in U.S. territories (H.R. 1278). This proposal was not particularly original—Montana and Wyoming had already granted women the franchise. Parker sought to extend that precedent to the remaining territories. But both bills, although dying in committee, reflected a more confident and assertive sponsor.[6]

Not surprisingly, Parker first demonstrated an interest in Indian affairs at this point in his career. On February 5, 1872, he presented a bill (H.R. 1376) entitled "For the Better Protection of Indian Tribes and Their Consolidation Under a Civil Government to be Called the Territory of Oklahoma." It was tabled. He reintroduced substantially the same legislation a month later; this time it died in committee. Not until nearly a year later, in January of 1873, did the bill (H.R. 2635) finally reach the House floor for discussion. The proposed legislation would create a civil structure in the Indian country similar to other territories, with appointed territorial officials such as governor and supreme court justices, and elected legislators. The unusual aspect of this bill, however, was that the elected officials would be American Indians—at least until the inevitable white majority established itself. By incorporating themselves into the governmental structure of the dominant culture, Parker reasoned, Indians could best defend their rights and "civilize" themselves. Although eventually unsuccessful, he worked for almost a year to pass the bill, then reintroduced substantially the same legislation in his second term, believing such measures to be the best way to assimilate American Indians.[7]

Yet his convictions, however heartfelt, were not the sole motivation for Parker's bill. H.R. 1376 and its successors combined assimilationism with party precedent; western Republicans had been unsuccessfully introducing similar legislation on behalf of an expansionist constituency for nearly seven years. From a Senate bill introduced by James Harlan in 1865 through the House legislation of Robert Van Horn in 1869 and Isaac Parker in 1872, the ultimate goals had been the same: the extinguishing of tribal sovereignty and the opening of the Indian Territory to white settlers. The "benefits" of "civilization" that Parker proclaimed may have had their merits, but they would be attained at the cost of American Indian autonomy.[8]

Although his rhetoric demonstrated faith that this bill protected the interests of Indians, Parker ignored critical problems in suggesting the measure; two decades later he would fight a similar proposal. In the first place, many American Indian inhabitants of the Indian Territory opposed the legislation. In 1872 delegations both from the Creek and Cherokee tribes traveled to Washington to denounce the bill as a violation of their 1866 treaties with the United States. Critics also pointed out that any immediate benefits to American Indians would soon disappear when waves of white immigrants inundated the new Oklahoma Territory. One opponent charged on the House floor that, once communal tribal titles were extinguished, the principal beneficiaries of the Parker bill would be railroad companies seeking land grants. In 1895, a more experienced Isaac Parker, educated by some twenty years of contact

with the inhabitants of the region, would testify against yet another
Oklahoma bill, citing many of the same arguments used against
his own legislation in 1872 and 1873.[9]

In November 1872, Parker was reelected to a second term in a
contest far less acrimonious than that of 1870. Unopposed in the
Republican Party, he received the endorsement of his former neme-
sis, the *Saint Joseph Daily Herald*. The Seventh District had swung
strongly to Grant since 1870, and the *Herald* had followed suit.
"Missouri had no more trusted or influential representative in the
National Congress during the past two years than Judge Parker," the
now-Stalwart editors opined. Characterized as "a friend to the laboring classes," he was a virtual certainty for reelection. Parker began
campaigning in his home district in August, and on November 5,
1872, voters returned him to Congress by a substantial majority.[10]

His second term built upon the successes of the first, bringing
him new responsibilities and attention. Parker continued his efforts
on behalf of his constituents and his advocacy of Indian rights,
introducing legislation that would permit some American Indians
to claim lands individually under the Homestead Act. Because of
his experience and party loyalty, Parker also achieved an appointment to the House Appropriations Committee, a position that
would bring him national recognition.[11]

On April 29, 1874, Isaac Parker rose in support of an appropriation bill (H.R. 2343) for the Bureau of Indian Affairs budget. This
speech highlighted his congressional career. Grandiloquently, he
presented his philosophy on government-Indian relations, conjur-
ing mental pictures of "the smoke of their wigwams," "the fires of
their councils," and other images calculated to arouse pathos for
"this once powerful race." He decried a litany of injustices endured
by American Indians in the face of American expansion, emphasizing the violence perpetrated by white settlers and troops. The
United States, he asserted, must pay a price—literally, in the care
and feeding of its charges—for violating natural law in this manner.
After all, he asserted, Indians could be civilized; the Cherokees had
proven this fact by successfully adopting the standards of the

dominant American culture. Not only was assisting assimilation "the cheapest plan" Congress could adopt, but "the most just and the most Christian." Thus the nation could ease its conscience and save money at the same time, Parker reasoned, if only Congress would pass this vital appropriation.[12]

But simply enacting the budget bill would not sufficiently protect American Indians. Just as importantly, Parker argued, the Bureau of Indian Affairs must remain under civilian control and not revert to the War Department. The seventeen years (1832–49) of military control over Indian affairs had been "a most lamentable failure," a period of "constant Indian wars," he asserted. And while commending "our gallant Army" for its valiant service during such conflicts, Parker recognized that "power alone can never civilize." Soldiers, both officers and enlisted men, were not suited for the work of inculcating white values in American Indians. Moreover, the presence of military camps near Indian communities almost inevitably resulted in "shameless concubinage" and the spread of "loathsome, lingering, and fatal diseases." Clearly peace had been better maintained, and assimilation would progress more rapidly and effectively, with the Bureau of Indian Affairs controlled by the civilians in the Interior Department.[13]

With this speech drawing national acclaim, Parker became a congressional champion for Indian rights. The *Saint Joseph Morning Herald* reprinted his oration in its entirety, citing favorable reaction from the *New York Herald*. Even the *New York Times* made note of the Missouri congressman and his impassioned rhetoric "from the point of view occupied by the Indians." On the House floor, Parker struggled resolutely with his opponents, showing a thorough understanding of the bill by patiently explaining each provision. He used parliamentary procedure, logic, appeals to justice—whatever tactics served his purpose to block amendments intended to reduce the budget. And his determination was rewarded; President Grant signed the bill into law at the end of the session.[14]

If Isaac Parker's emergence as an Indian advocate seemed surprising to colleagues, his ideology in that cause may have appeared even more puzzling to twentieth-century scholars. Despite his protestations to the contrary, the two Oklahoma bills in 1872 and 1873 had appeared to benefit settlers more than American Indians. Apart from introducing that unsuccessful legislation, he had not been involved much in related issues prior to the 1874 Bureau of Indian Affairs appropriation. His only comments in the House regarding American Indians had been to suggest that a proposed bill to protect bison from indiscriminate slaughter on federal lands would prolong Indian depredations, because native hunting parties usually clashed with other tribes and settlers. Even his leadership on the Bureau of Indian Affairs budget proposal seemed to stem as much from his position on the Appropriations Committee and his fealty to the Grant administration as from dedication to American Indian rights.[15]

Likewise, his paternalism, his insistence on assimilation, and his ethnocentric perspective all seemed to belie his position as an advocate; but such views actually represented the most progressive thought on Indian affairs of his era. The idea that American Indians could be "civilized" was a positive position in an age when some thinkers still advocated extermination as a viable option. Parker's image of Indians as a "dying race" was a common one in the United States during the latter half of the nineteenth century. Arguing for preservation by assimilation rather than for the course of "natural selection," clearly placed him on the American Indian side of societal debate.[16]

Perhaps the best proof that Parker genuinely supported American Indian rights could be seen in his tenacious efforts to pass legislation paying claims long overdue to the Choctaw and Chickasaw nations of the Indian Territory. These accounts, dating from 1830, represented compensation to the two tribes for the ten million acres in Mississippi ceded to the United States when they migrated under President Andrew Jackson's Removal policy. Despite a subsequent treaty in 1855, followed by a Supreme Court ruling in the Indians' favor, and Senate recognition of the claims in 1859, the two tribes remained unpaid in 1874. Parker began investigating the matter during the first session of the Forty-third Congress and concluded that "we cheated these people out of millions of dollars that justly belonged to them." Consequently, on June 12, 1874, he introduced an amendment attaching the accounts to a bill (H.R. 3600) "making sundry civil appropriations." Despite strenuous opposition, ranging from objections to the propriety of attaching an individual claim to a general appropriation to charges that the amendment was the work of "the most infamous set of jobbers ever connected with this house," Parker pressed his case. He settled for a substitute amendment directing the secretary of the Treasury Department to ascertain the specific amounts due individual claimants, then renewed his efforts during the next session. Seventy-two years before the United States established an Indian Claim Commission to adjudicate such cases, Parker continued to press for payment, not to support administration policy—he had initiated the matter himself—but to seek basic fairness for the Choctaw and Chickasaw peoples.[17]

The second session of the Forty-third Congress would proceed in much the same vein as the first, with Parker promoting the Indian cause even more vigorously than before. He introduced new legislation calling for federal assistance in the "government of Indians," shepherded the next Bureau of Indian Affairs appropriation through the House, and continued his agitation on behalf of the Choctaw-Chickasaw claims.[18]

The only real departure from previous sessions was a drop-off in the number of initiatives on behalf of his constituents in Missouri. Such a decline, however, was understandable, because Parker realized that this term would be his last. By autumn of 1874 the Democratic majority in the Missouri State Legislature had gerrymandered the Seventh District in such a fashion that no Republican could hope to win an election. A Senate bid was likewise out of reach. Isaac Parker at thirty-six, with a wife and a small child to support, suddenly found elusive the continuous political triumph, the rapid advancement that had marked his first thirteen years of public life. His only hope for continued government service now lay in a presidential appointment.[19]

Dozens of Republican congressmen sought executive commissions in the spring of 1875 as a result of Democratic victories in the previous November elections. Isaac Parker was one of the few credible applicants to receive one—and for good reason. He had proven his loyalty to the party and to the administration over the past four years, directing critical legislative efforts. He was, moreover, a westerner with a background in the law and experience in Indian affairs; therefore Grant could offer two positions to a favored candidate with such credentials. The first was in Utah Territory, as chief justice of the Supreme Court, the second as U.S. judge for the Western District of Arkansas.[20]

The Utah appointment was a substantial one, and Parker possessed the necessary qualifications to fill it. The term of office ran either for life or until Utah became a state. Parker's service as a state circuit judge in Missouri and knowledge of the law were sufficient to fulfill the duties of this position. His responsibilities in Utah would also utilize his Indian expertise, placing his assimilationist ideology in a setting where the American Indians and the Mormons already enjoyed amicable relations. Consequently, President Grant submitted Parker's nomination to the Senate on March 16, 1875.[21]

By this time, though, Parker had already applied for the second position. On March 9, 1875, he had submitted a letter to the Department of Justice requesting appointment to the bench of the scandal-ridden U.S. Court for the Western District of Arkansas. In this petition, he recited his long record of public service and loyalty to the administration, as well as his legal and Indian affairs experience.[22]

Although aware of the extreme corruption and controversy in the district—the issue had been debated in both houses during the Forty-third Congress—Parker still preferred the Fort Smith appointment; yet his reasons have remained somewhat obscure. Familiar surroundings may have played a role, since Fort Smith resembled his adopted hometown of Saint Joseph, a bustling and boisterous commercial center on the edge of the frontier. Surely Arkansas was geographically closer to his wife's family in Missouri—and to his political connections in Washington—than far-off Utah. Furthermore, a "firm-believing" Methodist would suffer social isolation as well as professional ostracism in the politically charged environment of Mormon Utah. More pragmatically, the Western District position virtually guaranteed employment for life (although Parker later claimed to have considered it a short-term appointment), and a salary double that of a U.S. representative; the lower-paying Utah office would expire as soon as the territory attained statehood. Certainly jurisdiction over the Indian Territory and its inhabitants—repeatedly the subjects of Parker's most earnest legislative efforts—appealed to him. But perhaps most importantly, the Arkansas appointment offered the potential of even higher prestige and greater prominence; the judge who reformed this infamously crooked court would no doubt garner favorable national attention and, consequently, gain political advancement.[23]

In two congressional terms from 1871 to 1875, Isaac Parker had thus built a respectable, if not spectacular, reputation, one centered on service to his home district, party loyalty, and a national reputation as an advocate for the American Indian. His dutiful attention to the manifold concerns of his constituents gave him the base of voters that secured his second term and thus made his most effective efforts on behalf of American Indians possible. If Parker proved more successful at demonstrating for Indian rights than at actually passing legislation on their behalf, it was not for want of effort; he seemed continually to be introducing some new bill. But four years was simply not long enough to gain backing for any major legislation. His efforts on behalf of the administration had, however, earned the support of President Grant, who would now direct Parker's interests and ambitions along a different path.

CHAPTER THREE

"MOST INTERESTING AND GREAT JURISDICTION"

To the Federal Bench

The judicial responsibilities facing Isaac Parker must have seemed daunting, even to an appointee of his abilities and ego. The sheer size of the Western District—74,000 square miles sprawling across eighteen counties and the entire Indian Territory—created unique problems. A small force of deputy U.S. marshals upheld federal statutes throughout that immense expanse, and witnesses often traveled hundreds of miles to testify before the district court at Fort Smith. As a consequence, government expenditures to pay these lawmen and attestants usually exceeded budgetary allotments. The American Indian inhabitants of the regions west of Arkansas further complicated the district's jurisdiction. Nomadic bands still roamed the western portions of the Indian Territory; the eastern third was divided among the Choctaw, Chickasaw, Cherokee, Creek, and Seminole peoples—the Five Civilized Tribes—each with its own tribal government and judicial apparatus. Indian courts held sway over their own subjects, while the district court at Fort Smith decided cases involving United States citizens and disputes between tribes. Because these delineations were not always clear, jurisdictional controversies arose frequently. In turn, administrative vagaries and the vast, rugged spaces of the Indian country enhanced the appeal of the region to criminal fugitives from surrounding states and territories. In addition to such endemic difficulties, the Western District had recently suffered major political upheavals. The "Brooks-Baxter War," a conflict among Arkansas Republicans over Reconstruction policy and gubernatorial succession, affected operations at Fort Smith from 1872 to 1874. In fact, the court was the subject of a national scandal after evidence had proved that widespread malfeasance involved officials from individual deputies to the district judge.[1]

The Western Judicial District of Arkansas evolved over a period of nearly forty years as a result of federal Indian policies and westward expansion. The Indian Intercourse Act of 1834 limited white contact with American Indians in the Indian country west of Arkansas and Missouri. For example, traders in the region were allowed to obtain only a restricted number of licenses; and providing liquor to American Indians was strictly prohibited, punishable by a fine of $500. United States courts would enforce all federal criminal statutes throughout the Territory, except for cases of "crimes committed by one Indian against the person or property of another." When Arkansas became a state in 1836, a single U.S. District Court held jurisdiction both over the state and the Indian Territory. In 1851, as westward expansion and growing population increased juristic business in the western counties, Congress established a separate Western District of Arkansas, including the Indian country, based in Van Buren; one judge, however, still presided both over the eastern and western district courts. In 1871, with rowdy railroad crews laying track across the Indian Territory, thereby increasing the burdens on the Van Buren court, Congress created a separate judgeship for the Western District and relocated its headquarters to Fort Smith, five miles closer to the Indian country.[2]

This administrative correction occurred amid the tumult of Reconstruction. Swiftly changing political alignments within the Republican Party led to violence across Arkansas in the "Brooks-Baxter War" of 1872–74. The conflict originated in January 1871, when the state legislature elected Reconstruction Governor Powell Clayton as United States senator. Following this action,

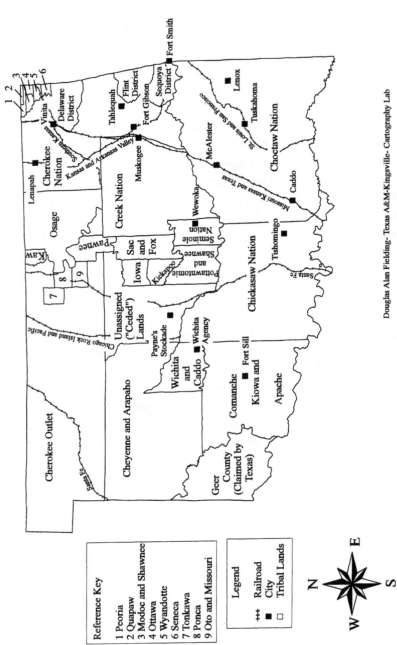

Reference Key

1 Peoria
2 Quapaw
3 Modoc and Shawnee
4 Ottawa
5 Wyandotte
6 Seneca
7 Tonkawa
8 Ponca
9 Oto and Missouri

Legend

+++ Railroad
■ City
□ Tribal Lands

1. Indian Territory jurisdiction of the Western District Court, 1875–83. *Map by Douglas Alan Fielding, Texas A&M at Kingsville, Cartography Lab.*

Douglas Alan Fielding- Texas A&M-Kingsville- Cartography Lab the lawmakers absurdly impeached the governor and—without a trial—replaced him with another Republican adherent while confirming his election to the Senate. Clayton supporters, equally dedicated to Grant and to the control of Arkansas patronage, committed widespread fraud during the 1872 balloting for state and federal offices by withholding opposition votes in three counties. Such blatant chicanery drew national attention when Congress threw out the fraudulent ballots. Behind-the-scenes maneuvering in Washington, supported by the Grant administration, finally produced a new, equally fraudulent count that declared Clayton functionary Elisha Baxter the gubernatorial winner over Liberal Republican Joseph Brooks.[3]

But this congressional solution failed to resolve the accelerating political strife in Arkansas. Once in office, Baxter proceeded to alienate his sponsors by pursuing a compromise policy with Democrats and former Confederates. Clayton and his supporters watched helplessly as the new governor vetoed their initiatives and dispensed patronage to their opponents. In March 1874, Clayton and Senator Stephen Dorsey joined forces with Joseph Brooks—the man to whom they had fraudulently denied the election in 1872— to oust their erstwhile ally from the governor's mansion. The Clayton-Brooks forces obtained a dubious ruling from a friendly state circuit judge that Brooks was indeed the rightful governor; at the same time, Baxter fortified the statehouse and reorganized the militia. But Brooks and his followers, armed with this judicial decision, as well as weapons from the Little Rock armory, occupied the statehouse without bloodshed, and on April 15, 1874, he took the oath of office.[4]

With the succession of Joseph Brooks, Arkansas teetered on the verge of civil war. The new governor and his supporters, barricaded in the statehouse, trained cannon down the street on the equally well-armed Baxter adherents. Disorderly mobs of both factions, calling themselves "militia," roamed the streets, firing their weapons at opponents and bystanders alike. Across the state, bands of "lawless men" used the political crisis in Little Rock as a pretext to pillage their enemies' properties. The death toll approached thirty as the violence spread and each side demanded official recognition by the president.[5]

In 1874 such disorders necessitated federal intervention; and President Grant, although vacillating at times, eventually succeeded in terminating the violence. At first the administration supported Brooks, yet refused to intercede beyond sending troops to Little Rock to prevent an all-out battle between the factions. But as negotiations continued through April and into May, Brooks's increasing intransigence and multiplying demands forced the administration to shift its support. In the end, the Arkansas State Legislature recognized Baxter as the legitimate governor, Grant supported the decision, and the violence, if not the accompanying tensions, abated. As a consequence, Baxter resumed his office on May 19, 1874.[6]

The Western District Court, despite its remoteness from Little Rock, did not escape the effects of the Brooks-Baxter affair. As early as October 1872, U.S. Marshal William Britton, fearful that the partisan proclivities of prospective jurors might interfere with their duties, wrote to Attorney General George Williams, describing their individual political leanings. In 1874, with Baxter still in office and a Democratic victory likely in November, the Clayton faction secured further federal patronage; in July, the senator's brother, William H. H. Clayton, accepted a presidential appointment as prosecutor of the Western District. And, in 1875, the aftermath of the Brooks-Baxter conflict also played a role in the appointment of a new judge for the Western District. With lingering animosities still dividing Arkansas Republicans, Senators Clayton and Dorsey advised President Grant to fill the vacancy with a candidate from outside the state.[7]

But the Western District Court faced problems far more vexing than ongoing political enmity; by March 1875, it was the most notoriously scandal-ridden of all federal jurisdictions. Officials left their posts under suspicion of malfeasance; questionable expenditures exceeded appropriations; and law enforcement was nil. Five U.S. marshals and three federal prosecutors had been dismissed over the previous eight years. In June 1874, District Judge William Story resigned after three years on the bench to avoid imminent impeachment. Then, early in 1875, a congressional investigation revealed long-standing, institutionalized corruption by court officials acting in concert with local businessmen. So outrageous were the abuses in the Western District that some legislators in Congress called for its abolition.[8]

The most flagrant corruption occurred during the tenure of William Story, an incompetent and unscrupulous jurist who personified the "carpetbagger" stereotype from 1871 to 1874. Born in Wisconsin and educated in Massachusetts, he migrated to Arkansas after the Civil War and quickly became the protégé of U.S. Senator Alick McDonald. Their relationship became so close that some Fort Smith wags later charged—but never confirmed—that the legislation creating a separate judgeship for the Western District in 1871 had originated to seal the impending wedding between Story and McDonald's daughter. Regardless of the genesis of his position, Story proved himself a contemptible judge. He fostered impropriety among deputies by approving a mileage schedule that grossly overstated distances, and thus allowed outrageous charges for travel expenses. Far more seriously, the judge routinely accepted bribes in exchange for dismissing pending cases. He seldom held court and, when he did, administered its affairs poorly. During the November term of 1871, for example, the grand jury indicted thirty-seven offenders for murder, most of them in absentia; Story offered bail to the five defendants who did appear. Only one of the accused actually stood trial. After a petit jury convicted this killer, the judge sentenced him to death, then released the condemned man on bond, which, not surprisingly, he forfeited to avoid hanging. Not one of the thirty-seven prisoners indicted received any punishment.[9]

Story's conduct soon drew the attention of a government agent who collected sufficient evidence to bring about his downfall. In December 1872, Secret Service agent L. B. Whitney arrived in Fort Smith to inquire into the rising expenditures of the Western District marshal. Although allies in Washington had warned Story of the probe and the local postmaster routinely opened and read Whitney's mail, the investigator nevertheless uncovered ample evidence of corruption, including bribery involving not only the judge, but also the district attorney. As a consequence, the House began preparations early in 1874 to impeach William Story. Eager to avoid the shame of a forced removal, the mendacious jurist struck a deal with Attorney General George Williams. On June 16, 1874, the House shelved its charges against Story, who resigned the next day.[10]

The evidence accumulated against Judge Story led to another investigation and to the disclosure of even greater corruption. On June 20, 1874, three days after Story's resignation, Attorney General Williams appointed Fort Smith lawyer Benjamin T. Du Val as special assistant U.S. attorney for the Western District of Arkansas and ordered him to examine the accounts of U.S. Marshal Logan Roots. In February 1875, Du Val's report to Congress demonstrated a pattern of pecuniary abuse dating back to 1870, implicating Roots and his three predecessors. In addition to the overstatement of deputies' travel expenses under Story, the U.S. Treasury paid fraudulent claims for expeditions into Indian Territory that never occurred. Court Commissioner W. A. E. Tisdale submitted phony expense claims by also listing himself as a deputy named Alvin Tisdale. All four marshals had also charged fraudulent claims by establishing accounts for fictitious deputies; authentic functionaries received two-thirds of the fees while turning the balance to the U.S. marshal.[11]

U.S. Marshal Logan Roots refined the practice of defrauding the government for juror and witness expenses, thereby profiting mightily by such swindles. "An energetic business man," he was the majority shareholder in the National Bank of Western Arkansas. As such, he paid attestants for their travel and lodging with promissory notes—"marshal's checks"—even though Congress had banned the procedure in 1868. Local businesses and banks, including Roots's own institution, honored these instruments at a discount ranging between 17 and 20 percent. The U.S. Treasury paid all witness and juror accounts in cash, at face value; Roots paid those holding his "paper" just over three-fourths of that amount and pocketed the remainder. During his fourteen months in office, he "earned" $54,650.35 through such speculation, and through phony expense claims.[12]

Du Val presented these findings to the Western District grand jury, who refused to indict any of the malefactors, because innocent former jurors and witnesses still holding "marshal's checks" might never receive compensation. Congress, on the other hand, took drastic, although unsuccessful, action to curb the corruption. During the second session of the Forty-third Congress, a bill to abolish the Western District of Arkansas (H.R. 3621) passed the House. On January 12, 1875, the Senate modified the legislation, accepting a substitute amendment by Powell Clayton that abolished the position of district judge, but retained the other court offices, including that of his younger brother, the new district attorney. Such an action, if successful, would have returned the court to the administrative arrangement employed before 1871, with one judge presiding over both the eastern and western districts. When the amended bill returned to the House, however, it languished. On March 2, 1875, the representatives voted 132 to 85 against a motion to submit the measure to conference committee; it remained in legislative limbo when Grant filled the Western District judicial vacancy less than three weeks later.[13]

Isaac Parker opposed sending H.R. 3621 to a conference committee just one week before he applied for the judgeship in the Western District. Regardless of whether his vote was self-serving, political considerations in Arkansas and Washington were as critical to his nomination as his four years of legislative service to the Grant administration. The aftermath of the Brooks-Baxter affair still lingered in Arkansas, necessitating the selection of a candidate unconnected with those events. In 1874, Democrats had gained control both of the House of Representatives and Arkansas; now Grant needed to ensure that federal patronage devolved on loyal—meaning Stalwart—Republicans. Senator Powell Clayton not only

shared the president's concerns but also hoped to strengthen his
own faction in Arkansas, which had already gained a foothold in
the Western District with the appointment of his brother as federal
prosecutor. A Grant loyalist since entering the Senate, Clayton
aided both the administration and himself by supporting a Stalwart
candidate like Parker and thus creating a long-lasting political
obligation. The court at Fort Smith desperately needed reforma-
tion, and Grant's appointee would be subject to national scrutiny
as a result of its widely publicized scandals; clearly the president
could not afford to appoint another William Story. Parker, a
Missourian loyal to Grant, untainted by corruption, experienced
in law, and knowledgeable in Indian affairs, met all the administration's political requirements.[14]

Thus on March 18, 1875, President Grant, after being made
aware of Parker's wishes and encouraged by both Arkansas senators, successfully re-initiated the judicial appointment process. He
sent two messages to the Senate. First he nominated Parker as
judge for the Western District of Arkansas, then withdrew his
previous designation as chief justice of the Utah Supreme Court.
The next day the Senate unanimously approved the president's
requests without debate.[15]

On Sunday, May 2, 1875, Parker created a minor sensation when
he disembarked from a steamboat at Fort Smith, a boisterous and
politically divided settlement on the edge of the Indian Territory.
Frontier conditions still prevailed in this small community of
less than three thousand as cowboys, gamblers, and prostitutes,
together with other curious residents, watched the new judge as he
rode in a carriage to temporary lodgings at the Le Flore Hotel.
Local Democrats—a majority in town—expected little improvement over William Story; like his predecessor, Parker was a Grant
appointee and an outsider, probably yet another corrupt carpetbagger. The local Democratic newspaper, the *Western Independent*,
doubted both his honesty and his capabilities. The Radical Republican *New Era*, on the other hand, praised Parker as "a staunch
republican . . . a conscientious man," and expressed hope that he

would "elevate the federal judiciary in Arkansas, so greatly debased in recent years."[16]

Keenly aware of such division in the community, Parker immediately launched a campaign to win over residents and to restore the tarnished image of his court. First, he appealed to civic pride by relating his favorable impressions of the town in an interview published in the *Fort Smith Weekly Herald*. Then he plunged into his judicial duties by appointing the first of two hundred deputy U.S. marshals who would police the vast Western District during the next twenty-one years, substantially increasing the force that his predecessor had maintained. Parker next hired a new clerk for the court. Then he issued orders for reluctant witnesses to appear and testify; directed that their expenses would now be paid in cash; and reopened unsolved murder investigations. And he promptly tackled the heavy backlog of cases remaining from Story's reign. On May 10, 1875, only eight days after arriving in Fort Smith, Judge Parker opened court.[17]

Despite such industrious efforts, Parker and his appointees remained open to suspicion that the new regime represented a continuation of "Carpetbag Rule" because of their links to the Clayton faction. Stephen Wheeler, the new clerk of the Western District Court, after migrating to Arkansas following the Civil War, was appointed tax collector and, later, quartermaster of the state militia by Governor Clayton; he then served in the Reconstruction legislature. District Attorney William H. H. Clayton was a brother of the senator and former "carpetbag governor," who had brokered his appointment as well as that of Judge Parker. Assistant District Attorney James Brizzloara, Virginia-born but raised in the North, had participated actively in the "Brooks-Baxter War." Even Parker's retention of executioner George Maledon, originally appointed by corrupt U.S. Marshal Logan Roots, could provoke doubts regarding the reform of the court.[18]

During his first few months on the bench, Judge Parker acted questionably but unsuccessfully to secure a court appointment for his brother-in-law, Thomas B. Burnett. On May 6, 1875, he wrote to

Attorney General Edwards Pierrepont, arguing the necessity for having a special federal attorney. Benjamin Du Val, although having conducted a thorough investigation of district financial irregularities, had left some matters unresolved; therefore another audit of court accounts was essential. Burnett was, Parker stated, the ideal candidate to conduct such an inquiry, "a good accountant," a man "of the highest character in every respect." Furthermore, he had just arrived at Fort Smith from Saint Louis, thereby remaining "entirely free from the bitterness of the factions in this community." Although such praise may have been justified, Parker failed to inform the attorney general of the familial link in any of his correspondence. The judge continued in his efforts until August 1875, when Burnett was rejected because of funding issues.[19]

Fortunately for Parker, details of his miscarried attempt at nepotism—a blunder less serious than the least of William Story's offenses—were not exposed. Digging in, he and his officers won over skeptics through diligent attention to their duties. In less than a year after his arrival in May 1875, the once-dubious Democratic *Western Independent* praised Parker effusively, declaring that he "had won . . . the confidence and respect of the members of the bar and our citizens, as well as of the law-abiding men of all races in the Indian Territory." By holding court from eight in the morning until sundown, six days a week; by trying, convicting, and sentencing miscreants swiftly; and by executing six murderers, Parker proved that, regardless of his political antecedents and alliances, his tenure would not continue past policies.[20]

CHAPTER FOUR

"A CERTAINTY OF PUNISHMENT"

"Hanging Judge"

On Friday, September 3, 1875, Isaac Parker showed his commitment to reforming the Western District Court when six killers,
condemned during the May term, lined up beneath coarse hemp
nooses on the rough oaken planks of the Fort Smith gallows. A
crowd of five thousand onlookers pressed around the base of the
gibbet, anxiously awaiting the awful spectacle. After preliminary
rituals—the reading of death warrants, the pronouncement of last
words, the singing of hymns, and the recitation of prayers—hangman George Maledon stepped forward to complete this grisly
work. He carefully adjusted the knots behind each doomed man's
left ear, then drew the slack over to the right side of the head, a
technique intended to break the neck and ease the death of each
victim. After shrouding their faces with black masks, Maledon
moved to the end of the platform, grasped a lever, and opened the
trap. The six bodies shot downward five-and-a-half feet, then
swung in midair, their necks snapped. The dangling corpses
demonstrated gruesomely, but unequivocally, that Judge Parker,
unlike his corrupt and lenient predecessor, would punish the
violent criminals under his dominion.[1]

This execution—and those that followed over the next twenty-
one years—firmly established a lasting, but distorted, image of

Parker as the "Hanging Judge." Carried out in public at a time
when most hangings around the United States had been moved
behind prison walls, the early executions at Fort Smith became
mass outings for families living up to fifty miles away. The grim
ceremonies followed a traditional, ritualistic pattern, with a solemn
procession to the scaffold followed by the condemned reading or
reciting final declarations of their guilt and penitence, the spectators joining them in hymns and prayers before the inevitable final
act. Local and national newspapers eagerly covered these proceedings, often in graphic detail. Such accounts, bolstered in later years
by books based upon them, created the prevalent image of Parker
as a stern jurist implacably dedicated to enforcing the law through
fear. But such a portrait ignored many complexities surrounding
the judge and his jurisdiction. Capital cases made up a small
percentage of the Western District docket; and federal statute, not
Parker, set the penalties. Moreover, this "Hanging Judge"
frequently exhibited ambivalence regarding the death penalty.

On May 10, 1875, Parker opened court. This initial term was
portentous, not only because the judge sought to prove his worth
as a federal magistrate but also because he now confronted and
punished the criminal outcasts of Indian Territory for the first time.
Long hours on the bench, combined with aggressive prosecution
and sentencing, demonstrated that Parker, unlike his unlamented
predecessor, would execute his responsibilities dutifully. The
federal "jail," a military stockade constructed before the Mexican-
American War, overflowed with prisoners awaiting trial, yet
another dubious legacy of William Story's reign and resignation.
Parker, in working through the backlog of cases, faced the wide
variety of criminals that infested his jurisdiction. Bootleggers,
whiskey peddlers, and thieves dominated the docket, mixed occasionally with bigamists, arsonists, and embezzlers. The number of
such offenders was shocking enough, but the crimes of those
charged with murder were truly appalling. During his first weeks
on the federal bench, Parker tried and sentenced killers who slew
their victims brutally and unrepentantly, their motives ranging

from theft to rage to reasons that only the defendants themselves understood. After petit juries had convicted eight of these murderers, Parker ordered their executions.[2]

The first accused killer to face justice under Parker was Daniel Evans, a young Texan charged with murdering a traveling companion in the Creek Nation. Although the case against him was largely circumstantial, a surprise witness assured his conviction during a second trial. In November 1874, Evans shot nineteen-year-old William Seabolt in the head, then stole the victim's horse, saddle, and boots. Tried at Fort Smith a month later by Henry C. Caldwell—judge for the Eastern District of Arkansas, serving as William Story's interim replacement—Evans escaped punishment because of a hung jury. No one had observed the actual crime, and the fact that the accused possessed his victim's horse and saddle when arrested seemed to some jurors insufficient evidence for a capital sentence. On May 17, 1875, a new trial began before Judge Parker. Two days later, after the defense had completed its closing arguments, District Attorney Clayton called another witness: the victim's father, who had reached Fort Smith only the night before. Parker allowed the testimony, which established that Evans and the younger Seabolt had left Texas together shortly before the murder, and that the boots Evans wore in the courtroom were a gift presented to the victim by his father. The jury returned a guilty verdict in thirty minutes, and, on June 26, 1875, "his eyes brimming with tears," Isaac Parker pronounced his first death sentence, ordering Evans to hang on September 3, 1875.[3]

Like Evans, quarter-blood Cherokee Samuel Fooey had mixed robbery with murder, and was still protesting his innocence after his appearance before Judge Parker resulted in the ultimate penalty. During the summer of 1872, Fooey robbed and killed itinerant schoolteacher John Neff in the Flint District of the Cherokee Nation. He confessed the crime to family members, but the district court did not file charges until a young boy discovered Neff's skeleton the following spring. Fooey remained free for another two years before finally standing trial in June of 1875. He quickly recanted his confession, but to no avail; on June 28, Parker sentenced him to hang with Evans.[4]

The six remaining murderers condemned during the first term were an equally brutal lot. Smoker Mankiller, an eighteen-year-old Cherokee who spoke no English, used sign language to convince a neighbor, William Short, to hand over his new Winchester rifle. He then turned the weapon on its owner and shot him dead; the young killer never explained his motive. In a drunken rage, William Whittington slashed his friend John Turner's throat and stole $100, while the victim's son watched in horror. Horse thief James Moore shot and killed Deputy U.S. Marshal William Spivey while resisting arrest; he claimed that the lawman was "the eight[h] man I've killed—niggers and Indians I don't count." Edmund Campbell and Frank Butler—both African Americans—resolved a personal dispute with a Lawson Ross and his daughter by shooting them to death after a prayer meeting. Young Oscar Snow and an accomplice, who remained at large, murdered George Beauchamps at the request of the victim's wife. Parker sentenced all six men to hang on September 3, 1875.[5]

Although the Fort Smith gallows could accommodate a dozen victims, only six of the first eight condemned would die there in 1875. Both Oscar Snow and Frank Butler avoided hanging, albeit by radically different means. On July 28, 1875, acting on a recommendation by Judge Parker, President Grant commuted Snow's sentence to life imprisonment. Butler, on the other hand, cheated the gallows but not the hangman. While awaiting execution, he arranged for his attorneys to schedule an evening hearing before Judge Parker. En route from his cell to the courtroom, Butler broke free of his guards and dashed for the wall surrounding the jail yard. Executioner Maledon, who also served as a guard, drew his pistol and felled the escapee with one fatal shot. Now six men would hang.[6]

As the sun rose on Friday, September 3, 1875, crowds poured into Fort Smith and court officers prepared for the sextuple execution. Whole families from forty and fifty miles distance converged on the little city, their numbers augmented by newspaper reporters from Little Rock, Kansas City, and St. Louis. By 9:00 A.M. over five thousand people jammed the jail yard around the gallows. George Maledon had completed his preliminary arrangements before the throngs arrived, dropping six two-hundred-pound sandbags through the trap on his well-oiled, custom-woven hemp ropes. Sixty special deputies, each armed with a heavy repeating rifle, patrolled the grounds to enforce the judge's order that no armed man be admitted. Even the local fire company participated, providing additional forces to police the crowd.[7]

Meanwhile, the condemned prepared for the end. Guards transported Daniel Evans and James Moore, both heavily shackled, to the Catholic Church, where Father Laurence Smyth heard their confessions, performed High Mass, and offered the doomed men Holy Communion. William Whittington consulted with his spiritual advisor, Reverend H. M. Granade. Edmund Campbell told a reporter that he would die in peace, knowing that he had received forgiveness when he joined the church; however, he remained unsure of precisely which denomination he now professed. Sam Fooey appeared relaxed and cheerful, relating to a guard a dream about his impending death. "I felt no pain," he said, "I just fell asleep and woke up in a beautiful garden."[8]

At 10:00 A.M. the guards opened the prison door and the condemned men followed Western District U.S. Marshal James F. Fagan into the jail yard for the deadly spectacle. The procession climbed the gallows stairs, and the prisoners seated themselves on a long wooden bench at the back of the platform, while Marshal Fagan read aloud each of their death warrants. This formality concluded, the chief lawman asked if the doomed men had anything to say. Surveying the crowd below him, James Moore announced: "There are worse men here than me." Sam Fooey said that he was as anxious to get out of this world as the crowd was to see him go. Edmund Campbell protested his innocence, as did Smoker Mankiller through an interpreter. Daniel Evans remained mute. William Whittington, too terror-stricken to address the assembly himself, had Reverend Granade recite a statement that he had prepared while awaiting this moment, entitled "How I Came to the Gallows." A long, rambling, and heartfelt message, it condemned demon rum and entreated the spectators to teach their children the ways of righteousness. Following this declaration of penitence, Reverend Granade led the audience in a hymn and a final prayer. With these rituals completed, George Maledon efficiently performed his lethal duties; all six men died "without a struggle."[9]

News of the macabre proceedings at Fort Smith spread rapidly across the United States via telegraph, justifying the spectacular hanging as a moral object lesson. On September 4, 1875, headlines in cities as distant as New York sermonized about "A Warning to Outlaws in the Indian Territory" and "The Cool Destruction of Six Human Lives by Legal Process," while others warned grimly of "The Gallows" or "The Scaffold." Most accounts included summaries of the crimes that resulted in the executions, emphasizing the religious conversion of the condemned as well as lauding their "nerve" on the gibbet. Fort Smith editor J. W. Weaver, a correspondent for the *New York Herald*, reminded eastern readers that, as pitiable as the condemned appeared on the gallows, they merited their fates; such felons, he asserted, were "preying wolves on the lives and property of their fellow beings, unfit to live and unsafe to remain at large."[10]

No one recorded Isaac Parker's reaction to this morbid publicity but it surely did not deter him. At the next session of the Western District Court he sentenced to death other violent felons, thus setting the stage for a second multiple hanging. During the November 1875 term Parker tried ninety-one criminal cases, eleven involving murders. While petit juries acquitted five of the accused killers, the judge ordered the remaining six to hang on April 21, 1876.[11]

The newly condemned seemed to exceed the first sextet in the brutality and callousness of their crimes. Aaron Wilson, for example, displayed trophies of his vicious deeds; such behavior resulted in his punishment. On October 12, 1875, Wilson, a black U.S. Army veteran, murdered merchant James Harris and his twelve-year-old son near the Wichita Indian Agency, south of Fort Sill. He split the unsuspecting peddler's skull with an ax while he slept. Awakened by his father's dying screams, the child pled for his life, but to no avail; Wilson cut him down with a double-barreled shotgun. The former soldier then scalped the corpses, helped himself to a new suit from their wagon, and rode away. Arriving at a nearby Comanche camp, he displayed his gruesome trophies to the village chief, who, in turn, reported the killer to the Indian agent at Fort Sill. On Saturday, February 5, 1876, Judge Parker sentenced Aaron Wilson to hang, exhorting him to seek Christian salvation.[12]

Two young Chickasaws—Gibson Ishtonubee and his nephew, Isham Seely—also used an ax in a robbery and murder committed nearly three years earlier. On May 10, 1873, Ishtonubee hacked to death an elderly white farmer named Funny, while Seely bludgeoned the old man's housekeeper, a Mrs. Mason, with a gun barrel. The pair escaped with a pair of boots, a dress, and the dead woman's pantaloons. Once captured, both offenders confessed to the murders. As a consequence, a Fort Smith jury convicted the duo and Judge Parker sentenced them to hang.[13]

The three remaining convicts that Parker ordered to hang were no better. Ossee Sanders, a Cherokee who fought for the Union during the Civil War, shot and killed Thomas Carlisle in full view of his wife and children. While the stricken family hid in the tall grass nearby, Sanders ransacked the house, then prepared and ate a hearty meal before riding away with his booty—$12 in cash, $1,000 in Cherokee national bonds, and a pair of shoes. Bootlegger William Leach killed and robbed wandering musician John Wadkins, then attempted to burn his body. But a traveler discovered the charred remains, and deputies arrested Leach when he tried to sell his victim's shoes. Orpheus McGee lured a neighbor, Robert Alexander, to his death by gobbling like a wild turkey, then shot the would-be hunter in the head, apparently for revenge.[14]

Thus Fort Smith prepared once more for a mass hanging, one that would draw yet larger, more expectant crowds and provide even greater drama for the papers. By 10:00 A.M. on Friday, April 21, 1876, over seven thousand spectators had rendered the streets virtually impassable. The onlookers comported themselves well, despite the fact that whiskey vendors circulated just outside the jail yard. The *Saint Louis Republican* reported one bystander "accidentally shot"; apart from this incident, no major problems occurred. As the appointed time neared, a rumor spread through the waiting multitude that a secret Cherokee society planned a daring rescue of the convicted Ossee Sanders, but no such deliverance occurred.[15]

A last-minute rescue of Sanders by his tribesmen would have been unnecessary at any rate. On April 19, 1876, President Grant issued a reprieve that temporarily postponed his execution. The telegram arrived on April 20, while Sanders ate breakfast with the other condemned prisoners. Now only five men, rather than six, would die before the throngs outside the jail.[16]

At 10:45 A.M. Marshal Fagan led the procession into the jail yard and up the scaffold steps to repeat the lethal ritual. Father Smyth accompanied Aaron Wilson, who had heeded Judge Parker's admonition and sought comfort in the Roman Catholic Church. Now the priest held an umbrella over the doomed man's head, shading Wilson from the sun as he enjoyed a final cigar while Fagan read the death warrants. At 11:15 A.M. the condemned sang "Other Refuge Have I None" and prayed with a Reverend Greathouse. Prisoners and spectators alike then joined in "Rock of Ages," followed by a recitation of the Lord's Prayer. At 11:27 A.M. Maledon and his assistants positioned the men over the trap. William Leach next delivered a penitent recitation, blaming his fate on liquor and resistance to Christian teachings. At 11:44 A.M., nearly an hour after the prisoners had ascended the gallows, Maledon took away Wilson's cigar and began the final preparations. He opened the trap at 11:48 A.M.[17]

Although George Maledon prided himself on his expertise as a hangman, later boasting that he had dispatched sixty men who "never even twitched," he botched this job badly. Of the five men executed, only Orpheus McGee was still after the drop. Even though his hands and arms were bound, Aaron Wilson struggled for eight minutes, convulsing so violently that the crucifix he wore around his neck was torn from the ribbon that secured it. Isham Seely moaned audibly for several minutes; the knot had slipped under his chin, strangling him slowly. Gibson Ishtonubee lingered for nine minutes, and the penitent William Leach for ten. Despite Maledon's skillful preparation and technique, hanging remained an inexact "science."[18]

Although unintended, the prolonged and ghastly death throes of the men hanged on April 21, 1876, underscored the most basic message of capital punishment, providing tangible proof of the dire penalties awaiting lawbreakers. But the centuries-old ritual of public execution served multiple purposes in nineteenth-century Arkansas, much as it had in England two hundred years before. Public hanging demonstrated incontrovertibly the ultimate power of the State. Furthermore, such rituals, with their carefully prescribed methods and religious sanction, symbolized the triumph of order—both civil and moral—over chaos. And, for the isolated residents of the Indian Territory frontier, a hanging provided one of the few opportunities for socializing, a kind of morbid holiday.[19]

The U.S. marshal, the highest-ranking peace officer in the Western District, organized and oversaw the execution ceremonies, representing the authority of the court and the federal government. He, not the judge, carried out the sentences. When the condemned proceeded from the jail to the gibbet, the marshal led the solemn parade, followed by the doomed men and their spiritual advisors. His deputies flanked the procession, isolating the condemned from society—the crowd—symbolically and literally protecting one from the other. Once atop the fatal platform, the marshal further demonstrated the power of civil authority by reading aloud each death warrant, announcing to all the unruly offenses that had justifiably led the criminals to these orderly executions.[20]

The custom of allowing the condemned to make final declarations from the scaffold, a tradition inherited from the English and intended to provide admonition to the onlookers, continued in Fort

Smith with varied results. Some, like William Leach and William Whittington, provided the expected morality lesson, blaming drink or some other personal frailty for their unhappy ends and praising their new-found Christian faiths for saving their souls. Others, however—Edmund Campbell and Smoker Mankiller, for example—used the gallows to protest their innocence one last time. Still others affected a posture of brave indifference and "died game," a practice by no means restricted to frontier desperadoes. James Moore's cool observation, "there are worse men here than me," would have played equally well to the urban masses that congregated to watch condemned thieves hang outside Newgate Prison in eighteenth-century London as to the Fort Smith crowds a century later. But most of the men facing Maledon's nooses remained mute on the scaffold, too overcome by their circumstances to feign bravado or to proclaim penitence. Although a majority of the condemned subverted its purpose, the ritual of allowing time for a few last words continued through the last execution under Parker in 1896.[21]

The participation of local clergymen, likewise a long-standing execution tradition, provided multiple messages for onlookers. On a practical level, the divines ministered to the condemned, offering spiritual comfort with the promise of salvation for those about to "spring from the gallows to glory." Father Smyth even offered temporal comfort by shielding Aaron Wilson from the sun with an umbrella. The presence of clergy on the scaffold further legitimized the proceedings, confirming Christian sanction for the death penalty. The clerics also used the executions to advance their evangelical purposes; Reverend Greathouse made pious object lessons of the condemned, directing them in "Other Refuge Have I None" at the moment when the truth of that lyric was most painfully obvious. Moreover, the ministers symbolically united the condemned with the onlookers, who became participants through communal hymn-singing and prayers. Someday those assembled before the gallows would also face death, so they too needed to consider the status of their souls.[22]

The onlookers implied approval of the death ritual by their presence and participation. Contemporary accounts of their behavior have indicated that the spectators were relatively orderly, but less solemn than the occasion that brought them together mandated, not unlike the masses that had assembled in Boston or Philadelphia to view public executions earlier in the century. A "picnic atmosphere" prevailed among Fort Smith crowds, enhanced, no doubt, by the whiskey vendors just outside the jail yard. Albeit a grim occasion, the hanging provided the opportunity for association and relaxation to the isolated inhabitants of the Indian Territory frontier. The actual execution proceedings occupied only an hour or so, and were concluded by midday, allowing plenty of time for fraternizing before beginning the journey home. But Parker and his officers recognized the possibility of disorder inherent in such a large crowd and appointed extra deputies to ensure tranquility; on April 21, 1876, the accidental shooting of one spectator proved such precautions justified.[23]

As the public executions at Fort Smith exhibited multiple purposes, so they served Isaac Parker in a variety of ways, demonstrating the efficacy of his new regime as well as building his reputation. The first two mass hangings confirmed that this new judge would conduct the affairs of the Western District honestly, efficiently, and fairly, thus winning over more Fort Smith skeptics. Clearly, Isaac Parker was no William Story. In less than a year on the bench he had ordered more executions than had been carried out in Fort Smith since 1871, when the court had moved there. And, unlike his disreputable predecessor, Parker never freed condemned prisoners on bond pending execution. Of the eight men hanged during Story's tenure, seven were American Indians, only one was white. The first eleven executed by Parker, on the other hand, reflected the mix of the races present in the Indian Territory: three whites, five American Indians, and three African Americans. The ethnic composition of the condemned indicated to some observers that court proceedings under the new regime were less biased than under Story. Certainly the speed with which the Western District arrested, tried, and executed these men pointed to a more efficient administration. Such improvements, demonstrated to a far wider audience through the public hanging spectacles, persuaded some to lessen their criticism of Parker. After the second mass execution, even Democratic editor J. W. Weaver praised Republican Judge Parker for his "determination . . . that the laws shall be firmly and faithfully administered."[24]

The mass executions also helped to establish the image of Parker as a stern, intractable jurist who remorselessly enforced the law: as the "Hanging Judge." Newspaper accounts and thousands of eyewitnesses spread the news of a harsh jurist dispensing lethal justice, a perception that Parker did little to dispel. During his twenty-one years at Fort Smith, Parker sentenced 161 men to the gallows, 79 of whom were executed. They continued to hang, alone and in pairs, in trios and quartets, until 1896, when Congress extinguished the Western District's jurisdiction over the Indian Territory; two more quintettes "swung off" together, one in 1881 and the other in 1896, as well as another sextet in 1890. National and local newspapers persisted in covering the executions, borrowing the traditions of "gallows literature" dating from the eighteenth century. These moralizing accounts emphasized the cruel brutality of crime and the awful finality of justice at Fort Smith. A firm believer in the deterrent value of punishment, Judge Parker never responded publicly to the macabre publicity during his years on the bench. If fear of the Hanging Judge discouraged crime, then so much the better for the deputies serving his overburdened court.[25]

Although Parker ordered the executions that built his reputation, the Hanging Judge image was incomplete at best. His 161 death sentences—156 for murder, 5 for rape and murder—represented less than 1 percent of the Western District Court docket from 1875 to 1896. Many of these orders resulted from the inflexibility of federal law, not from Parker's zeal for "stretching hemp"; death was the only penalty available under a statute that included no distinction between degrees of murder. Similarly, rape carried a mandatory death sentence; neither judge nor jury could exercise

discretion in such cases. Parker also frequently supported successful petitions pleading clemency for the condemned felons. Shortly
before his death, the notorious Hanging Judge even asserted that
he would support abolishing the death penalty, "provided there
[was] a certainty of punishment."[26]

Regardless of his personal feelings, Parker continued to ensure
"a certainty of punishment" to the Indian Territory killers convicted in his court. On September 6, 1876, four more died in public
for their deadly crimes. Ossee Sanders, the recipient of a temporary reprieve the previous April, failed to gain a permanent commutation and hanged for the murder of Thomas Carlisle. Sinker
Wilson had been convicted of murdering one Datus Cowan and
sentenced to death at Van Buren in 1867, but escaped before he
could be executed; he remained at large for nearly nine years
before Parker deputies returned him to Fort Smith for his date with
the hangman. John Valley had robbed and murdered a traveler
named Eli Hackett in the Cherokee Nation; and Samuel Peters had
sexually assaulted, then stabbed to death one Charity Wilson at
her cabin in the Choctaw Nation. On June 24 and 27, 1876, Parker
ordered their deaths; the quadruple execution raised his grisly total
to fifteen in just over a year.[27]

Despite the supposed deterrent effect of public hangings, capital offenses continued to appear on the Western District docket,
resulting in twenty-four convictions and nine executions over the
next five years. In December 1876, Parker sentenced three killers
to the scaffold and, during the May 1877 court term, ordered the
deaths of seven more convicts—six murderers and a rapist. Yet all
ten succeeded in obtaining executive clemency. On December 28,
1878, the next executions at Fort Smith, those of John Diggs and
John Poastoak, occurred. Again in 1879, Judge Parker ordered five
hangings, but one of the condemned died awaiting execution, and
two received commutations. On August 29, 1879, the remaining
two—William "Colorado Bill" Elliot and Henri Stewart, a Harvard-
trained physician—died together at the end of Maledon's ropes.
In 1880, only two convictions resulted from eleven murder cases,

whereupon President Rutherford Hayes commuted both sentences to life imprisonment. But the next year marked a resurgence in capital activity; on September 9, 1881, five men perished simultaneously in the second quintuple execution at Fort Smith.[28]

Unlike the first such event, however, this five-man hanging occurred within a small enclosure before an audience of less than fifty witnesses. Bowing to years of pressure from the Justice Department, Parker and his officers began conducting their executions in relative privacy. On June 11, 1878, Attorney General Charles Devens responded favorably to a letter from Western District Marshal D. P. Upham suggesting construction of a fence around the scaffold prior to a hanging scheduled for ten days later. Devens authorized the expenditure and instructed Upham "to conduct the execution . . . with as little public display as is consistent with duty." Executive clemency prevented the planned hanging and, apparently, the immediate construction of a fence. But by 1881 a barricade kept out the huge crowds that had attended previous spectacles. Thus on September 9, 1881, "only 40 or 50 persons" witnessed the deaths of George Padgett, William Brown, Patrick McGowan, and brothers Amos and Abner Manley. Then, in 1882, although Western District officials had already constructed the fence, the Justice Department finally ordered Parker to build a more substantial wall around the gallows because his executions had "taken on the aspects of a carnival."[29]

Thus the sixty future executions ordered by Parker would be conducted privately, conforming to a trend in American capital punishment over forty years old. No matter how tardy the orders of the Justice Department or the actions of the Western District, the concerns that had prompted the movement for private executions before the Civil War applied in Fort Smith forty years later. The sickening spectacle of botched hangings had prompted many reformers to advocate their seclusion. Surely the ghastly death struggles of the condemned on April 21, 1875, supported such arguments; the wall around the Fort Smith scaffold would spare many potential spectators the hour-long strangulation of Edward

Fulsome in 1882 and the near-decapitation of John Thorton ten years later. Some early proponents of private execution had decried the loss of labor when stores closed and thousands abandoned their work to attend hangings; others had asserted that such spectacles lionized the condemned; still others had feared disorder from the assembled masses. All of these conditions were present at the Parker executions. The journey to and from Fort Smith could mean up to three workdays lost for some spectators, and most local businesses closed their doors for the hangings. Newspaper coverage, although demonstrating "the wages of sin," also frequently praised the courage that doomed men displayed before the huge crowds. And Parker's ban on weapons, enforced by extra, heavily armed deputies, proved that he recognized the potential for disorder among the throngs that attended his public executions. Moving the proceedings behind walls eliminated such concerns, yet maintained their presumed deterrent value via the newspapers.[30]

Conducting executions out of public sight also revealed ambivalence toward the death penalty. Such hangings were just, lawful retribution, yet they were unfit for public viewing. Isaac Parker's behavior belied similar contradictions. Seventy-nine men died by his order, nineteen of them before huge crowds; the hangings moved behind walls only through the continued prodding of his superiors in Washington. Yet Parker never attended an execution, and he wept in court the first time that he sentenced a man to die. Still, the Bible sanctioned the death penalty—"an eye for an eye"— and the law demanded it. Hanging was, Parker had been taught, a just punishment, a necessary deterrent, an important shield for society. If the brutes he ordered to the gallows—child-killers, rapists, men who killed for no reason—did not merit the ultimate price, then no one did. But his Bible also ordained mercy. Thus Parker could order seven men to hang, exhort them to find salvation, then seek clemency for anyone that he thought deserving, and be reasonably satisfied that he had fulfilled his duties both to God and the law. But enough doubt remained that, by the end of his career, he advocated abolition of the death penalty.

Ultimately, the law prescribed the penalty and Parker sentenced convicts accordingly; federal statute obviated any ambivalent feelings on the part of the judge. Hanging criminals was the most distasteful aspect among the many obligations of his station, and Isaac Parker seldom, if ever, shirked his duties. His primary function at Fort Smith was to uphold federal law in the Western District of Arkansas, and he did so tirelessly for twenty-one years. As will be shown, the majority of the cases he tried did not involve murder, or even crimes of violence. That he has been most remembered for less than one percent of his official activities reveals far more about Americans' ongoing fascination with violent crime and punishment than about the man behind the popular image of the Hanging Judge.

CHAPTER FIVE

"THE INTERESTS OF JUSTICE"

Pardons, 1876–1880

From May of 1875 to September of 1876, Isaac Parker secured judicial preeminence over the Western District of Arkansas. He increased the efficiency of his court by improving administrative procedures and redoubling law enforcement efforts in the Indian Territory. More deputy marshals now patrolled "the Nations" west of Fort Smith, following Parker's admonition to "bring [outlaws] in alive— or dead!" Such men now faced vigorous prosecution; the public spectacles of four mass hangings illustrated clearly that those convicted faced certain punishment. And Parker's authority seemed virtually absolute. Because the Fort Smith tribunal also exercised collateral circuit court powers, Parker ruled as U.S. circuit judge on applications for new trials stemming from his own district court decisions; not surprisingly, he rarely granted such motions. Such dual powers arose from congressional oversight; when establishing the Eastern and Western Judicial Districts of Arkansas, lawmakers neglected to create a separate circuit court for the districts. Thus, the only viable refuge from Parker's sentence was executive clemency.[1]

But such complete command of the Western District would not remain unchallenged. Over the next five years, a majority of Parker death sentences were unexecuted. From 1875 to 1880, local attorneys successfully sought commutations and pardons for condemned prisoners in cases that have provided a more complex and more complete picture of the federal judicial system, the Western District Court, and its mercurial judge. Surviving documents, illustrating local responses to Parker decisions, have demonstrated the strengths and weaknesses of federal judicial procedures and criminal statutes. These records also have provided insights into the judge himself: his relationship with superiors in the Justice Department, his reactions to those who challenged his judgment and authority, and his peculiar sense of justice.[2]

The Hanging Judge lent his wholehearted support to the first commutation application arising from one of his sentences. The youthful defendant, Oscar Snow, had been convicted of murder in a case that illustrated the inflexibility of contemporary federal laws. Late in 1874, Snow and his accomplice, Henry Lewis, conspired to murder George Beauchamps at the request of the victim's wife. Although Lewis fired the fatal shots, Snow, who had loaded the murder weapon, was equally culpable under federal law, and, on June 26, 1875, Parker sentenced him to hang—the only course available to him under a statute that included no distinction between degrees of murder and no penalty other than death.[3]

Following standard procedures to secure executive clemency, Snow and his attorneys received unexpected support in their successful efforts from Judge Parker. On July 6, 1875, the Fort Smith law firm of Duval and Cravens—headed by Benjamin T. Du Val, who had investigated Western District corruption in 1874—submitted a request for clemency to Attorney General Edwards Pierrepont, citing as grounds for commutation Snow's youth, his inability to secure counsel before trial, and the fact that he had not been present when the murder occurred. Pierrepont, in turn, requested reports from District Attorney Clayton and Judge Parker. Clayton responded favorably on July 19; he confirmed that the defendant was not present at the murder scene, and wrote that the Beauchamps woman had swayed the youth. Judge Parker, although absent on personal business, had concurred in the opinion that commutation to life imprisonment served "the interests of justice."

A week later, on July 27, Parker, who was visiting Washington, personally filed his opinion with the attorney general. He stated that Snow had been "under the influence of a bad woman" when conspiring to kill Beauchamps; and, had the law permitted, he would have sentenced the youth to life in prison rather than to death. The next day Pardon Attorney William Edwards French, the Justice Department official charged with scrutinizing clemency applications, reviewed the case and advised commutation. Consequently, the attorney general recommended clemency; and on July 28, 1875, President Grant commuted Snow's sentence to life at hard labor in the Illinois Penitentiary at Joliet.[4]

Since Oscar Snow was the only convict in the first three terms of the Parker court to receive a commutation, Fort Smith lawyers and residents reacted to the executions of fifteen men in just over a year by joining forces to ameliorate the severity of Parker's sentences. Beginning with the November 1876 court term, applications for clemency from the Western District increased dramatically. Hundreds of residents from Fort Smith and the Indian Territory—often including the jurors who had convicted the condemned—signed petitions supporting commutations or pardons. And their efforts were remarkably successful: not one of the criminals that Parker sentenced to death between December 1876 and February 1878 was hanged.[5]

The crime for which Parker condemned Irving Perkins in December of 1876, as well as his sexual conduct, outraged nineteenth-century sensibilities and virtually guaranteed conviction. Perkins, an African-American, lived in the Indian country with his wife and a stepdaughter, Vina Washington. After he "became too familiar" with the girl, she bore him a daughter. His wife understandably resented the infant and complained incessantly about her. In the autumn of 1876, Perkins, believing Vina Washington incapable of raising the child and hoping to restore his relationship with his wife, poisoned the baby and disposed of its body. He later confessed to the crime, informing a Parker deputy that "he thought one way was as nice as another and he gave it some camphor and it went to sleep." Perkins, however, recanted the next day. "Perhaps you misunderstood me last night," he told the lawman; "I meant to say that the child was sick and I gave it the Camphor as medicine." A Fort Smith jury, however, discounted the second version of events and convicted him. In December 1876, Judge Parker sentenced Perkins to hang on April 27, 1877.[6]

On March 30, 1877, less than a month before the scheduled execution, thirty-six influential Fort Smith attorneys and citizens used legal technicalities, emotional appeals, and logical arguments in petitioning President Hayes to pardon Irving Perkins. Benjamin Du Val, the former special U.S. attorney, and William H. Sandals, future Western District prosecutor, signed the document, as did John H. Rogers, a young lawyer who would one day successfully sponsor legislation allowing those convicted by the Parker court to appeal. Thomas Marcum, who had defended Perkins, argued that the government case was "entirely circumstantial, except for the prisoner's confessions." Both admissions remained suspect, Marcum continued, because the unfortunate Perkins "was chained to a post when he made these statements." Furthermore, the prosecution never produced the body of "the alleged deceased." The judgment was also improper because the jury convicted on a faulty indictment. Moreover, Vina Washington, who testified against Perkins and "did not know that it was wrong to tell a lie upon an oath," had "as good an opportunity to commit the crime" as her stepfather. Consequently, the signatories "entertain[ed] doubts of the gravest nature" regarding Perkins's guilt.[7]

District Attorney Clayton, in contrast, harbored no such reservations, and Judge Parker concurred; both officials opposed any form of clemency. Although deputies never found the body of the murdered infant—Clayton surmised that Perkins threw the corpse into a creek and it had washed away—the district attorney voiced "no doubt" that Perkins had "murdered his own child" and urged that "clemency ought not to be extended to him." Judge Parker was more succinct, writing that "I have no recommendation . . . to make in the case of Perkins."[8]

Accepting the prosecution version of events, Pardon Attorney Alexander F. Gray argued successfully for commutation rather than a pardon, but his reasoning ignored the issues raised by petitioners. On April 19, 1877, Gray submitted his report on the Perkins application to Attorney General Charles Devens. He repeated the version of events contained in Clayton's report without mentioning any of the misgivings—concerning the circumstances of Perkins's confession, the possibility that Vina Washington had killed her own baby, the missing body—that had initially prompted this plea for pardon. Still, Gray wrote, "A commutation of sentence to imprisonment at hard labor for life might be proper in this case." Perkins had obviously murdered the child, but he was "ignorant" and had lived "without regard to decency or morality." "It seems almost a pity," he continued, "to deal with one so low in the scale of humanity as if he were to be charged with full moral responsibility." Life in prison would thus be "sufficient for punishment and . . . example." Attorney General Devens accepted this reasoning and forwarded a recommendation for clemency to the White House. On April 21, 1877, President Hayes commuted Perkins' sentence to life at hard labor.[9]

The next clemency applicant in the Western District was scheduled to die on the same day as Irving Perkins. The facts in his case were clear, the legal issues cloudy. After the Civil War, African Americans Charley Thomas and Lewis Adams migrated to the Chickasaw Nation from Texas. Adams married and soon thereafter began beating his wife. Thomas fell in love with the abused woman and, together, they hatched a scheme to escape Adams. He hired a wagon and driver to transport her secretly to the Wichita Indian Agency, planning to join her there. The rescue effort failed, however, when Adams, armed with a revolver and a double-barreled shotgun, overtook his fleeing spouse. After pistol-whipping her, he ordered the driver: "You tell Thomas that I intend to kill him on sight," then turned back with the battered woman.[10]

Returning home ahead of the pair, the driver encountered Thomas en route to the planned rendezvous at the Wichita Agency.

He repeated Adams's threat and thus set the stage for a deadly confrontation. Rather than fleeing, Thomas immediately set out to challenge Adams. After riding about three miles farther, he hid beside an abandoned house along the road that Adams and his wife would travel. As the couple approached, Thomas stepped forward, "his pistol cocked in his hand." Pointing the weapon at Adams, he demanded, "I understand you intend to kill me on sight—did you say so?" He shouted this challenge three times, but received no reply. Adams may have reached for his shotgun, slung over the pommel of his saddle—testimony conflicted on this point—but Charley Thomas definitely fired his revolver, twice. The first shot killed Adams's horse, throwing the rider. The second struck Adams in the left side; he died within an hour.[11]

Thomas, certain that he had committed a justifiable homicide, surrendered to U.S. Deputy Marshal A. S. Fowler. Instead of vindication, however, he soon faced the death penalty in a case that hinged on the legal definition of self-defense. Common law, both English and American, traditionally required an individual confronted with lethal force to retreat to "the wall at his back," to flee the aggressor until no other option presented, before responding violently. Thus, even though Lewis Adams had demonstrated a propensity for violence by repeatedly abusing his wife and had threatened to kill him, Charley Thomas could not claim self-defense. He sought, rather than avoided, the fatal confrontation and challenged his adversary with a drawn, cocked revolver. That Thomas assumed the threat to be genuine and feared legitimately for his life held no legal consequence. On November 7, 1876, Judge Parker instructed the jury accordingly. They returned a verdict of "guilty," and he ordered Thomas to hang on April 27, 1877.[12]

Once again, lawyers and interested citizens appealed to the president to prevent another hanging, presenting petitions, affidavits, and personal entreaties for the pardon of Charley Thomas. On March 24, 1877, Valentine Dell, editor of the *Fort Smith New Era* and future U.S. marshal for the Western District, wrote directly to President Hayes, describing Thomas as a victim of "the prejudice against his race and color in a community . . . thoroughly imbued by proslavery" attitudes. "A white man," he continued, "charged with having killed another white man . . . under the same circumstances . . . would be declared 'not guilty' by a southern white jury within five minutes." A. S. Fowler, the deputy marshal to whom Thomas surrendered, vouched for his industriousness and declared the killing "justifiable . . . in order to save his own life." Despite Judge Parker's jury instructions regarding the law, the petitioners emphasized self-defense in their pleas. They also included an affidavit attesting to Thomas's previous good character and concluded that "it would be doing violence to strict justice to take the life of the accused, and . . . this is the general view of the community."[13]

On April 9, both Judge Parker and District Attorney Clayton recommended against a pardon, suggesting that "executive interference ought not extend further than a commutation." Pardon Attorney Gray opposed even that much clemency, and his findings led Hayes to reject the application. Thomas, Gray reported to Attorney General Devens, "was the aggressor . . . from the beginning"; when informed of Adams's threat, "he did not turn back, or aside, but sought to meet him, and coolly . . . shot him to death." Countering assertions of the applicant's sterling character, Gray contended—erroneously, as adultery and fornication did not become federal crimes until 1887—that Thomas had engaged in "criminal interference" with the "domestic and conjugal relations" of his victim. The moralistic Gray thus found no "sufficient considerations to justify the exercise of clemency." Attorney General Devens concurred in this opinion and reported his findings to the president. On April 21, 1877, Hayes refused to "interfere" with the sentence.[14]

With death looming less than a week away, Charley Thomas finally escaped the gallows through the surprising intercession of an unlikely advocate: Isaac Parker. On April 23, 1877, the judge dispatched a brief telegram to Attorney General Devens, stating that "I think the ends of justice will be met by the commutation of the sentence of Charlie [sic] Thomas to imprisonment for life."

Although he had advised against a pardon less than three weeks before, Parker probably had expected President Hayes to reduce the sentence to life at hard labor. While an inflexible federal statute mandated the death penalty, many contemporary state laws permitted extenuating circumstances to reduce either the charge or the sentence in a murder case. Outside the federal courts, the facts that Adams had beaten his wife and threatened Thomas, as well as the defendant's previously law-abiding habits, could have mitigated against a capital sentence. Parker, although stopping short of a recommendation of leniency, had hinted at such a course by suggesting that clemency not extend "beyond commutation of sentence to hard labor for life" in his initial report. When Hayes failed to intervene, the judge formally endorsed mercy, and his opinion overruled that of Pardon Attorney Gray. On April 25, 1877, just two days before the scheduled execution, President Hayes commuted Charley Thomas's sentence to life in prison at hard labor.[15]

Other commutations continued through 1877. Black Crow, another murderer condemned during the November 1876 term, also received executive clemency. On September 18, 1877, Parker sentenced murderer William Meadows to hang. Eleven days later, he ordered killer Thomas Robinson and rapist Joshua Wade to die with Meadows. But President Hayes reduced the sentences of all three men.[16]

Four more condemned killers escaped the gallows in 1878, their case demonstrating flaws both in the federal murder statutes and the pardon process. On August 15, 1877, Carolina Grayson, his brother Peter, Manuel Lewis, and Robert Love, all African Americans, participated with five others in a dispute over stolen hogs that resulted in the murder of Henry Ross—and still more death sentences from Parker. Carolina Grayson led these neighbors to the Ross farm in the Cherokee Nation, demanding that they be allowed to search the premises for some missing swine. After a lengthy row over the implied accusation of theft, Grayson shot the farmer, who presumably was running to his cabin for a gun, "in the back part of the head." Two days later, Western District deputies arrested all nine; and then a grand jury indicted them. Even though evidence proved that Carolina Grayson fired the fatal shot, the others were equally culpable because testimony indicated that they had discussed killing Ross if he was discovered to be the thief. But a petit jury found only the Graysons, Lewis, and Love guilty of the murder. On February 25, 1878, Judge Parker sentenced all four to hang on the following June 21.[17]

Petitioners, while seeking clemency for the four defendants in the usual manner, gained support not only by challenging the right of the court to try the case, but also by contradicting the evidence that had convicted the men. Several familiar names graced the petition for pardon. Attorneys Thomas Marcum and Thomas Barnes, as well as courthouse janitor Tillman Knox, had signed similar requests for Oscar Snow, Irving Perkins, and Charley Thomas. In addition to these persistent individuals, former Assistant U.S. Attorney James Brizzolara, a commissioner—or magistrate—of the Western District Court, who was running for mayor of Fort Smith, signed the document, along with the jury that convicted the quartet. Their application charged that the Graysons, Lewis, and Love were all subjects of the Creek Nation and that Henry Ross claimed Cherokee citizenship; therefore, the Western District Court held no jurisdiction in the case. They further contended that the evidence showed a "clear case of self-defense," an argument ignoring the fact that Ross was shot from behind.[18]

Despite such a distortion, the petitioners, aided by the recommendations of Judge Parker and District Attorney Clayton, achieved their purpose for three of the four men. On June 5, 1878, Clayton related the facts of the case in a letter to Attorney General Devens, suggesting commutation for Peter Grayson, Manuel Lewis, and Robert Love "if the sentence . . . is interfered with at all," but agreeing to no clemency for Carolina Grayson. Judge Parker concurred. On June 14, the attorney general submitted his report to President Hayes, who, in turn, reduced the sentences of all the defendants, except Carolina Grayson, to life at hard labor.[19]

Rather than accept this partial victory, however, the supporters of Carolina Grayson circumvented the standard pardon
process—and Judge Parker—to save his life. Through continued
entreaties, they secured a series of respites, postponing the execution until July 19, then August 16, and, finally, August 23, 1878.
On August 16, a delegation from Fort Smith, led by Tillman Knox
and bearing a letter of introduction to President Hayes from attorney Thomas Marcum, arrived in Washington. On August 20,
Knox presented to the chief executive a final plea for the life of
Carolina Grayson. After flattering Hayes by crediting his "inter-
position" in capital cases with reducing "the number of murders
in the Western District," the delegates offered new arguments for
clemency. Grayson, because of a "lack of means," had been unable
to procure witnesses who would have "clearly proved" that he
was "not more guilty" than his codefendants who had been
spared. Furthermore, the victim, Henry Ross, "was a bad man
and provoked this murder." Thus, "all the Colored citizens of
Fort Smith . . . and many of the most respectable" white residents,
Knox concluded, requested that the punishment be reduced from
death to life in prison, a sentence that Hayes agreed to that same
day.[20]

The next day, August 21, 1878, an outraged Isaac Parker protested in vain to the attorney general, complaining of the "false . . .
statements made to you and the President" by the Fort Smith delegation. This irregular procedure—bypassing Parker, Clayton, and
the pardon attorney—prevented the judge from presenting further
arguments against clemency. The delegates must have presented
evidence that overrode Parker's rationale. What misrepresentations might they have fabricated? "I have a right to know," he
wrote angrily, "in regard to statements . . . concerning me . . . and
the trial of a case in my court." He therefore demanded that the
attorney general send him "all letters and papers . . . touching the
application for pardon or commutation in said case of Carolina
Grayson." But the president had already decided the matter, and
the documents remained in Washington.[21]

On December 20, 1878, two more condemned killers, James Diggs and John Postoak, died on the Fort Smith gallows in the first Parker-directed hanging in over two years. Yet this event did not signal a return to wholesale convictions and executions. In 1879, Parker condemned only four killers, two of whom, Henri Stewart and William Elliot, were hanged on August 29. Of the remaining two, Jackson Marshal died in jail awaiting execution and Uriah M. Cooper secured executive clemency.[22]

The Cooper litigation originated with a minor offense, but the defendant's words resulted in a capital case. A professional photographer born in North Carolina, Uriah Cooper migrated to Caddo, in the Choctaw Nation, where he augmented his legitimate income by selling whiskey. As a consequence, in the autumn of 1876, he found himself in the custody of a Parker posse, en route to Fort Smith to face a charge of "retail liquor distribution." He became abusive in camp one night, requiring posseman Robert Donnelly to shackle him. As the temporary deputy affixed the leg irons, Cooper threatened to kill him. But such a dire warning seemed pure bluster, and without further incident the party reached Fort Smith, where, on December 19, 1876, Judge Parker sentenced Cooper to pay a hundred-dollar fine and serve thirty days in jail. The death threat remained forgotten until March 1879, when a party of men murdered Robert Donnelly in the Missouri, Kansas, and Texas Railroad Yard at Caddo.[23]

On April 7, 1879, a grand jury indicted Cooper, along with Lum and Jap McGee, and "one Scott," for murder, setting the stage for a long and contentious trial that resulted in the death sentence. Only Cooper faced the judge and jury, his codefendants having eluded capture. The proceedings lasted for six days, over twice the length of most murder trials in the Parker court, and featured highly contradictory testimony. All prosecution witnesses placed Cooper at the shooting, with some stating that he fired the fatal shotgun blast. Yet the defense produced even more testimony—from twenty-five attestants—that placed Cooper in a billiard hall at the time that Donnelly was shot. Judge Parker, favoring the government case, characterized such contradictions as irrelevant. Even if the defendant was not present at the actual shooting, the judge instructed the jurors, Cooper shared equal guilt if he had conspired with them. Parker also charged the jury to consider that the defense witnesses, but not those for the prosecution, might have fabricated their testimony. Not surprisingly, in light of his instructions, the jurors returned a guilty verdict and he sentenced Uriah Cooper to hang.[24]

By 1879, such biased jury instructions were a fading remnant of preindustrial legal culture in the United States. Thus Parker's continuance of the practice provided grounds for ongoing criticism of him. Before the Civil War, jury charges truly "instructed" the jurors as to what their verdict should be. Judges commented not only upon the specific points of law involved, but also on the merits of the evidence, thereby exercising considerable control over the final outcome of a case. In the decades between 1875 and 1900, however, written charges pertaining only to specific points of law replaced the long harangues of judges throughout the nation. But Parker clung to his early training, convinced that juries "must be led." Attorney Thomas Marcum, by objecting to Parker giving "undue prominence . . . to all the testimony for the prosecution" in the Cooper trial, foreshadowed the grounds for dozens of reversals after 1889, when appeals from the Western District finally gained hearing in the United States Supreme Court.[25]

But in 1880 inappropriate jury charges held little significance in the federal pardon system. Other factors were more likely to sway the pardon attorney, and in the Cooper case they all favored a commutation. Both District Attorney Clayton and Judge Parker supported clemency, as long as it did not extend beyond reduction of sentence to life imprisonment. Pardon Attorney Alexander Gray, after reading the "voluminous" documents associated with the case, favored mercy, if only to guarantee punishment. The fact that the panel convicting Cooper signed the petition for pardon did not affect Gray's decision, however; such behavior had become, he argued, "a very usual thing with juries in the Western District."

The contradictory testimony established that "if [Cooper] did not fire the fatal shot . . . he was in a conspiracy" to kill Robert Donnelly. But, Gray continued, "owing to a strange deficiency in the statutes"—a requirement all the conspirators in such a case be proven guilty—he could not be punished for planning the crime. Therefore, Gray concluded, the "expedient" course was to accept the advice of Parker and Clayton to commute the death sentence. Cooper would thus remain in prison, although reasonable doubts remained as to whether or not he actually participated in the shooting, thereby saving the government the cost of a second trial on conspiracy charges that might never be proven. Attorney General Devens and President Hayes agreed. On June 8, 1880, Cooper received clemency, a life sentence in the House of Corrections at Detroit, Michigan.[26]

The gibbet at Fort Smith remained idle throughout 1880, despite ten capital indictments. Juries acquitted eight accused of murder, with the remaining two, James Heaslett and Lum Smith, receiving commutations. During the lull in hangings, court officials coated the gallows with whitewash.[27]

Young James Heaslett, a twenty-year-old farmhand, never denied committing murder; yet his defense, which was insufficient for acquittal, created enough doubts to spare him from a death sentence. On June 1, 1879, he brutally murdered his stepfather, Chauncy Legard, in a cornfield near Okmulgee, in the Creek Nation. After shooting his victim twice from behind, he "literally beat his head to a jelly" with "a large Colt's six-shooter." Detained by neighbors the same day, Heaslett told them that "if you knew as much as I did, you would have killed him long ago." Once on trial and pleading insanity, he related a frightful tale of family abuse that led to the killing. The defense argued that Chauncy Legard had repeatedly "ravished" his eldest stepdaughter, resulting in her death four years earlier. Heaslett and his mother both testified that the deceased had begun sexually assaulting his own daughter, who was not yet ten years of age, about a month before the murder. The defendant further asserted that his mother, although aware of such abuse, "kept it a profound secret" until she told him, "about a week" before he took vengeance on his stepfather. The knowledge of these shameful "outrages" had driven him to murder.[28]

The jury was not convinced, however. Nor were Judge Parker or District Attorney Clayton, both of whom nevertheless supported a commutation after the jurist had sentenced Heaslett to hang. Clayton challenged the sexual abuse defense in his report, pointing to the mother as the real source of the crime. Medical evidence regarding assault of the youngest daughter belied the charges of rape, he asserted. Two doctors examined her before the trial, one finding her hymen intact, the other finding it "ruptured but present." "Three or four weeks" later, two different physicians found "no trace" of the membrane, but all agreed that the child had never been penetrated. The interval between the examinations, Clayton noted, provided "ample time" for the defense "to tamper with her." Finding unbelievable the fact that the mother would allow such abuse to continue, the district attorney posited that she had concocted the story to spur Heaslett to dispose of her husband, who was "old and worn out." Because of this "possibility" that the mother influenced Heaslett with an outrageous fabrication, Clayton suggested a commutation to life at hard labor. Judge Parker concurred, stating that "I have no confidence in the defense of insanity . . . in this case less in the alleged cause of it." "The mother of Heaslett instigated the murder," he continued, and the defendant "was an instrument in her hand." Thus his sentence could be justly reduced "to life imprisonment," but "no greater clemency . . . should be extended to him."[29]

Others advocating mercy accepted the insanity defense and its "alleged cause," successfully seeking the aid of prominent local and national politicians to save Heaslett. On April 14, 1880, Attorney J. K. Pratt, representing the Fort Smith law firm of Du Val and Cravens, wrote to Arkansas Congressman L. M. Gunter and reminded him that Heaslett's relatives were neighbors of the representative's brother. On April 22, five more Arkansas congressmen wrote to President Hayes requesting clemency and asserting that the facts of the case "by the common verdict of mankind demand[ed] leniency." The same day, Ohio Senator (and future president) James A. Garfield presented a letter from one William Brown, "a trustworthy man" who had once lived in his home district and now resided in Bloomfield, Arkansas, outlining the Heaslett case and requesting a pardon. Pardon Attorney Gray never mentioned such correspondence in his surprisingly brief report, instead simply restating the opinions of Judge Parker and District Attorney Clayton and recommending commutation to life imprisonment. On June 8, President Hayes reduced the sentence to life at the Detroit House of Corrections.[30]

Previous accounts of the Parker court have characterized its authority as absolute until the onset of Supreme Court appeals in 1889. The commutations granted between 1875 and 1880 reveal, however, that Parker, even at the pinnacle of his considerable powers, never exercised total control in capital cases. Lawyers and citizens succeeded in preventing fourteen of thirty-four scheduled executions through the pardon process. Thus executive clemency provided a check on the judge and on his application of an inflexible system of federal statutes. Clearly, Parker wielded more power, both in influencing the outcome of trials and recommending for or against clemency, than the petitioners. But in 1878 the emotional pleas of a delegation from Fort Smith overruled his most strident arguments for hanging convicted killer Carolina Grayson.[31]

Parker supported most of these applications, sometimes clearly stating his reasoning, other times cryptically obscuring his motives. In the cases of Oscar Snow in 1875 and James Heaslett in 1880, the judge pointed to the youth of the defendants, as well as the influence of "bad women" in their crimes as grounds for mercy. Public support for clemency seemed not to influence him, no matter how often petitioners claimed to represent the "general view of the community." Parker, in those cases where reasonable doubt existed as to the direct culpability of the defendants—Peter Grayson, Manuel Lewis, Robert Love, and Uriah Cooper, for example—remained officially convinced of their guilt; yet he advocated sparing them, offering a vague rhetorical appeal to "the interests of justice." He also never acknowledged technical grounds, such as errors in his jury charges, as criteria for leniency. To admit misgivings regarding a conviction or to acknowledge procedural deficiencies in reports to his superiors would have been professionally dangerous and personally abhorrent to a jurist of Isaac Parker's ambition and pride.

The recommendations of the judge and district attorney held great significance in securing clemency through a pardon process subject to personal caprice and political influence. Most recipients of commutations from Parker death sentences initially requested full pardons, but, based largely on his reports, succeeded only in obtaining reductions of their sentences. In the case of Charley Thomas, Parker secured a commutation simply by stating his preference to President Hayes. The Western District officials, however, did not exclusively determine the outcome of such cases. Each functionary who reviewed the pleas, from the district judge to the president, tended to accept the recommendation of his immediate subordinate. Thus the biases of the pardon attorney could spare or condemn an applicant, as when Alexander Gray successfully suggested a life prison term for Irving Perkins, contrary to the advice of Parker, because he considered the defendant "so low on the scale of humanity" and therefore not entirely accountable for poisoning his own child. And the president could ignore all the reports if he so chose, as Hayes did in the case of Carolina Grayson; until 1885, the chief executive bore no obligation to explain his reasons for granting a pardon or commutation. Politics, too, played a role. Although not cited in the reports of the attorney general or his subordinates, letters from prominent politicians requesting mercy remained part of the official pardon file that Justice Department officials—all of them political appointees—reviewed before writing their reports on the application of James Heaslett.[32]

Responding to the political aspect of the pardon process, the lawyers directing petitions for clemency often appealed to the political instincts of the president; their motives varied as much as

the individuals who signed the documents. At times they emphasized "the general view of the community" and the support of
"respectable citizens"—meaning potential voters—in the applications. If the defendants were African Americans, then the letters
accompanying the application would report that "all the colored
citizens" of Fort Smith, an important Republican constituency,
supported clemency. A solid core of defense attorneys also initiated and supported such attempts, aided by other citizens either
connected with the cases or seeking gain from their participation.
Attorney Thomas Marcum, for example, signed virtually every
petition, whether he had represented the applicant or not; lawyers
Ben Du Val, Thomas Barnes, and his brother, James, were also
perennial signatories. Successful applications enhanced professional stature and justified increased fees, and furthered justice as
well. U.S. Commissioner James Brizzolara, on the other hand, lent
his name to the dubious self-defense claim of Carolina Grayson,
apparently motivated by his desire to gain votes in his campaign
for mayor. Courthouse janitor Tillman Knox signed all the petitions
for fellow African Americans and led a delegation to Washington
that saved Grayson from the gallows in 1879.

The Grayson commutation, one of only two ordered against the
specific wishes of Parker through 1880, revealed the judge's growing frustration with the use of the pardon process. In 1877, when
President Hayes reduced the sentence of Irving Perkins, Parker
stoically accepted the decision. Three years later, however, he
lashed out at the attorneys and delegates seeking commutation for
Carolina Grayson, condemning their statements as false without
knowing what they had said. He had supported most of the pleas
for clemency, but this one evaded the established procedures and
excluded him. By addressing the president directly, the delegation
to Washington had defied Parker's authority, an act that he found
intolerable. But his anger over the Grayson case only foreshadowed his response to similar future challenges. The applications
for pardons and commutations would increase with the continuing influx of criminals into the Parker court.

William H. H. Clayton, Parker's trusted prosecutor, shown here in his later capacity as federal judge in the Indian Territory. *Archives and Manuscripts Division, Oklahoma Historical Society.*

"Bandit Queen" Belle Starr "robbed" Judge Parker in a mock stagecoach holdup in 1886, shortly after her release from a prison term the judge imposed for horse theft. *Archives and Manuscripts Division, Oklahoma Historical Society.*

The execution of Cherokee Bill, March 17, 1896. *Archives and Manuscript Division, Oklahoma Historical Society.*

Judge Isaac Parker in his later years. *Fort Smith National Historic Site.*

Old jail and courtroom, a former barracks, where Parker presided from 1875 to 1889. *Fort Smith National Historic Site.*

Judge Parker presiding in the new federal courthouse in Fort Smith, where he held court from 1889 to 1896. *Cravens Collection, University of Arkansas at Little Rock Archives.*

CHAPTER SIX

"ALWAYS DRUNK WHEN HE COULD GET WHISKEY"

Criminal Enforcement

On Tuesday, May 3, 1881, the United States Court for the Western District of Arkansas convened its second session of the year at Fort Smith. Early that morning a cross-section of the frontier population, many of them inhabitants of the Indian country, filled the courtroom on the first floor of the former enlisted men's barracks to act out their roles in the legal dramas about to unfold. On the south side of the chamber waited anxious witnesses and curious spectators, the friends and families both of the victims and the accused in cases ranging from hog theft to murder. Journalists from the Fort Smith newspapers also sat beside them, gathering material for their local columns and looking for a story of regional, or even national, interest. Across the wooden railing dividing the room, attorneys and court officials busied themselves with their final preparations before the proceedings began. And in the foul, dank cellar directly below them that served as the federal jail, the main actors in this morality play—the prisoners—waited to appear.

At 8:00 A.M., court crier Joshua P. Clark rose and announced: "Oyez, oyez! The Honorable District Court of the United States for the Western District of Arkansas, having criminal jurisdiction of the Indian Territory, is now in session." As he spoke, Judge Parker occupied his seat on the raised bench along the north wall and called to order the busiest criminal tribunal in the federal system. All U.S. district courts prosecuted statutory offenses—violations of legislation passed by Congress—such as revenue infractions, counterfeiting, civil rights infringements, and interference with the postal system. They were additionally charged with enforcement of all federal laws enacted to protect American Indians, such as the Indian Intercourse Act of 1834. Furthermore, district courts held common-law jurisdiction, based on judicial precedents that had evolved since the Magna Carta, over U.S. citizens in any "unorganized tract" within the borders of the United States. The Indian Territory fit this description. Thus the Parker court, owing to its authority over this fugitive-infested region, tried more common-law offenses, such as murder, rape, and larceny, than any contemporary federal bench. Liquor offenses in violation of Indian Intercourse and Trade acts, as well as revenue enforcement, greatly increased its burdens. But, as records of one day's proceedings illustrates, the operations of the "Court of the Damned" were far more prosaic than the image of the presiding Hanging Judge might suggest.[1]

On May 3, 1881, the judicial process proved less than dramatic, although the first action that Parker took concerned a murder case. The defendants, Thomas Faelis and Tulwa Harfs, charged with murder by the previous grand jury, did not even appear in court. Instead, their attorney, James K. Barnes, presented a motion requesting the court to subpoena six people to testify for the defense at government expense. Judge Parker granted this routine motion— a common procedure in light of the vast distances that witnesses in the Indian Territory often crossed to reach Fort Smith—ordering the six to appear on June 1, 1881, and binding the court to pay their travel and lodging costs.[2]

The court next attended to administrative matters. On the motion of local lawyer James A. Yantis, Parker enrolled Michael J. Casey as "attorney and counselor" in the Western District. The judge then received five indictments from John J. Hill, foreman of the newly selected grand jury. Parker ordered the documents filed and Hill returned "to further deliberate" with his panel.[3]

One of these indictments charged James W. Henderson with embezzlement from the United States mails. Appearing before the court in the custody of U.S. Marshal Valentine Dell, the accused needed a lawyer but claimed that he could not afford legal representation. As a consequence, Parker appointed attorneys Thomas A. Barnes and Evan F. Tilles as his advocates.[4]

The next case presented charges of "assault with intent to kill" resulting from a churchyard brawl. The facts in *U.S. v. Thomas Triplett* were clear and undisputed. On Sunday, April 24, 1881, Triplett attended church at North Coffee, Choctaw Nation. According to elder George Varnum, who conducted services that day, the accused came to church drunk, seated himself at the rear of the congregation, then left after a brief conversation with a Peter Campell. A few minutes later, screams and curses from outside disrupted the worshipers. Elder Varnum ran to the door in time to see Thomas Triplett advancing with a knife toward Peter Campell, whose father, Edmund, attempted to intervene. Triplett slashed the old man's throat, inflicting a serious but not mortal wound. He next menaced Peter Campell, who backed away from his assailant, then "brained" him with a heavy board lying in the yard. Triplett fell unconscious, his part in the fight—which had escalated into a melee involving eight other participants—concluded.[5]

The victims and witnesses in this violent episode promptly sought justice through the Western District Court. On Monday, April 25, the injured Edmund Campell swore out a complaint in Fort Smith (the charge was preprinted on the form, so common were such assaults in Parker's jurisdiction), as did his son. Three days later, both Campells, the elder Varnum, and all of the participants in the previous Sunday's disturbance gave testimony before U.S. Commissioner James Brizzolara, who in turn passed his findings on to the grand jury. On May 2 Triplett was indicted, and on May 3, only ten days after the disturbance at North Coffee Church, he appeared before Judge Parker in the custody of Marshal Dell, represented by the law firm of Marcum and Buckley, to plead not guilty and prepare for trial.[6]

In the next case on the day's docket, Parker accepted a plea in another deadly assault. Again the evidence was uncomplicated, although disputed. According to Indictment 1807, Leonard Fulsome attempted to kill Peter Johnson, "a Negro," on the night of December 8, 1880, in the Choctaw Nation. Fulsome and Johnson had been acquainted before the incident, which occurred after a dance, but neither had expressed any prior enmity toward the other. As Johnson and his companions returned from the promenade in his wagon, the defendant allegedly rode beside the travelers and fired two shots at Johnson. Fulsome adamantly denied these charges. He retained the services of attorney Thomas Barnes and entered a plea of "not guilty." A jury acquitted him when he was finally tried.[7]

Yet another assault indictment followed Fulsome's plea, this one originating with a mere verbal threat. On December 26, 1880, Frank Webster and John Bell spent the evening relaxing at the Eli Luman home in the Indian country. The conversation turned unpleasant when Webster cursed his employer (who was not present), vowing to "wring his neck." When Bell suggested that he could not successfully perform such an assault, Webster pulled a pistol. Mrs. Luman separated the combatants and expelled Webster from her home. Then, just after 2 o'clock the following morning, someone fired two bullets at Bell as he attempted to repair his wagon. Just after the shots, the intended victim claimed, Frank Webster rose from concealment nearby and fled into the darkness.[8]

Webster soon faced trial and punishment. On January 13, 1881, U.S. Deputy Marshal C. F. Heffington swore out a complaint against the accused assailant and arrested him. Represented by the Fort Smith law firm of Marcum and Buckley, Webster appeared before U.S. Commissioner Brizzolara on March 3. As a result of this initial inquiry, the case went to the grand jury, and on May 3 the panel returned Indictment 1808, charging the defendant with "assault with intent to kill." Webster pled not guilty, but to no avail. On May 26, 1881, despite his attorney's novel defense that the defendant was merely target practicing in the dark, a petit jury found Webster guilty. Two days later, Parker sentenced him to thirty months at hard labor in the Detroit, Michigan, House of Corrections.[9]

The next defendant had prior experience before the district court, but now returned on a less serious charge. On May 27, 1875, Isaac Morris had appeared before newly appointed Judge Parker, indicted for attempting to shoot one Richard Wilson. Apparently the jury accepted his explanation of the assault as an accident, for no records revealed a conviction. Now he answered to one of the most common charges in the Western District: "introducing" liquor into the Indian Territory in violation of the Indian Intercourse Act of 1834. Represented by Marcum and Buckley, he entered a plea of not guilty and then, unable to raise bail, returned to the basement jail to await trial.[10]

Judge Parker next diverted the court's attention briefly from indictments and pleas, pausing to confirm the appointment of bailiffs for the May term. Marshal Dell recommended five men— Samuel Peters, George H. Williams, John McCaldwell, Samuel Dean, and George Winton—whose duties would be to escort prisoners and witnesses, as well as to maintain order in the courtroom. The judge administered their oath of office and the new officials began their duties immediately.[11]

Following this administrative interlude, accused bootlegger Frank Woods entered his plea to a series of charges in a case that eventually required over a year to resolve. On August 9, 1880, U.S. Deputy Marshal Hugh Simpson charged Woods with "introducing"; Fort Smith officials issued a writ the next day. Then, early in November 1880, the Western District grand jury indicted Woods for "retail liquor distribution without the proper license," a charge that federal prosecutors frequently appended to such cases to ensure more severe sentencing. On May 3, 1881, perhaps unaware of this stratagem, the accused pled not guilty upon finally appearing before Parker. His trial, although delayed to gather witnesses for his defense, nevertheless ended in a guilty verdict. On September 5, 1881, Judge Parker sentenced him to fifteen months in the Detroit House of Correction and fined him one hundred dollars.[12]

The postponements in the Woods prosecution were minor, however, compared with those encountered by accused killer I. C. Miller. Charged with a murder committed during a New Year's Eve spree, he entered his plea during the May 3, 1881, proceedings after a series of delays and continuances; the case ultimately concluded even later. Miller, a sizable man fifty years of age, "talkative and always drunk when he [could] get whiskey," joined four others in the Chickasaw Nation, bibulously celebrating on December 31, 1878. When one of the revelers became too drunk, Miller and the others suggested leaving him at the homestead of C. S. Hughes. But the besotted companions grew angry when Hughes refused them hospitality. Shouting a string of foul oaths, they tore down his fence and challenged him to come out and fight. Then they were silent. A moment later Matthew Fletcher, a guest at the Hughes home, went to the door to see if the disturbance had subsided. A shot rang out and Fletcher staggered back, shot in the chest. Before dying the next morning, he identified Miller as his assailant.[13]

Miller fled the region after the shooting, thus beginning a series of proceedings that culminated over two years later. On January 7, 1879, U.S. Commissioner Stephen Wheeler issued a warrant for Miller's arrest, based on the testimony of I. C. Hughes. Deputy Marshal C. C. Ayers then tracked the accused murderer for three hundred miles, capturing him on July 7, 1880. Proceedings before Commissioner Wheeler began on September 29, 1880, and continued on October 2; on November 4 the grand jury charged Miller with murder. Requests by his attorneys for witnesses at government expense and a for continuance further delayed progress of the case; Miller entered his "not guilty" plea nearly two and a half years after the crime. When the case was finally tried, a petit jury acquitted I. C. Miller despite the deathbed testimony of Matthew Fletcher.[14]

In the next order of business, Judge Parker castigated several individuals whose failure to appear in court as promised delayed proceedings, first applying stern measures to prosecution witnesses in a Choctaw Nation larceny case. District Attorney William H. H.

Clayton moved for a continuance because his two principal com-
plainants, Robert Coleman and Charles W. Pryor, were not present.
Parker granted the motion, then issued writs of *serra facias*, demanding that the witnesses show cause for not appearing or face additional penalties. Additionally, he ordered an attachment on each,
confiscating as collateral the property that they had posted (a
common practice to guarantee the appearance of witnesses) and
mandating that they be brought before him "forthwith" to answer
contempt charges.[15]

This minor larceny case was, however, a simple one—and soon
to be resolved. On November 2, 1880, Eastman Jones, who "pass[ed]
for a nigger" but was more likely of "mixed" heritage, stole a hog
"worth four or five dollars" from Robert Coleman. Charles Pryor,
a neighbor, saw Jones with the animal. On January 26, 1881, Coleman and Pryor testified before Commissioner Stephen Wheeler,
and on February 2 the grand jury indicted Jones for larceny, now
valuing the purloined pig at ten dollars. Jailed since December 13,
1880, to await trial, the accused did not need to face his accusers to
know that their testimony would convict him. Thus Eastman Jones
pled guilty and, on May 28, 1881, received a three-month sentence.[16]

The next case of nonappearance on May 3 involved charges
against a colorful defendant and his hapless surety. Italian immi-
grant Francesco "Frank" Rocco was no ordinary bootlegger; the
scope of his criminal operations set him apart. He led a "desperate
band" of alcohol smugglers and horse thieves so successfully that
one Fort Smith newspaper dubbed him "King of the Whiskey
Dealers." Arrested earlier in the year with a confederate named
Satterfield, Rocco had posted bond and disappeared to plan his
retirement to Italy, vowing that "he would not be taken alive." His
unfortunate surety, Thomas H. Thomas, had also offered $500
bond to guarantee Rocco's presence in court; unable to locate his
erstwhile associate, he forfeited the money. Rocco lost $1,000—$500
on each of the two liquor charges for which he had posted bond.
In addition to confiscating the collateral, Parker issued an arrest
warrant and a writ of *serra facias* for "the King."[17]

But the missing whiskey peddler would soon appear before Judge Parker. Unfazed by Rocco's bravado, U.S. Deputy Marshal D. H. Layman captured the bootlegger. With a small posse, he set an ambush in a wooded area of the Indian Nations that Rocco and his gang frequented. After several days the outlaws finally appeared and a "terrible combat" ensued. Although severely wounded—a bullet struck Layman in the head, ranging downward into his neck—the deputy captured his quarry. Remarkably, he survived his injury to escort Rocco (who apparently had reconsidered his oath never to surrender) back to Fort Smith to face Judge Parker.[18]

Once before the district court, "King" Rocco found himself in the decidedly unregal accommodations of the overcrowded Fort Smith jail, where he faced harsh justice. Technically a first offender, the bootlegger might have received leniency; but District Attorney Clayton forestalled such an attempt. As a result, the grand jury handed down five separate indictments, charging Rocco with illegally introducing spiritous liquors into the Indian country and with acting as an alcohol retailer without first paying the required taxes. Thus, by filing as many charges as possible, federal officials hoped to imprison him for a term commensurate with his offenses. For his part, Rocco may have realized how fortunate he was to have avoided further charges in the wounding of Deputy Layman. Whatever his reasons, on Wednesday morning, August 3, 1881, Francesco "Frank" Rocco pled guilty to all counts. Judge Parker ordered him to serve five consecutive sentences of one year each and to pay fines totaling $350.[19]

On May 3, 1881, Judge Parker next disposed quickly of five minor liquor cases. A suspect named Green B. Parker, charged with one count of retail liquor distribution, changed his plea from not guilty to guilty; the judge suspended sentencing until the November term. He then dismissed "introducing" accusations against Tobias Ward and Charles Farley on the recommendation of District Attorney Clayton, while recording a similar charge against one Joseph Davis. Finally, Parker accepted a guilty plea for the same offense from Thomas J. Ray and sentenced him to thirty days in jail and a twenty-dollar fine.[20]

The next accused alcohol violator required more attention. Parker therefore presided while District Attorney Clayton and defense counsel James K. Barnes selected a jury and presented conflicting testimony in the case of Bill Blue. According to Indictments 1616 and 1617, sometime in January 1881, Blue, together with one Gabe Underwood, brought an unspecified amount of whiskey to Stonewall, Cherokee Nation. He denied the imputation strongly, stating that he had been raised to avoid spirits. Blue also avowed that Celias Ceanter—who had brought the charge—invented the complaint merely to divert attention from his own theft of horses from Underwood. The defense offered the testimony of Blue's father, King Blue, as well as that of his employer, "Old Man" Bradshaw, to support this version of the events. The prosecution, on the other hand, only repeated the charges in the original complaint. After hearing the presentations of both sides, Parker adjourned the matter until eight o'clock the following morning, when the jury acquitted Blue.[21]

Judge Parker next approved $1,389.25 in travel expenses incurred by Marshal Dell while escorting convicts to prisons in Detroit and Little Rock; then he attended to the last case of the day, yet another violent assault. On August 30, 1880, Elias Jenkins and his son visited the homestead of Samuel Kuhns near Vinita, Cherokee Nation, to borrow some corn. While gathering the grain, they discovered in Kuhns's field the bones of a sow that they believed to be theirs. Jenkins demanded immediate payment for the loss. But the "sodbuster" refused and a fistfight ensued. After being smashed in the eye and knocked to the ground, Kuhns angrily drew a pistol from his pocket and tried to shoot Kuhns, but the weapon misfired. As Kuhns advanced toward him with a club "four or five feet long." Jenkins called out to his son, "Shoot the son of a bitch—shoot him." Although armed with a double-barreled shotgun, the boy did not fire. Meanwhile, as Jenkins futilely snapped a pistol at the advancing farmer, Kuhns's dog attacked him, tearing viciously at his legs. Finally, on the fourth attempt, Jenkins's gun discharged, striking his opponent in the left breast and frightening the canine away. "You have shot me through the heart," Kuhns gasped as he stumbled into his house. "Damn your heart," Jenkins replied. "Look at what your dog done."[22]

Fortunately, Kuhns was mistaken about the severity of his wound; therefore, Jenkins faced only a charge of assault before the Parker court. Prior to adjournment on May 3, 1881, the judge oversaw the case of *United States v. Elias Jenkins* from jury selection to verdict. After twelve men had been chosen, all the participants in and several witnesses to the confrontation gave their accounts. The prosecution portrayed Jenkins as the aggressor. The defense, in turn, described the incident as mutual assault. By advancing with a deadly weapon, they argued, Kuhns had deliberately engaged in combat rather than retreat to avoid the use of lethal force, the traditional duty under common law. All witnesses agreed that the homesteader had moved toward Jenkins; the case therefore turned on the club itself. If it was a potentially lethal weapon, then two armed opponents had faced each other on relatively equal terms. If not, then Kuhns was a defenseless victim. Although he described the club as "an old rotten . . . ash limb," incapable of seriously injuring anyone, others described it as a solid "stick . . . two and one-half inches in diameter . . . about the size of a chair post." Believing the cudgel was a deadly weapon, the jury acquitted Jenkins. With the conclusion of this case, Judge Parker deferred further proceedings until the next morning.[23]

The court had performed an impressive amount of work for one day, demonstrating the ability to clear its caseload efficiently; yet such performance was unusual. Parker attended to seventeen cases in addition to receiving indictments, registering a new attorney, swearing in bailiffs, and approving travel expenses. Five of the seventeen criminal actions—nearly one-third—had been disposed of through dismissals, guilty pleas, and a trial; a sixth would be resolved the next morning. Judge Parker also oversaw one complete jury trial, and most of a second, after acting on some aspect of fifteen other cases. Yet such a pace was actually well above average for the Western District Court. Based on 290 working days annually for the 21 years that Parker presided, to clear the approximately 12,800 cases docketed required resolution of just over two cases per day. Of course, the speedy disposal of relatively minor offenses such as those heard on May 3, 1881, was necessary to allow for the additional time that serious offenses required. In 1882, for example, the court met for 291 days, 116 of which were devoted to murder trials alone.[24]

Compared with the overall statistics for the Parker years, some of those for May 3, 1881, corresponded relatively closely; others did not. Nonviolent crimes outnumbered violent crimes in both cases, but the single day's figures reflected a greater proportion (36 percent) of violence than the overall figure (23.1 percent). Murder, for example, made up 11.8 percent of the proceedings on May 3, 1881, as opposed to 9.4 percent of the total (including manslaughter) for all years. As in the total figures, liquor violations exceeded all other crimes, but by a far wider margin. Alcohol crimes made up 52 percent of the May 3 caseload while accounting for just over 30 percent of the total.[25]

Parker's battle to stem the flow of alcohol to the Indian Territory continued for twenty-one years, with varying success. The case of Arkansas whiskey peddler W. T. Sellars illustrated some of the frustrations involved in prosecuting such minor offenders. Charged in November 1881 with four counts of illegal liquor retailing, Sellars and his attorneys secured a postponement to obtain witnesses at government expense. His attestants, however, eluded court officials; therefore, on February 22, 1882, Judge Parker dismissed two of the charges for lack of evidence. Nearly eight months later, with other counts still pending, a bootlegger named William Fairn testified that he had been providing corn whiskey to Sellars in twenty-gallon batches since the spring of 1880. Court officials finally possessed sufficient evidence to convict the alcohol dealer. But by the time officers prepared and served the appropriate writs, W. T. Sellars had fled the Western District after diverting its resources from more important matters for over a year.[26]

Some liquor violators fled to avoid prosecution, some escaped charges completely, but nearly four thousand faced the varying consequences of their acts between 1875 and 1896. Because the law permitted Parker some discretion in sentencing, the punishments differed as much as the convicts. A hardened criminal like Francesco Rocco received the maximum penalty of three years—which was extended by manipulation of the charges—while a minor offender, William Tramel, served merely one hour in jail and paid a paltry five-dollar fine for "introducing." Overall, first convictions earned approximately six months per offense. Such Indian offenders as Henry Bearpaw and his brother Daniel, Union Bearhead, and the Creek bootlegger Siller fared no better or no worse in court because of their ethnicity. Parker usually determined sentences based on the severity of the crime, as well as the character and background of the perpetrator. However, he sometimes took liberties with his powers. For example, on November 29, 1875, one Charles D. Miller pled guilty to violating revenue retail liquor laws, and Parker sentenced him to six months confinement. The next day a jury found Columbus Gentry—who cost the court extra time and money by exercising his right to a trial—guilty of the same offense: yet he received eight months. The federal jail was unusually overcrowded at the time, and trials in such minor cases clogged an already jammed docket. Thus the additional sentence served as an inducement for attorneys to expedite lesser proceedings by pleading their clients "guilty."[27]

The attention of the federal government to the intent and execution of liquor restrictions indicated the importance of such regulations in the nineteenth century. Supporters of the laws contended that alcohol was ruinous to health and a catalyst for violence. In 1881, the editors of Fort Smith's *New Era* praised Parker for "coming down pretty heavily on these whiskey fellows," who were "the indirect cause of a majority of the murders committed in [the Indian] country." The Western District docket for May 3, 1881, provided support for such an assertion. Thomas Triplett, for example, arrived at church drunk the morning that he assaulted

Edmund and Peter Campell; I. C. Miller and his rowdy companions all drank heavily in the hours prior to the shooting of Matthew
Fletcher. More recently, historians have concurred in the relationship between alcohol and frontier mayhem. One has described the
brutal chaos that often ensued from "the whiskey menace."
Another has explained how, throughout the frontier, "drink
enhanced self-importance, impaired judgment, generated heed-
less courage, and encouraged unreasoning resort to violence." Yet
another has pointed out the significant role liquor played in violent
confrontations across the West, from saloon brawls to the legen-
dary "Gunfight at the O.K. Corral."[28]

Fueled by the liquor trade, violent crime constituted nearly
one-fourth of the Western District Court's business, with capital
offenses—murder and rape—making up 42 percent of the brutality. Some slayers killed for no better reason than to acquire their
victim's boots or a bottle of bad whiskey; they raped because the
urge struck and no one prevented them; they resorted to gunplay
at the slightest perceived insult—and shot to kill. Frank Webster
and Elias Jenkins, for example, quickly resorted to lethal force after
minor verbal confrontations—one over a difference of opinion and
the other over the bones of a sow.[29]

And such offenses continued to clog the Western District docket
as long as the court held jurisdiction over the Indian Territory.
Although federal prosecutors achieved a ratio of approximately
five convictions for each acquittal, crime perpetually exceeded
punishment in Parker's jurisdiction. Between 1875 and 1896, Fort
Smith grand juries issued 3,942 indictments for murder alone. Only
161 of the alleged killers were finally convicted and sentenced.
Many suspects escaped, others died resisting arrest, still others
won acquittal. The unavoidable fact remains that many of the
worst criminals in the Indian country avoided punishment despite
the best efforts of Parker and his officers.[30]

The size and complexity of the Western District jurisdiction
worked against efficient enforcement. To uphold all federal
statutory and common law in an expanse of 74,000 square miles,

overrun by innumerable criminal intruders of every stripe, was too massive a responsibility for any court, especially when its proceedings occurred hundreds of miles away from the crime scenes. Even with a small army of federal deputies, Parker could only hope to capture a percentage of the malefactors. Further complicating such efforts was the system of coexisting jurisdictions that enticed lawbreakers to the region. No American Indian court could pass judgment on a white perpetrator, and the Fort Smith court held no authority over the worst Indian offenders unless their crimes involved U.S. citizens; thus the vagaries of tribal citizenship often preempted federal authority. But despite such insurmountable obstacles, Parker and his officers continued their battle against crime in the Western District, resolutely if not efficiently, until 1896.

CHAPTER SEVEN

"Indian Invaders"

American Indian Issues

Most of the business transacted in the Parker court resulted from its jurisdiction over the Indian country. Defined by "an act to regulate trade and intercourse with the Indian tribes and preserve peace on the frontiers" of June 30, 1834, the new Indian Territory served the federal policy of Indian Removal. Sincere humanitarians, convinced that American Indians' best chances for survival lay in isolation from the dominant culture and its vices, joined with avaricious speculators and harassed government officials to relocate eastern tribes west of the Mississippi. These unsettled lands offered a refuge for dispossessed natives to escape the encroaching armies of settlers and thereby avoid conflict. Living in a region that white homesteaders would never want, proponents theorized, American Indians could follow their traditional ways under their own legal systems. Only when an Indian committed a crime against a white man, or vice versa, would federal rule intrude.[1]

By 1875, however, circumstances had changed dramatically. Westward expansion had continued unabated and the Indian Territory, no longer isolated from American rapaciousness, had become a refuge for criminals from the surrounding states and a lure for land-hungry homesteaders. Swarming in with the crews building the transcontinental railroads, lawbreakers of every description found haven in "the Nations." The Indian courts were ineffective in such cases, completely powerless to try white offenders. In addition, bills to open the region to increased settlement, establishing a territorial government and thereby extinguishing traditional native systems of law and land tenure, continued to be introduced in Congress. Thus the rightful American Indian inhabitants now confronted threats from criminal intruders within and expansionist forces without.[2]

As early as 1851, the Western Judicial District of Arkansas maintained a responsibility to protect the native population that Judge Parker would continue to uphold. On May 10, 1875, upon assuming his duties at Fort Smith, he emphasized this role as guardian of law-abiding Indians, while charging the grand jury with its duties. The laws governing the Indian country existed "for the purpose of protection," he told them, and "they [would] be enforced by this court with that purpose alone in view." In fact, both he and the grand jury shared "the responsibility of seeing to it that the laws for the protection of that country [were] so enforced, that the good shall be protected from the bad."[3]

Parker further clarified to the grand jury its authority over felons of varied citizenship. "You have jurisdiction of all offenses of an Indian against a white man or a colored man," he explained to the panel. The reverse was also true of crimes "committed by those persons against an Indian." Oftentimes, however, the official nationality of a prisoner determined the punishment. If the white or African-American defendant claimed citizenship in an Indian tribe—and proved it—then the Western District Court was powerless to act.[4]

Two bigamy cases before the Parker court in 1886 illustrated the effects of citizenship on jurisdiction. Although both actions involved white perpetrators and Cherokee spouses, the outcomes contrasted sharply. The facts of the Matthew Flannigan case appeared simple enough, complicated mainly by his attempts at concealment. In July 1886, he eloped with Louisa Hendrix, a fourteen-year-old Cherokee girl. Unfortunately, Flannigan had another wife, whom he had married under Cherokee law four years earlier. This was a clear-cut case of bigamy. In order to create the appearance of a valid second marriage, he drew up a property settlement, dated it prior to the July wedding, and asked his first wife, N. J. Flannigan, to sign it. While awaiting her decision, he placed a petition for divorce on the September docket of the Circuit Court for the Delaware District of the Cherokee Nation.[5]

But such attempts at obfuscation were of little use. Flannigan, although having married and sought divorce under Cherokee law, remained a citizen of the United States. The Western District Court was already investigating him, and its ongoing proceedings sent his case before the grand jury. On August 28, 1886, Mary Weaver, the legal guardian of Louisa Hendrix, wrote to U.S. Commissioner John Q. Tufts at Muskogee, Creek Nation, describing both the July wedding and Flannigan's marital status. Tufts convened a hearing at Muskogee on October 19, 1886, taking testimony from the accused bigamist as well as from Louisa Hendrix, Mary Weaver, a Parson Tucker who had performed the illegal ceremony, and Deputy U.S. Marshal L. P. Isabel, who had investigated the case. The evidence confirmed that Flannigan had married Louisa without the consent of her guardian and that the second marriage had occurred before the defendant began attempts to dissolve his first union. Commissioner Tufts therefore sent the case to the Western District grand jury at Fort Smith.[6]

Once the case reached the grand jury, it concluded quickly. On Saturday, November 6, 1886, Indictment 1624 charged Flannigan with one count of bigamy. Then, on the following Monday morning, he appeared before Judge Parker to plead "guilty." His plea, saving the court the time and expense of a trial, probably mitigated in his favor. At any rate, Parker sentenced him to serve only six months in jail at Fort Smith and pay a fine of $100, a light sentence for such an offense.[7]

On the other hand, Indian citizenship completely saved Ally Baily from punishment, despite the parallels between her offense and Flannigan's. She likewise married a Cherokee, Mark Christian, on May 1, 1886. Her first husband, Jack Baily, filed a complaint with Commissioner Tufts on May 10. In the proceedings the following day, Ally produced a certificate confirming her citizenship in the Cherokee Nation. Since a marriage between two Indians, bigamous or otherwise, was outside Western District jurisdiction, Tufts ordered her discharged, pencilling on the complaint: "guilty of bigamy but is a Cherokee—white as anybody!" The color of her skin, however, was of no consequence; her legal status as a Cherokee spared her the punishment that Matthew Flannigan faced for similar actions.[8]

The most commonly prosecuted offense in the Western District Court, providing ardent spirits to American Indians, had been forbidden since the earliest laws governing Indian-white relations. Parker enforced this embargo with the support of the tribes inhabiting the Indian Territory—and for good reason. The Indian Intercourse acts passed in 1802, 1832, and 1834 banned the introduction, sale, or manufacture of distilled beverages among American Indians, and Congress reaffirmed this policy with further legislation in 1864, 1877, and 1892. Indians, as well as whites concerned with their welfare, decried the effects of liquor on native culture. Whiskey demoralized American Indians, they contended, breaking down their health as well as their resistance to other vices, and rendered them more pliable in negotiations with land swindlers. As a consequence of these ill effects, temperance movements evolved within many tribes. As early as 1820, the Choctaws appointed an agent to confiscate any alcohol imported into their lands. By 1836, hundreds of Cherokees had "taken the pledge"; in 1841, prohibition became law on all their tribal lands. At a meeting in 1856, held at Lenox Church, Indian Territory, 238 Choctaws promised total abstinence; twenty years later, 120 more followed suit at Big Lick Church, Choctaw Nation. And in March of 1879, Creek Chief Ward Coachman dispatched a company of Indian police to Muskogee with orders to force "all engaged in the whiskey traffic . . . to leave, bag and baggage, within two hours."[9]

Although such criminal cases filled most of Judge Parker's docket, his authority extended into other areas of jurisprudence.

He held collateral circuit court powers over all federal equity cases arising within the Western District; any lawsuit involving interstate commerce, for example, came before the Fort Smith bench. Parker also exercised the right to rule on the constitutionality of any incarceration in his district through writs of habeas corpus. During his long judicial career, Parker decided cases concerning American Indian rights in each of these areas.[10]

In 1879, an apparently minor criminal violation produced a ruling by Parker on the legal status of Indian land tenure. On January 8, 1879, Cherokee Lighthorse police arrested Ben Reese, an African American, chopping wood just south of the Kansas border in the Cherokee Nation. Forbidden to try Reese in their judicial system, the Lighthorsemen turned him over to federal authorities at Fort Smith and charged him with cutting timber on government lands. On April 4, 1879, the defendant cheerfully admitted before U.S. Commissioner Stephen Wheeler that he had been cutting timber on Cherokee lands for several months, hauling it back to Kansas and selling it for $2.50 a load. His attorneys also acknowledged such actions, but insisted no violation of law had taken place. Consequently, they filed a demurrer with the court, stipulating that Reese's acts "[did] not constitute a public offense" and that the court had "no jurisdiction of the offense charged."[11]

Judge Parker upheld the demurrer and dismissed the case, but not without an acid commentary. Technically, he conceded, Ben Reese had not violated the law. Indian holdings were not defined as "government lands" under the criminal statutes; therefore, Reese had not broken federal law. The Western District accordingly exercised no authority over American Indian landholdings. Of course, Native American tribunals could still enforce property rights, but only against other Indians. In other words, the Cherokees—and by extension, all American Indians—maintained no legal remedy against U.S. citizens who expropriated their common property. But Parker was livid. Handing down his decision, he railed that he held no power over a whole "class of men . . . who revel[ed] in the idea that they [had] an inherent right to steal from the Indians." Parker, although believing Reese to be an ordinary thief, was forced to uphold the law and discharge him.[12]

In 1881, guardianship over federal possessions presented the central issue in another Parker decision. The lands in question totaled 1,675,000 acres of prime farmland, a magnet to colonizers despite their disputed status: the "Ceded" or "Unassigned Lands" of the central Indian country. As a consequence of their Confederate allegiance during the Civil War, the Creek and Seminole nations ceded the western portions of their landholdings to the United States in 1866 as a future home for Plains Indians. By 1879, a few members of the Sac, Fox, and Kickapoo tribes had settled in the region, but a large portion of the territory remained unassigned. The image of over a million acres of arable soil lying fallow incensed potential homesteaders in adjoining states—1,600,000 acres amounted to a potential of 10,000 homesteads. Under the treaties of 1866, they reasoned, American Indians had surrendered their titles for the express purpose of locating conquered western nomads there. If thirteen years later the government had not yet populated the area as intended, then the lands surely belonged in the public domain and thus ought to be opened to settlement under the Homestead Act. Federal officials contended, however, that the unassigned portions remained part of the Indian Territory—and therefore exempt from white incursion—until Washington determined their final disposition.[13]

In 1880, led by promoter David L. Payne and the mixed-blood Cherokee lawyer Elias Boudinot, the homesteaders forced a pair of confrontations that eventually brought the status of the Unassigned Lands before the Western District Court. Boudinot—probably employed as a publicist by the Missouri, Kansas and Texas Railroad—outlined the case for occupying the lands. In articles for regional newspapers, he painted glowing pictures of fertile, well-watered fields awaiting the farmer's plow. Hundreds of homesteaders, drawn by these rosy descriptions and a hunger for free land, flocked to southern Kansas, establishing tent cities near Baxter Springs and Arkansas City. In response, the U.S. Army sent

troops under Generals Philip Sheridan and John Pope to keep the
migrants out of the Indian Territory. But on the evening of April
26, 1880, David L. Payne, a former Indian fighter, Kansas state
legislator, and most recently assistant doorkeeper of the U.S. House
of Representatives, quietly led a small party of "boomers" (as the
settlers were nicknamed) across Bitter Creek from Kansas into "the
Nations." With scouts in advance and flankers posted along their
line of march, the intruders encountered no opposition; within a
week, they were staking claims and constructing a stockade on the
Canadian River, a few miles west of present-day Oklahoma City.
Payne dispatched a messenger to Wichita, Kansas, with an announce-
ment dated May 3, 1880, boastfully declaring the "public lands in
the Indian Territory . . . not only open to settlement, but settled."[14]

The Army viewed the situation differently. On May 15, 1880,
Lieutenant G. H. G. Gale and a squad of Fourth Cavalry troopers
arrested Payne and his associates, then escorted them to the Kansas
border—where they received a hero's welcome on June 6. Only a
month later, on July 6, the Payne boomers launched a second foray
into the Ceded Lands. Once again the Army captured the interlopers, who this time were not merely ejected. On August 12, the
"Indian Invaders," as one newspaper called them, rode into Fort
Smith under military escort to face Judge Parker.[15]

On August 13, 1880, U.S. District Attorney William H. H. Clayton
filed a civil complaint against Payne; the resulting stratagems on
both sides delayed a decision in the case until the following spring.
In the summons that Clayton issued, the United States requested
that the Western District Court order Payne to pay damages of
$1,000 for his illegal presence in the Indian country on May 3 and
August 10, 1880. In essence, the government was suing the boomer,
rather than charging him with a crime. Judge Parker set a trial date
of November 3 for this civil action. Payne failed to appear in court
on that day, but his attorney, none other than Elias Boudinot,
unsuccessfully filed a motion to dismiss the case "for want of jurisdiction." Thus, on December 31, 1880, the defendant and his
lawyer presented a full answer to the government suit. Payne

denied that he owed the United States any money, asserting that he had not been in the Indian Territory on the dates in question, but rather on public lands belonging to the U.S. government and its citizens. Contrary to the federal charges, Payne asserted, he was the injured party; he demanded $25,000 in damages. On March 7, 1881, District Attorney Clayton filed a demurrer, whereupon Payne filed an amended answer, which in turn triggered another government response. Both sides having exhausted their arsenal of maneuvers, Parker was finally able to render a decision.[16]

On May 2, 1881, nearly a year after Payne had first been ejected from the disputed area, Judge Parker ruled against the boomers. First, he attacked the legitimacy of Payne's homestead claim in the Unassigned Lands. Even if the region were subject to the Homestead Act of 1862, the intruder had staked a claim far exceeding the 160 acres allowed by law. But the lands were not, Parker determined, open for settlement. The original American Indian owners had ceded their property to the United States in 1866 "to locate other Indians . . . thereon." Although the government had not settled the entire region, it had never disavowed its original purpose in acquiring the land. Therefore, the area remained part of the Indian Territory; white intruders faced expulsion; and David Payne owed the United States of America $1,000.[17]

Although Parker had taken a firm position against white encroachment, his decision resolved little. The majority of American Indians opposed to opening the Indian Territory for settlement now had a legal precedent to point to, but their rivals, with more capital backing them, continued to test the status of the Ceded Lands in other courts. Railroads sought lucrative land grants, boomers free homesteads, and mixed-bloods like Elias Boudinot prestigious positions that territorial status would engender; one judicial decision could not turn aside their cupidity. Parker failed even to collect the forfeiture he had ordered: Payne owned no assets to attach, and the law provided no other means of enforcement. He continued his colonization efforts, continued to be arrested, and continued to be defended by railroad lawyers, until his sudden death from a pulmonary blood clot in November, 1884. His followers, however, persisted in their efforts to settle the Indian Territory.[18]

Late in 1884, Indian frustrations with boomer activities led to a habeas corpus case in the Western District Court. The facts of *Ex Parte Rogers* were relatively uncomplicated. In addition to the Unassigned Lands, boomers also claimed access to the Cherokee Outlet—or "Strip"—in the northwestern Indian Territory despite the objections of the Cherokees, who profitably leased over six million acres of the region for grazing land. In the fall of 1884, Lighthorse policeman Connell Rogers proceeded beyond mere eviction; he burned an interloper shack in "the Strip." The owner therefore charged Officer Rogers with arson, and officials of the U.S. District Court at Wichita, Kansas, claiming jurisdiction under an 1883 redistricting law, issued a warrant for his arrest. Knowing that Judge Parker had ruled against boomers in the Payne case, Rogers fled the bailiwick of the Kansas court to Fort Smith. On December 30, 1884, he surrendered and thereupon petitioned for a writ of habeas corpus to avoid extradition to Wichita.[19]

As a consequence, the boomers provided Parker the opportunity to rule on Indian land tenure, and once more he supported the majority of American Indians. On April 27, 1885, the jurist granted Rogers—who had been at liberty on bail since January 20—the desired writ. He ruled that the Cherokee Outlet, like the Ceded Lands, remained closed to settlement and a part of the Indian country. As such, the region fell under the jurisdiction of the Western District; therefore, the Kansas district court had issued an invalid warrant. Even if the burned-out homesteader had filed charges in the proper venue, Parker would have dismissed the case. Rogers had acted within his authority as a police officer in burning the squatter's shanty and ejecting the intruder from Indian lands. Consequently, he went free, and American Indians pointed to one more small victory in their struggle against encroaching settlers.[20]

Such habeas corpus cases frequently afforded Parker an occasion to rule on some facet affecting the legal status of Indians. In

1877, for example, his decision on the case *Ex Parte Reynolds* had narrowed the jurisdiction of American Indian courts and had further incurred the wrath of expansion-oriented whites. Issuing the writ in December of that year, Parker ruled that the mixed-blood petitioner Reynolds, by virtue of his white ancestry, was "amenable to the laws of the United States" and hence not subject to the authority of Indian tribunals, despite his adoption as a Choctaw. Although the decision—which was later reversed—temporarily diminished the authority of Choctaw courts, the expansionist editors of one Fort Smith newspaper, *Wheeler's Western Independent*, were outraged by Parker's decision. His ruling lent legitimacy to "petty Indian governments," which should "be set aside by Congress," the *Independent* opined, "and a territorial government [should be] established over the whole Indian country west of Arkansas" to pave the way for settlement.[21]

In a third habeas corpus case, Parker ruled on the ability of Indian courts to extradite criminals who had fled their jurisdiction. The facts seemed relatively straightforward. On April 25, 1883, Frank Morgan fatally shot Albert Johnson, who was sheriff of the Sequoyah district of the Cherokee Nation, claiming self-defense. Both men were Indians, and thus under the authority of the Cherokee judicial system. Morgan, fearing retribution from his victim's friends, many of whom occupied prominent positions in district government, fled to Arkansas. On July 13, 1883, Dennis W. Bushyhead, principal chief of the Cherokee Nation, signed a requisition, entreating Arkansas Governor James H. Berry to issue a warrant for Morgan's arrest and return to tribal authorities. Berry complied on August 18, sending a copy of the document to every county sheriff in the state. Then on September 11, Sebastian County Sheriff H. I. Falconer arrested Morgan at Fort Smith and notified the Indian officials to collect their prisoner.[22]

Morgan, fearing for his life if returned to Cherokee custody, retained attorney Thomas Marcum to plead in federal court for his release. A petition dated September 11, 1883—the day of Morgan's arrest—requested a writ of habeas corpus on the grounds that

Sheriff Falconer held his prisoner illegally. Dennis Bushyhead had no authority, the attorney contended, to ask any governor of any state to arrest criminals on his behalf; such extradition authority rested with the executive of a state or territory, and the position of principal chief of the Cherokee Nation did not meet that qualification. Governor Berry had therefore acted improperly in issuing the arrest warrant, Marcum asserted, as had Sheriff Falconer in executing it. Citing additionally the prisoner's fear for his safety, his lawyer requested that Morgan be discharged from custody immediately.[23]

Parker partly granted the petition, issuing a writ of habeas corpus on September 12 and thereby setting the stage for a final ruling. Attorney Marcum had filed a meritorious petition, one that would require further evaluation. In the meantime, Sheriff Falconer was forbidden to turn his charge over to the Cherokees; furthermore, he was ordered to file a response to the charges made in the petition, showing just cause for Morgan's arrest. On October 1, 1883, the sheriff complied with the order of the court, claiming Chief Bushyhead's requisition and Governor Berry's warrant as his authority. Then Marcum filed an answer similar to his original petition, charging those documents to be extralegal and improper.[24]

Judge Parker, who had been carefully studying a California decision on extradition, was now ready to issue a decision. His ruling upheld every point in the Marcum petition, thus further limiting the powers of Indian courts. Citing the California Supreme Court decision in *Ex Parte James Romaine, et al.,* Parker agreed that a valid extradition must originate with the executive of a state or territory. As principal chief of the Cherokees, Bushyhead represented only one tribe in the Indian country and, therefore, he could not claim to be the political leader of the entire region. Hence the requisition, the warrant, and the arrest were all improper, and the petitioner should be released. Parker's decision extended far beyond Frank Morgan, however; it wholly denied the authority of Native-American tribunals to extradite. Without a territorial or state governor to issue requests on behalf of the whole region, the individual tribes possessed no legal means to compel fleeing criminals to return and face trial.[25]

Judge Parker had defined the limits of Cherokee judicial authority in *Ex Parte Morgan;* he clarified their sovereignty with his decision in *Cherokee Nation v. Southern Kansas Railway.* Congress unwittingly initiated the controversy. On July 4, 1884, members passed an act granting the Southern Kansas Railway Corporation permission to build a line across the Cherokee Nation and allowing the Indians to be justly compensated. The law specified the exact route for the railroad, instructing that no unnecessary permanent structures be erected along the right of way. A panel of referees, appointed by the president, would determine proper recompense to the American Indians, who, in turn, could challenge the arbiters' decision in federal court.[26]

The Cherokees protested even before the commissioners could determine the appropriate payment, and eventually they brought their objections to the Western District Court. On December 12, 1884, the tribe sent its first notice of disapproval to Washington. Two more followed: on April 14, 1886, and on December 17, 1886. Although the presidential referees had awarded the Cherokees $7,352.94 for the right of way on October 29, 1886, Chief Bushyhead and the National Council found the offer inadequate.[27]

Consequently, on February 18, 1887, the Cherokee Nation filed suit against the Southern Kansas Railway Company in the U.S. Court for the Western District of Arkansas. The Indians contended that as a result of a series of treaties from 1785 to 1866, the United States recognized the Cherokees as a sovereign nation; accordingly, Congress had no authority to grant the right of way specified in the act of July 4, 1884. The American Indians therefore asked the court to enjoin the Southern Kansas from further construction and to order the railroad to vacate Cherokee lands. If Parker refused to grant the injunction, then they asked that he fix and award compensation for the tribe as stipulated in the 1884 law.[28]

On February 21, 1888, after more than a year of motions and countermotions by each side, Judge Parker ruled in behalf of the railroad. Despite the treaties cited by the Cherokees in their complaint, he asserted, the United States maintained ultimate sovereignty over all lands within its borders, including the Indian country. American Indian governments exercised their powers at the pleasure of the United States. In assigning the right of way through Cherokee lands, Congress had acted properly; the complaint was groundless. The Indians had also improperly sought both equitable and legal damages in their suit, instead of filing separate actions for each remedy as required. Parker dismissed the case, further ordering the Indians to pay the legal fees of the railroad.[29]

The Cherokees, upon appealing their case to the U.S. Supreme Court, won an incomplete victory. On May 19, 1890, the high court reversed Parker and ordered him to set and to award compensation for the tribe. The decision did not take issue with his pronouncements on sovereignty, only with the failure to award recompense as intended by the 1884 law. On January 19, 1892, after nearly eight years of legal wrangling, Judge Parker concluded the matter by awarding the Cherokee Nation $7,502, the original amount set by the referees, plus the cost of the Supreme Court appeal.[30]

Although biographers would later describe Parker as "a friend to the Indian[s]" citing his public praise of their virtues, most of his rulings on American Indian issues reduced tribal authority in favor of the federal government, hastening the dissolution of traditional cultures among the Five Tribes. His decision in the Cherokee-railroad dispute upheld United States sovereignty over their lands; his habeas corpus pronouncements in the *Reynolds* and *Morgan* cases limited the powers of tribal courts. Even when the decisions seemed to favor American Indians, as in *U.S. v. Payne* and *Ex Parte Rogers*, federal dominion was the basis for his edicts. Parker, in situations requiring him either to recognize the jurisdiction of native tribunals or expand that of the Western District Court, typically opted in favor of his own power. His duty was to interpret and apply federal law, which overwhelmingly served the interests of white Americans over those of Indians. Bound by the rule of law,

Parker necessarily set aside his own feelings toward American Indians and applied the law as it existed.[31]

Yet such decisions supported the crusade for territorial status in the Indian country, a movement Parker had come to oppose during his years on the Fort Smith bench. Many advocates of expansion targeted the tribal judicial and landholding systems as obstacles to settlement. Communal property rights, and the courts that upheld them, would need to be extinguished before homesteaders could survey and claim individual plots. Thus, each Parker decision that chipped away at American Indian sovereignty aided expansionism. The judge argued paternalistically against the creation of a new territory in "the Nations," charging that the Five Tribes were not yet ready for full assimilation; their "ignorance" of Anglo-American land tenure customs rendered them too susceptible to fraud. He never challenged the goals of the territorial movement, only the timing of its implementation.[32]

American Indians in "the Nations," keenly aware that their traditional way of life was at stake, participated actively in the cases affecting them in the Parker court and reacted strongly to his rulings. Full-blooded members of the Five Tribes generally opposed territorial status; mixed-bloods tended to favor it. Thus, while Elias Boudinot, the son of a Cherokee father and a white mother, represented boomer David Payne in his 1881 civil action, full-blood delegates from all five "Civilized Tribes" met to raise $4,820 for American Indian lawyers willing to assist the prosecution. In 1878, after Parker ruled in the *Reynolds* case that adopted citizens of Indian tribes remained under federal jurisdiction, Choctaw lawyers appealed to the attorney general and won. In 1882 the Cherokee National Council instructed its representatives in Washington to protest "the encroachment and abuse" of Western District officers who continued to assume authority over adopted Cherokees "in plain violation of the plain letter of the treaties."[33]

From his second term in Congress to his last days on the Fort Smith bench, Isaac Parker remained involved with American Indian issues. Although he frequently praised Indians, his actions often injured their interests. Such ambivalence reflected white attitudes in the nineteenth century. Like many more active reformers, Parker presumed that his duty was to help American Indians assimilate into a superior culture, not to preserve their traditions. Virtually all the Indian legislation that he introduced or supported in the House of Representatives facilitated that goal. He approached his role as judge over the Indian Territory in much the same light, as a protector of a less-evolved people. Although some of his decisions weakened tribal rights, he believed that such rulings at least prepared American Indians for the time when they would participate fully in white society. Still, a basic sense of fairness influenced his positions. He agitated for payment of Choctaw and Chickasaw claims in Congress because the government owed the debt; he opposed a rush to settle the Indian Territory to prevent the inhabitants from being swindled. Surely his attitudes were paternalistic and ethnocentric, but his actions afforded the most legal protection available to the native inhabitants of the Indian Territory under a system that favored the white citizens of an expanding nation.

CHAPTER EIGHT

"STARVING WITNESSES"

Reform and Retrenchment, 1883–1889

On August 5, 1882, Hiram Price, commissioner of Indian Affairs, received an unusual request from the president of the Fair Association of Western Arkansas—Isaac Parker. For one of the "attractions" in the annual exposition at Fort Smith, he wrote, "we want to have some Osage Indians, say twenty." Although the Osage agent in the Indian Territory had already approved the appearance, Parker "thought it best" to secure the permission of Commissioner Price as well. He promised to "take good care" of the Osages and argued that their "visit" would "have a good effect on the Indians." Price replied favorably the same day, and American Indians became fixtures in the Western Arkansas Fair for the next several years.[1]

This request illustrated Parker's growing participation in Fort Smith affairs and demonstrated his importance to the community. As president of the fair association, he promoted Fort Smith and the surrounding counties. At the 1886 exposition, he even participated in a mock stagecoach robbery in which convicted horse thief Belle Starr, recently returned from a Parker prison term, led the theatrical "outlaws." Other civic activities also reflected his stature as an influential citizen. Parker served for four years on the school board and was president of the Social Reading Club; in addition,

he aided in establishing the first library and the first hospital at
Fort Smith. He also joined the Grand Army of the Republic, the
Union veterans' organization, as well as fraternal associations such
as the Odd Fellows and the Knights of Honor. By the 1880s, Parker
had become a prime example of the substantial citizen, dedicated
to his family, involved in his community, and prominent in his
profession.[2]

But from 1883 to 1889, Judge Parker, despite such social status
in his adopted hometown, faced mounting challenges. The U.S.
Justice Department continually badgered him to reduce expenditures for his court and the federal jail. Criticism of his methods
increased in Washington and in Fort Smith; by 1889, new legislation permitted the U.S. Supreme Court to review his capital
sentences. Parker argued with superiors over the prisons to which
he sentenced convicts, and contended with judges from adjacent
bailiwicks regarding authority in the Indian Territory. And, beginning in 1883, Congress initiated a series of reductions in the Parker
court's jurisdiction that would culminate in the complete removal
of its powers over the Indian country by 1896.

The contraction of the Western District originated with a bill to
establish a federal court in the Indian Territory. Late in 1881, U.S.
Senator George Vest (D-MO.), an expansionist opponent of tribal
sovereignty, and a harsh critic of the Fort Smith court, sponsored
a bill that would create a separate federal judicial district within
the Indian Territory. The legislation stalled, only to be replaced by
a House measure redistributing the western half of the region
between existing district courts in Kansas and Texas. Vest initially
opposed the House bill, delaying its enactment for nearly a year.
But eventually he relented, and the Courts Act of 1883 entered the
statute books on January 6.[3]

This legislation reduced Parker's jurisdiction by half. Under the
new arrangement, all lands in the Indian Territory north of the
Canadian River but west of the Cherokee, Creek, and Seminole
nations were now part of the Judicial District of Kansas, with courts
at Wichita and Fort Scott. The region west of the Chickasaw Nation

and south of the Canadian fell under the jurisdiction of the Northern District of Texas; proceedings would be held at Graham. The Fort Smith court retained federal authority only over the eastern half of the Indian country, in the lands of the Five Civilized Tribes.[4]

But such redistricting did little to reduce the burdens of the Parker court or to increase those of the Kansas and Texas districts. The reassigned lands were the least populated regions in the Indian country. The immense distance from Fort Smith and the sparse settlement of the western Indian Territory had always hindered enforcement activity by Parker officers; deputies seldom ventured beyond the domain of the Five Tribes even before their jurisdiction was reduced. The new arrangement thus failed to shrink the case-load substantially or to increase the efficiency of the Western District court dramatically.[5]

The reassignment of federal authority did, however, set the stage for a jurisdictional dispute between two of the district courts holding sway over the Indian country. In 1885 Judge Parker ruled in *Ex Parte Rogers* that his court maintained control over the Cherokee Outlet, although the region had been assigned to the Kansas district under the Courts Act of 1883. The law granted the Western District of Arkansas jurisdiction over the lands of the Five Civilized Tribes. Parker therefore argued that his district encompassed all lands controlled by the Cherokees, including the Outlet—which lay outside the borders of their Nation—so long as the tribe held title to the area. As a consequence, he granted a writ of habeas corpus against an arson indictment issued by the federal court at Wichita. But his decision failed to resolve the jurisdictional question. Shortly after the *Rogers* case, U.S. Supreme Court Justice David Brewer, ruling for the Eighth Circuit, reaffirmed that the Outlet was part of the Kansas district. But this decision ignored the issue of Cherokee title and, therefore, did not directly overturn Parker's pronouncement. Federal jurisdiction over the disputed region remained nebulous until May 2, 1890, when President Benjamin Harrison placed the Cherokee Outlet under the authority of courts in the new Oklahoma Territory.[6]

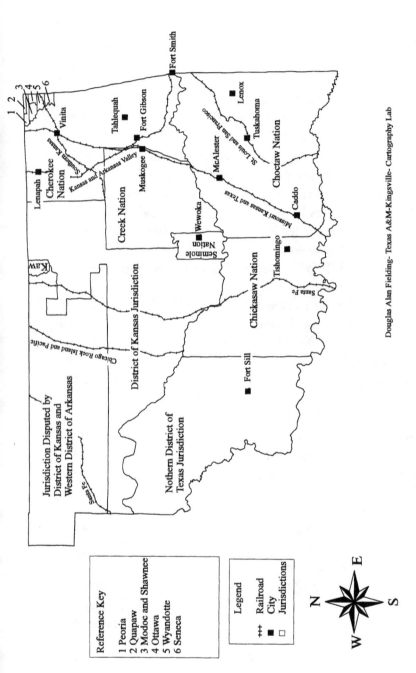

Reference Key

1 Peoria
2 Quapaw
3 Modoc and Shawnee
4 Ottawa
5 Wyandotte
6 Seneca

Legend

+++ Railroad
■ City
□ Jurisdictions

N
W E
S

Jurisdiction Disputed by
District of Kansas and
Western District of Arkansas

District of Kansas Jurisdiction

Nothern District of
Texas Jurisdiction

Kaw

Cherokee
Nation

Lenapah

Creek Nation

Muskogee

Seminole
Nation

Wewoka

Chickasaw Nation

Tishomingo

Fort Sill

Vinita

Tahlequah

Fort Gibson

McAlester

Caddo

Choctaw Nation

Lenox

Tuskahoma

Fort Smith

Southern Kansas

Kansas and Arkansas Valley

St. Louis and San Francisco

Missouri Kansas and Texas

Chicago Rock Island and Pacific

Santa Fe

Santa Fe

Douglas Alan Fielding- Texas A&M-Kingsville- Cartography Lab

2. Indian Territory jurisdiction of the Western District Court, 1883–89. *Map by Douglas Alan Fielding, Texas A&M at Kingsville, Cartography Lab.*

Although the Western District territory had diminished, its case-load and expenses multiplied during the 1880s, due in large part to the growing population in the Indian Territory. The Parker court, always the most expensive domain in the federal judicial system, increased its expenditures from $160,000 in fiscal year 1882–83 to $250,000 in 1885–86. The number of criminal cases completed in the same time periods rose from 517 to 724. The Fort Smith court, despite losing half its territory to other tribunals, tried more cases in 1886 than it did before the Courts Act of 1883. The cause was simple enough: the population of the Indian country tripled between 1871 and 1889. An influx of white residents, including railroad workers, coal miners, farmers holding leases from the Five Tribes, and illegal "squatters," increased business for an already overtaxed criminal justice system. Expanding population meant more crimes committed, additional cases tried, further witnesses procured, new jurors seated, and extra funds required for all such operations.[7]

The Department of Justice offered little assistance beyond exhortations to cut costs. As early as 1878, Attorney General Charles Devens had cautioned Parker to curtail the "vast expenditures" in his district, implying that deputies were overstating their fees, as they had under Judge Story, and advising that "stern supervision" of their accounts "would reduce this expense decidedly." But padded accounts were not the source of rising costs during the 1880s; expanding fees for jurors and witnesses corresponded with the increasing number of criminal cases on the Fort Smith docket. In 1886, Justice Department auditors suggested a cutback in the amount spent "for the subsistence of prisoners" and a reduction of the "force of deputy marshals employed in the Indian Territory" to save money. They also recommended that officers from the Northern District of Texas cease arresting outlaws in the Indian Territory and holding hearings at Graham before transporting the criminals to Fort Smith for trial, a practice that resulted from the 1883 redistricting act. In 1888, another examiner proposed completely eliminating Parker's jurisdiction over the Chickasaw Nation to further trim costs. By 1890, Attorney General William H. H. Miller advised Western District officials to cut expenses by bringing only the most serious cases to trial and "letting the other ones go."[8]

The system established by Congress and administered by the Justice Department for payment of juror and witness fees further hampered financial matters in the Western District, forcing Judge Parker to respond drastically. U.S. marshals received expense allotments for each court session and were required to exhaust the full amount before applying for the next installment, which, in turn, arrived after approval by the U.S. Treasury. This procedure often stranded witnesses who had traveled hundreds of miles to testify; since the fees could be paid only to the attestants, they had to stay in Fort Smith until Washington released their money. And throughout the period from 1875 to 1896, appropriations for such fees typically fell below actual expenses. On occasion, Congress passed a deficiency bill to cover additional expenditures. More often, however, when court funds were exhausted, they remained depleted until the next fiscal year. Parker, when confronted with such circumstances, necessarily closed court until additional resources became available. Expenses exceeded appropriations during the February 1887 term, forcing him to suspend operations and discontinue all cases until July, the first month of the new fiscal year. The same situation repeated itself during the May term of 1888. The *Arkansas Gazette,* in reporting "STARVING WITNESSES" at Fort Smith, declared "the strong arm of justice" to be "paralyzed . . . because Congress failed to appropriate sufficient funds to run the courts." Western District officials resorted to the old method of paying witnesses with vouchers (now legal, provided that they were used only by the individual attestant), but the "marshal's paper" was "worth nothing and [could not] be sold for 25 cents on the dollar." Thus, "nearly four hundred witnesses, nearly all of whom [were] without means" faced a long summer awaiting their payment. Despite the publicity attending such hardships, funding remained a perennial problem for the court.[9]

Parker, frequently lacking sufficient funds to carry on normal court operations, encountered similar obstacles in attempting to improve the deplorable conditions of the Western District jail. In 1875, upon arrival at Fort Smith, he found prisoners jammed into the old military stockade. Soon thereafter, he ordered the conversion of the old enlisted men's barracks into a courtroom, with its basement to serve as the federal jail. Two stone-floored chambers, each fifty-five by twenty-nine feet with seven-foot ceilings, vermin-infested and without plumbing or ventilation, occasionally housed up to two hundred prisoners. Sanitation facilities consisted of buckets, emptied twice daily; confiscated whiskey barrels, sawn in half, served as bathtubs. When summer heat grew oppressive, guards soaked the flagstone floors, producing a steamy mist in the dank dungeon. Prisoners of all descriptions—men and women, old and young, sick and well, murderers and petty thieves—shared the dark, crowded space that Attorney General Augustus Garland called "the most miserable prison, probably, in the whole country."[10]

Yet political considerations delayed building a new jail for years. The U.S. House of Representatives always faced more demands for funding than it could meet. And the Indian Territory, home of most of the "guests" in "Parker's Hotel," was unrepresented in Congress. Representatives from Fort Smith were Democrats, while Parker and most of the appointed federal officials—except during the presidencies of Grover Cleveland, 1885–89 and 1893–97—were Republicans. In addition, advocates of judicial reform in the Indian country opposed the continued jurisdiction of the Parker court and therefore were against any measure that might improve conditions in the Western District. But in 1885, with Cleveland in the White House and Democrats serving as district attorney and marshal at Fort Smith, Congress finally authorized funds for a new jail.[11]

The new facility, begun in 1886 and completed in 1889, was a vast improvement over the basement dungeon. Attached to the old barracks-courtroom building, the three-story brick structure boasted seventy-seven cells, each containing two iron bedsteads, enough to accommodate 144 occupants. Four "swinging water closets," one for each floor of cell blocks and a separate one for guards, provided for sanitation. Prisoners were now segregated by offense, with the worst consigned to "Murderers Row" on the first floor. The middle range of criminals occupied the second tier—those charged with assault, burglary, and various forms of larceny. The third floor housed alcohol violators and those convicts serving sentences of less than one year.[12]

But conditions in the new jail, as well as the expense of its operations, soon caused contention between Judge Parker and his superiors. Like its predecessor, the recently completed prison quickly became overcrowded. As a result, federal inspectors soon recommended methods to reduce costs. On November 16, 1889, Western District officials countered this report with a glowing account from the grand jury that praised the "good, cleanly condition" of the facility, the absence of "stench or odor," and the "wholesome, well-cooked food" provided for inmates. A month later, however, two inspectors complained of tobacco-stained walls, poor discipline, and overpriced meals. Justice Department officials continued such complaints, usually accompanied by advice to cut expenses, while Parker relied upon favorable local reports, without producing any appreciable improvement in jail conditions, until 1896.[13]

Judge Parker reflected contemporary reform philosophy by devoting his attention not only to prison conditions under his immediate control in Fort Smith but also in those penitentiaries around the United States to which he sentenced convicts; such concerns again led to a conflict with his superiors. Parker, despite his stern image, argued that prisons must rehabilitate, not merely punish, criminals. In 1885 he wrote to Attorney General Garland that the purpose of imprisonment should be "to lift the man up, to stamp out his bad nature . . . and so govern and direct him that he becomes a good citizen, of use to himself and his fellow men." Despite having sentenced "hundreds of men" since 1875, he asserted that "not one of them, no matter how depraved, had entirely lost [the] better part of human nature." He determined, after investigating penitentiaries throughout the South and West, that only those at Detroit, Michigan, and Chester, Illinois, fulfilled the rehabilitative requirement. All the others, he insisted, operated on the "purely speculative principle of getting the most dollars and cents out of the transaction," rather than functioning "for the good of the men sentenced." As a consequence, Parker ignored Justice Department instructions to send convicted felons to other institutions until 1886, when the state of Michigan forbade the reception of out-of-state prisoners at Detroit. A year later he determined that the Arkansas State Penitentiary at Little Rock was acceptable, "if I have not been entirely misled as to its present management."[14]

Parker, in addition to such administrative dissension with his superiors over costs and procedures, sensed his influence in pardon cases waning as more commutations were issued or denied contrary to his recommendations. In 1884, for example, Justice Department officials ignored his advice in the case of Fannie Echols. Although two witnesses were present when she shot John Williams, conflicting accounts cast doubt on the exact circumstances of the crime. On July 20, 1883, just before retiring for the night, Echols and Williams, who lived as man and wife without benefit of clergy in the Creek Nation, quarreled. At one point he threatened her: "You damn bitch, I'll kill you." A few hours later, two guests sharing their cabin awakened to the sound of a gunshot and found that "both Fanny and John had hold of the pistol." Williams, shot through the stomach, died within minutes. Although Echols claimed she fired in self-defense, the ball had passed through her victim and lodged in a floorboard, indicating that Williams had been attacked while lying down.[15]

A jury found the location of the fatal bullet a telling fact and convicted Echols; Parker therefore ordered the death sentence. But despite strong local sentiment for commutation and the favorable report of Prosecutor Clayton, an adverse reaction by the attorney general necessitated extraordinary measures to save Echols from the gallows. Over three hundred residents of Fort Smith and the Creek Nation, including the jury that convicted her, signed the petition requesting executive clemency. Clayton concluded that, although her claims of self-defense were "probably untrue," the threat Williams made on the night of the crime created "enough doubt to justify" sparing her life—and Judge Parker agreed. But Attorney General Benjamin H. Brewster opposed any interference, asserting that Clayton and Parker merely sought to avoid hanging a woman. On the contrary, Brewster wrote, the execution of a female like Fannie Echols would help "subdue . . . if not civilize," the inhabitants of the Creek Nation. On June 21, 1884, acting on the attorney general's report, President Chester Arthur "decline[d] to interfere" with the sentence.[16]

Once aware of this outcome, Parker circumvented standard procedure by writing directly to the chief executive to spare Fannie Echols's life. He "most earnestly but respectfully" asked Arthur to reconsider his decision. Life imprisonment, he argued, was sufficient punishment for Echols, who had received "no moral training" as a child. "The certainty of punishment rather than its severity" deterred crime, Parker argued, a theme that he would echo frequently in later years. The judge had tried "hundreds, yes thousands" of criminal cases, "pronounced the death penalty on over a hundred criminals"; and he would "never" recommend a commutation unless he believed "from all the facts and circumstances it [was] warranted," as he now did. Consequently, President Arthur reversed his decision and reduced the sentence to life imprisonment.[17]

On June 21, 1884, the same day that Chester Arthur initially declined to commute Fannie Echols's sentence, the president granted a full pardon to another Parker defendant, Mat Music, who had been sentenced to death for a heinous crime on dubious evidence. During the summer of 1882 Music and his wife were caring for Fannie Whitlow, the six-year-old daughter of a neighbor in the Chickasaw Nation. After accompanying Music on a visit to Texas, the child developed an "inflammation of her private parts," which a local doctor diagnosed as gonorrhea. On October 14, 1882, Fannie, her parents, and the physician testified in proceedings before United States Commissioner Stephen Wheeler; on November 8, the grand jury indicted Mat Music for raping the little girl. The testimony presented at the trial was highly contradictory: the defense portrayed Music as an industrious family man, while the prosecution introduced disputed evidence that he had suffered from some venereal disease several years earlier. Although the alleged victim—with her mother at her side—described the attack vividly, medical evidence remained inconclusive as to whether she actually had been penetrated, if the inflammation of her genitals was in fact the result of gonorrhea, or if such an assault had even taken place. Despite the doubts raised by such testimony, an outraged petit jury convicted Music and, on April 28, 1884, Judge Parker sentenced him to hang.[18]

But the pardon process revealed further flaws in the government case and raised even greater misgivings regarding the defendant's guilt. Attorneys Thomas Barnes and James Millette contended that Fannie Whitlow's testimony was inadmissible because of her age; she was too young, they insisted, to understand the meaning of an oath. Furthermore, they produced evidence that her mother, angered by Fannie's condition after being in Music's care, had coached the child on her statement. The inflammation of her genitals had followed a fifty-mile journey on horseback, during which she rode astride the mount. Chafing followed by poor medical care seemed to be the most likely cause of her complaint, especially considering that the symptoms did not appear until six weeks after the alleged rape, rather than within the usual ten days expected for a sexually transmitted disease. District Attorney Clayton substantiated many of these charges in his report, especially the defects of the girl's testimony. He concluded that, given Fannie Winslow's "tender years" and "the immaturity of her intellect . . . it would be better to commute the sentence to imprisonment for life." Judge Parker concurred.[19]

Attorney General Brewster, however, was angered by the "loose and peculiar way" that Parker and Clayton had conducted the case; he argued successfully for a full pardon. Clayton's recommendation for commutation, he asserted, indicated that the prosecutor was "conscious of the impropriety of conviction." The facts, "even as presented by [Clayton]," offered "more than reasonable doubt as to the guilt of the defendant." After noting that no crime was "more easily charged and more difficult to disprove" than rape, the attorney general expressed his "official censure" at the "laxity" that the judge and district attorney exhibited in prosecuting such a weak case. Brewster recommended a full pardon for Mat Music, and President Arthur complied on June 21, 1884.[20]

Although his reaction to such censure by superiors went unrecorded, Judge Parker became more and more critical of the clemency process as the number of commutations and pardons increased during the 1880s. The murder case of Jack Spaniard produced a response more vituperative than any the judge had previously issued. On April 15, 1886, Spaniard and a confederate murdered United States Deputy Marshal William Erwin while freeing their partner, Felix Graham, from custody in the Choctaw Nation. Erwin was the twentieth deputy marshal killed in the Western District since 1881, a fact Parker emphasized repeatedly during sentencing. Spaniard "wickedly took [Erwin's] life because he was an officer and in the discharge of his duty," the judge declared. Anticipating an attempt at clemency, Parker concluded that, when twenty such "gallant, brave" officers had died at the hands of "bloody-minded" felons like Jack Spaniard, then "it [was] well high time . . . that those in authority . . . stand by the courts . . . and not permit themselves to be deceived . . . to the extent of overthrowing the findings of juries and the solemn judgment of the courts."[21]

When attorney Thomas Marcum launched an unsuccessful attempt to save Spaniard from the gallows, Judge Parker shifted his invective from the condemned to the defense counsel and his perceived misuse of the pardon process itself, lashing out at both the counsel and the process in a local newspaper and in private letters to his superiors. On August 1, 1889, the *Fort Smith Times* reported Parker's charge that "abuse" of the pardon power "lessen[ed] the influence of the Court and fear of its power [was] dying out." In a letter to Attorney General William H. H. Miller, he asserted that "this game of fraud and falsehood" had produced an "increase of murder in the Indian Country" and that the lawyers who sought pardons and commutations were "corrupt." To President Benjamin Harrison he described Marcum—who had countered Parker's published opinions in an editorial letter critical both of the death penalty and the Western District Court—as a "drunken lawyer," a "pardon broker" who associated with the "baser classes," and who conducted his "practice . . . in the saloons." Regardless of such character assassination, President Harrison respited Spaniard's execution date from July 17 to August 30, in order to examine all available evidence, but refused to interfere further. On August 30, 1889, Spaniard died on the Fort Smith gallows.[22]

In his vilification of Thomas Marcum, Judge Parker revealed an unfortunate character trait, one that he would demonstrate increasingly throughout the remainder of his career—a tendency to portray opponents as malevolent rather than misguided. Since 1875, he had viewed his court, its officers, and himself, as the rightful protectors of justice in the Indian Territory. A lawyer like Marcum, who successfully sought pardons or commutations for evildoers that merited punishment, thus became "corrupt" in Parker's eyes, part of a conspiracy to undermine justice and see the wicked escape warranted retribution. That the convict and his attorney acted under a constitutional right mattered little to the judge. If Parker opposed a commutation, he believed that the criminal deserved capital punishment—the law demanded it; to resist his judgment was to obstruct justice itself.

But Judge Parker would soon face opposition far more powerful than defense lawyers who manipulated the pardon process; Congress was about to curtail his powers drastically. In 1888, legislative reformers introduced a bill stripping three federal district tribunals of their concurrent circuit court powers and authorizing the U.S. Supreme Court to review their death sentences. Although two other courts—the Northern District of Mississippi and the Western District of South Carolina—fell under the proposed law, Parker was its obvious target. Both of the bill's sponsors, James K. Jones in the Senate and John Rogers in the House, were Arkansans; Rogers had been among the first to sign pardon applications at Fort

Smith ten years before. Surely the capital sentence provision applied
to Parker, because the other courts transacted minimal criminal
business. Senator George Vest (D-MO), speaking in favor of the bill,
criticized Parker, arguing that he had executed men "for years . . .
without any right to ask the Supreme Court of the United States
whether it be judicial murder or not."[23]

Despite such rhetoric, the bill almost failed to become law.
Although both houses passed the legislation at the end of the first
session of the Fiftieth Congress, President Grover Cleveland, a
Parker supporter, "pocket-vetoed" the measure by refusing to sign
it before Congress adjourned on October 20, 1888. Senator Jones
reintroduced the bill in the next session, however; the combined
votes of reformers and expansionists guaranteed its passage despite
Cleveland's refusal to sign. The Jones-Rogers bill became law on
February 6, 1889, and went into effect on May 1.[24]

Passage of this judicial reform marked a turning point in Parker's
career. Fifteen years, almost to the day, after his arrival in Arkansas,
his unique status as the most powerful judge in the United States
ended. Although his authority had never been as absolute as his
public image—executive clemency always provided a check—he
had operated his court with greater independence than any other
federal magistrate, forcefully ruling over an unparalleled jurisdiction. As of May 1, 1889, he was subject to the same appeals process
as any other district judge. Supreme Court justices, unfamiliar with
the frontier conditions of the Indian country and less experienced
in criminal trials, would now pass judgment on him.

The Jones-Rogers bill represented both a culmination of judicial
reform during the last half of the 1880s and a harbinger of larger
conflicts between Parker and his superiors in the 1890s. To secure
passage of the court reform bill, Senator Jones and Congressman
Rogers had joined forces with George Vest, a vocal proponent of
opening the Indian Territory to white settlement. The ongoing
pressure for colonization of the region resulted in the reduction of
Parker's jurisdiction in 1883, and such agitation would continue
during the 1890s, with the Western District Court as a prime target.

And Parker, as the number of appeals under the 1889 law grew, would react much as he had when Justice Department officials complained about expenditures or jail conditions, or when his authority was challenged by pardon applications: at first he ignored his critics and then he attacked them. The last seven years of his tenure would not be happy ones.

CHAPTER NINE

"Disposed to Be Insubordinate"

The Last Years

Late in 1889 and throughout the first half of 1890, Isaac Parker, his
official powers considerably reduced, wrestled with the prospect
of stepping down from the Western District bench to accept two
additional judicial appointments. Early in December 1889, he acqui-
esced to the wishes of "friends" in Washington by allowing them to
submit his name to President Benjamin Harrison for consideration
as judge of the Eighth U.S. Circuit Court, based at St. Louis.
Attorney General William H. H. Miller wrote to Parker that "I take
pleasure in presenting your name" to the president. But as soon as
the possibility of such a selection became public, congressional critics of Parker reacted forcefully and sought to block the nomination.
On January 18, 1890, Parker forwarded an opposing newspaper
editorial to the attorney general, who responded three days later
with the assurance that "whoever may be appointed . . . the determination will not . . . depend upon evidence so unreliable" as a
biased editor's opinion. Unmollified and eager to preserve his reputation, the judge further defended himself in two letters to President
Harrison, characteristically attacking one of his critics as "a natu-
ralized judas." Then, in March 1890, Attorney General Miller offered
Parker a transfer to the Eastern Judicial District of Arkansas, head-
quartered at Little Rock. Both appointments promised a reduced

workload with fewer criminal cases to be tried; moreover, the Eighth Circuit position offered closer proximity to Parker's son and in-laws at St. Louis. But Parker had established himself at Fort Smith; over the past fifteen years he and his family had become part of the community. And he was also convinced that no one else could preside as well over Indian Territory lawbreakers. Thus, on July 23, 1890, he removed his name from consideration for either post.[1]

As a consequence of this decision, Parker faced growing challenges in a shrinking bailiwick. Less than a month after Congress had subjected his capital sentences to Supreme Court review, President Cleveland signed the Courts Act of March 1, 1889, which further reduced the Western District jurisdiction and established a federal court specifically in the Indian Territory. It represented a concession both by the court-reform and expansionist forces who sought total extinguishment of "outside" judicial authority over the Indian country as a precursor to opening the region to settlement; this compromise legislation was another step toward their ultimate goal. Under the act, the Parker court relinquished authority over the entire Chickasaw Nation and nearly two-thirds of the Choctaw Nation to the newly created Paris division of the Eastern Judicial District of Texas. The law also installed a federal tribunal at Muskogee, within the Creek Nation, to adjudicate civil disputes and criminal misdemeanors involving U.S. citizens. Although the Arkansas, Kansas, and Texas districts continued to handle more serious offenses, the creation of the Muskogee court foretold the end of jurisdiction for "outside courts" in the region.[2]

Judge Parker subsequently clashed with officials in the adjacent district, as he had after the initial diminution of his jurisdiction in 1883, this time over the dubious removal of a prisoner. On March 6, 1891, Eugene Marshall, U.S. attorney for the Eastern District of Texas, complained to Attorney General Miller after the U.S. marshal of the Fort Smith court, Jacob Yoes, paid a Texas sheriff twenty-five dollars to deliver a felon to him in the Indian Territory, thereby circumventing the required written application for assistance to the U.S. marshal of the Texas district. The Justice Department responded with a letter admonishing Parker that "if [Marshall's] statements are true, such practices ought to be stopped." Yet Parker fully supported Marshal Yoes, who denied any impropriety, even though his actions clearly had bypassed the usual process for the transfer of prisoners between districts. On March 18, 1891, the judge denied all charges in a letter to the attorney general, stating that "I would not permit a practice such as is complained of by the District Attorney of Texas." Parker concluded that he was "entirely satisfied" with the marshal's explanation, considering it to be "correct" and "true in every respect."[3]

Although Texas officials did not pursue their complaint, Parker continued to contend with his superiors over other administrative concerns. In 1891, he protested again the treatment of federal prisoners sent to the Arkansas State Penitentiary at Little Rock. But expenses dominated the disputes, with the judge typically requesting funds for additional jail guards or a Secret Service man to conduct investigations, and Washington usually denying the expenditures. In 1894 Parker asked for a telephone specifically for his chambers, complaining that the only one in the new federal courthouse at Fort Smith was in the marshal's office two floors below. Attorney General Richard Olney refused this request, pointedly reminding the judge that the five-story Department of Justice building in Washington also was equipped with only one telephone. Later that year Parker further antagonized Olney by sending youthful offenders over the age of sixteen to a federal reformatory rather than to penitentiaries, as required by law. Although the judge argued that the reform school better served the interests of such young convicts, the attorney general ordered him to comply with regulations.[4]

The worst disputes, however, centered on Supreme Court reversals of Parker death sentences. Beginning in 1890, the justices in Washington remanded nearly two-thirds of the capital appeals from Fort Smith for new trials. The high court ruled that Parker explained the law incorrectly and commented too freely on evidence in his jury charges, and that he favored the prosecution to the point of denying defendants fair hearings. Parker, however, balked at

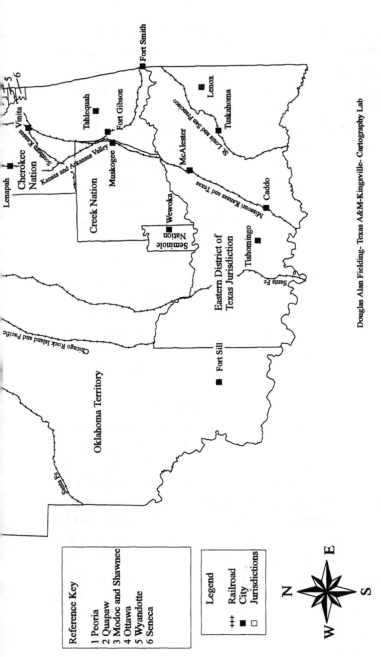

3. Indian Territory jurisdiction of the Western District Court, 1889–96. *Map by Douglas Alan Fielding, Texas A&M at Kingsville, Cartography Lab.*

these decisions instead of simply accepting them and modifying
his courtroom practices. His frustration mounted as cases on appeal
grew in number and the reversals became more critical of his methods, leading to an embarrassing public feud with his superiors that
marred his last years of federal service.

Surprisingly, Judge Parker ordered ten hangings—after May 1,
1889, when the legislation permitting Supreme Court review
became effective—before the first case was appealed in 1890. It
hinged on "entirely circumstantial" evidence. On October 21, 1889,
William Alexander and David Steadman rode into a remote area of
the Creek Nation with several horses acquired in Arizona. Alexander
returned alone, but in possession of his partner's animals and
saddle. A few days later he consulted with Attorney R. G. Rawles
regarding ownership of the mounts, declaring that Steadman had
fled the area with a married woman. Early in November, however,
passersby discovered and identified the decomposed body of David
Steadman. The corpse had been partially devoured by hogs, but
enough remained to determine that he had been shot to death. As
a result, on February 7, 1891, a Western District grand jury indicted
William Alexander for murder.[5]

Despite the absence of any direct evidence, District Attorney
Clayton secured a conviction and Judge Parker decreed yet another
death sentence, prompting defense lawyers to appeal to the U.S.
Supreme Court. On August 29, 1890, J. Warren Reed, a newcomer
to Fort Smith legal affairs, who quickly developed a formidable
reputation, filed a Bill of Exceptions listing thirteen errors by
Parker. Reed contended that the judge improperly admitted the
testimony of R. G. Rawles, the lawyer with whom Alexander had
consulted regarding ownership of the deceased's property; such
conversations between attorneys and clients were confidential and,
therefore, inadmissible. Parker, Reed continued, also unfairly
excluded testimony supporting the alibi that Alexander offered
and charged the jury in a manner "misleading . . . and prejudicial
to the defendant." For example, the judge began his instructions
to the panel by stating that Alexander was "charged with being

guilty of murder because on the 21st day of October, 1889, in the Creek Nation, he took the life of David C. Steadman," thereby presenting as a fact the central, disputed issue of the trial.[6]

On February 2, 1891, the Supreme Court handed down its decision in *William Alexander v. United States.* Judge Parker, the justices ruled, had erred by admitting the testimony of the defendant's attorney. Justice Henry Billings Brown, author of this unanimous decision, stated that "whatever facts are communicated by a client" to a lawyer "solely on account of that relation," attorneys were "not at liberty, even if they wish, to disclose." Even though the conversation between Alexander and his lawyer may have demonstrated a motive for the murder, according to Justice Brown, it did not "necessarily" do so, and was "perfectly harmless upon its face." Therefore, the high court overturned the verdict and ordered Parker to grant Alexander a new trial.[7]

The justices did, however, affirm the death sentence of Boudinot "Bood" Crumpton, who was executed at Fort Smith on June 30, 1891. Yet, before the Supreme Court ruled on the growing list of Parker cases pending, a new piece of legislation provided further appellate recourse from the Western District Court. In an effort to relieve the backlogged Supreme Court docket—numbering 1,816 cases in 1890, of which the court could reasonably dispose of 450—Congress passed the Circuit Court of Appeals Act early in 1891. This law created an intermediate level of federal tribunals to hear appeals in citizenship and patent cases that previously had been directed to the high court. It also permitted review of convictions for any "infamous crime" tried in the U.S. district courts. As a result, the level of criminal appeals to the Supreme Court expanded, but the reduction in civil cases compensated for this increase, thereby reducing the backlog.[8]

Now any conviction in the Parker court was subject to Supreme Court review—even a minor alcohol violation. For example, during the May 1892 term of the Western District Court, a beer peddler named Sarlls was found guilty of introducing ten gallons of lager beer into the Indian country. This conviction was unlawful, argued his attorney, former U.S. Attorney General A. H. Garland, because statutes prohibited only the introduction of "spirituous liquor or wine," and not beer, which was a malt liquor produced by fermentation. Judge Parker overruled the argument. The intent of the Indian Intercourse Laws, he maintained, had been to prevent the debilitating effects of alcohol on American Indians. Beer contained alcohol, and was as capable of producing drunkenness as whiskey. The intent of the statute, if not the actual wordage, he reasoned, was to prevent such behavior; therefore, lager beer was as prohibited in the Indian Territory as whiskey.[9]

But the Supreme Court disagreed. On April 9, 1894, Associate Justice George Shiras stated that Parker had surrendered to "the temptation . . . to stretch the law to cover an acknowledged ill." The statute notified the public of legislative intent in "the common and popular significance" of the language employed. In other words, a law written to ban wine and liquor could not include beer without saying so explicitly, even if the same behaviors could result from overindulgence in one as in the others. Although the original act had since been amended to include beer, it could not be enforced retroactively; the Court ordered the indictment quashed and the defendant discharged.[10]

Meanwhile, the reversal of Parker death sentences increased. In 1892, the Supreme Court overturned the murder convictions of John Boyd, Eugene Standley, and Alexander Lewis. The next year, convicted killers John Brown and John Graves escaped the gallows, while the justices affirmed the sentence of Frank Collins. In 1894 the Court ordered new trials for John Hicks and Sam Hickory, but confirmed the judgments on John Pointer and Lewis Holder.[11]

All of these reversals resulted from Judge Parker's courtroom conduct. In the *Lewis* case, he permitted the prosecution to question potential jurors without the defendant being present. Each side was permitted to challenge eight panelists in the proceeding; thus Lewis unwittingly lost two such opportunities—and the chance for a fair trial, the Supreme Court ruled—by challenging jurors that the prosecutors had already rejected in his absence. But lengthy jury charges, ranging from forty to seventy typed pages and read aloud for each case, caused most of the reversals. In these rambling instructions, Judge Parker frequently moved beyond simply stating the law and its application to the evidence presented during the trial. In the *Hickory* case, for example, he included among the legal requirements for a valid claim of self-defense the ancient doctrine of duty to retreat, which was falling from legal favor in state courts. He then described anyone who killed an attacker as "judge . . . jury . . . and . . . executioner," further asserting that society would not tolerate the application of such powers even by "the chief executive officer of this government." In reversing the verdict, Chief Justice Melville Fuller noted that "such instructions . . . could not but have a decided influence" on the jurors. Rather than explaining legal principles, Parker had assumed the role of advocate for the prosecution.[12]

But the judge would not be dissuaded by such commentary. In 1895, when Sam Hickory returned for a second trial, Parker disparaged the reversals while using the emotional power of Scripture and an unproven imputation of corruption to sway the jury. While explaining how jurors could infer culpability from the actions of a suspect, he noted the rising number of appeals from his sentences. "There are a great many exceptions filed here to almost everything said by the court," he complained. Reaching for the Bible that rested on his desk, he continued: "I apprehend the [defense lawyers] won't take any exceptions to reading from this book," whereupon he perused the story of Cain and Abel for the jury, drawing parallels between the defendant and the first murderer of Genesis. Then, before concluding his charge, the judge implied that defense witnesses could have been bribed.[13]

Contrary to Parker's expectations, defense attorneys did object to his Biblical tutelage, and the U.S. Supreme Court agreed. In writing the majority opinion, Justice Edward D. White conceded that "acts of concealment by an accused" were "competent . . . as tending to establish" wrongdoing. But such actions, by themselves, were not sufficient in "creating a legal presumption" of culpability.

Judge Parker's comments, however, had "practically instructed that [such] facts were, under both divine and human law, conclusive proof of guilt." The charge, Justice White concluded, "crosses the line which separates impartial exercise of the judicial function from the region of partisanship." The Court ordered a third trial.[14]

Judge Parker did not resist the adverse rulings of the Supreme Court merely by continuing reversible errors, however. In at least one case he altered the trial record of a pending appeal, and he may have sought to do so on another occasion. In March of 1892, during the murder trial of John Brown, the Supreme Court ordered a new trial in the *Alexander Lewis* case, citing improper jury selection procedures. On October 7, 1893, hoping to avert another reversal on similar grounds, Parker called a special hearing to amend the transcript of the Brown trial—which already had been submitted to the high court—by including a description of jury selection using language that met the criteria set out in *Lewis v. United States*. Over the objections of Brown's attorneys, Parker inserted a lengthy paragraph stating unequivocally that the defendant had been present throughout the empaneling of the jury.[15]

Less than a year later, Judge Parker raised suspicions at the Justice Department with another irregular action regarding trial documents. On August 20, 1894, he wrote to Solicitor General Lawrence Maxwell, asking that the clerk of the Supreme Court send proof sheets of the transcripts in two pending appeals to Fort Smith so "that I may correct them, as a great many errors have heretofore occurred in the printed record." Two weeks later Clerk James H. McKenney refused this entreaty curtly, writing that the "records must be preserved . . . as certified . . . by the clerk of the lower court without correction." Parker, in response, denied any intent beyond revising printing errors, which "were mostly of a typographical nature," and acknowledged that altering the certified record without a court order would be "a crime." The dispute probably amounted to nothing more than poor communication, but Washington officials nevertheless were becoming increasingly wary of this problematic jurist.[16]

In 1894 an application for bail brought Parker into open conflict with the Supreme Court. During the May term of the Western District Court, after a petit jury found Lafayette Hudson guilty of "assault with an intent to kill," Judge Parker sentenced him to four years in prison. On August 14, 1894, the defense attorneys, ex-Attorney General A. H. Garland and former federal prosecutor William H. H. Clayton, filed an appeal with the U.S. Supreme Court, further requesting that Associate Justice Edward D. White issue a writ granting Hudson bail pending a decision on his appeal. White granted the writ, ordering the defendant to post $5,000 bond "to be approved by the district judge." But at a hearing on September 3, Parker denied bail, citing a lack of authority on the part of Justice White to issue such an order and thereby setting the stage for a confrontation.[17]

Anticipating an opportunity to argue this case personally before the high court, Judge Parker prepared a lengthy brief while pressing for a speedy hearing of the Hudson appeal. Throughout the autumn of 1894, Parker badgered Solicitor General Lawrence Maxwell with entreaties to advance the assault case because Hudson, "a lawless and desperate character," remained confined in an overcrowded federal jail, where he was a "disturbing element" among the prisoners. On November 12, 1894, the judge wrote to Attorney General Olney, insisting that he be allowed to argue, orally, his position on the bail question. Four days later, the attorney general replied that such a request was "entirely unusual" and "would be deemed inadmissable by the Supreme Court." On December 3, the Court ordered that Parker show cause why a writ that offered bond should not be issued. He responded with a twenty-page document asserting that only federal circuit and district courts could grant bail to convicts awaiting appeals; Congress had never given such authority to the Supreme Court. He also argued that Justice White, who was assigned to the Fifth U.S. Circuit, lacked jurisdiction over the Western District of Arkansas, part of the Eight Circuit. Therefore, Parker concluded, the order for bail was without legal foundation.[18]

In January 1895, Judge Parker traveled to Washington, where he joined Solicitor General Maxwell in presenting written briefs on the Hudson bond dispute to the Supreme Court. On February 4, the justices overruled Parker, but their decision failed either to free Hudson or to hasten his appeal. The Court upheld Justice White's writ, dismissing Parker's arguments with the caustic comment that the judge misapprehended "the powers of this court . . . and his own duties." But, with the authority for bond now established, Lafayette Hudson was unable to raise the required $5,000. Late in July of 1895, while his assault appeal still languished, the convict found a more direct means of securing freedom—he escaped from the federal jail at Fort Smith. Nearly two years later, on April 22, 1897, with the plaintiff still at large, the high court finally dismissed his appeal.[19]

While in Washington for the *Hudson* case, Judge Parker also lobbied unavailingly against legislation that would soon eliminate his jurisdiction over the remnant of the Indian Territory under his control. On January 10, 1895, he testified before the House Judiciary Committee, extolling the virtues of the tribal governments and stating the necessity of his continued dominion. The next night he dined with President Cleveland and recommended that the chief executive not open the Indian country to settlement until its native residents were ready to exercise full civic responsibilities. Such politicking, however, proved fruitless. On March 1, 1895, Cleveland signed a new Courts Act, which divided the Indian Territory into three federal judicial districts and ended the jurisdiction of the "outside courts" in Arkansas, Kansas, and Texas over the region, effective September 1, 1896.[20]

The year, 1895, did not begin well for Judge Parker. In the first two months of 1895, the Supreme Court had chastised him harshly and Congress had passed a death sentence on his jurisdiction. Within a few months his relations with Washington worsened further when he publicly criticized the high court for its handling of an Indian Territory outlaw named Crawford Goldsby, better known as "Cherokee Bill." Already a hardened criminal at age nineteen, Goldsby, who described himself as "half white, half negro, and half Indian," had robbed and murdered in the Indian country for over two years before brought to trial by Judge Parker and a Fort Smith jury early in 1895. On February 26, the jurors found him guilty of killing Ernest Melton, an innocent bystander who was shot during the robbery of a dry-goods store at Lenapah, Cherokee Nation. On April 13, Cherokee Bill returned to court for sentencing. As Parker ordered his death, the young killer's mother and sister, who had attended the entire trial, burst into tears. "What's the matter with you two?" Goldsby scolded. "I'm not a dead man yet."[21]

Both Cherokee Bill and his attorney, J. Warren Reed, intended to keep the convicted murderer alive, albeit by radically different means. Although Judge Parker had delivered one of shortest jury charges of his career—fifteen minutes, as opposed to the usual hour-and-a-half or more—Reed nevertheless discovered fourteen errors on which to base an appeal. Goldsby, while awaiting Supreme Court action, laid more concrete plans for his freedom, persuading the wife of a fellow prisoner to smuggle a pistol and "a hatful of cartridges" into the federal jail. He secreted the weapon behind a loose brick in his cell, awaiting an opportunity to escape.[22]

On Friday, July 26, 1895, Goldsby made a violent but futile bid for freedom. At 7:00 that evening, turnkey James Eoff and guard Larry Keating conducted their usual rounds, confirming that all prisoners were present in locked cells. Upon reaching Goldsby, however, they found his door blocked open and a pistol in his hand. The killer demanded that Eoff give up the keys and ordered Keating to surrender his revolver. Instead, the guard reached for his gun, whereupon Cherokee Bill shot him in the stomach and then again in the back. Upon hearing this gunfire, guards and deputies rushed to the jail to thwart the escape. A two-hour gunfight ensued within the prison corridors, lasting until Goldsby exhausted his ammunition. Finally subdued, he returned to his cell in handcuffs and leg irons to await another murder trial.[23]

Judge Parker, who was visiting relatives in St. Louis, erupted when he learned of the attempted jailbreak and resultant murder.

On July 29, 1895, he "freely" expressed his outrage to a reporter for the *St. Louis Globe-Democrat*, blaming the Justice Department and the Supreme Court for the death of Larry Keating. Recalling his repeatedly rebuffed entreaties for more guards, he ascribed this violent incident to "the fact that our jail is filled with murderers and there is not a sufficient guard to take care of them." Many convicted killers remained in the Fort Smith lockup, he contended, because of the Supreme Court. In fact, Parker argued, the high court was responsible for an upsurge in murder across the United States. "I attribute the increase to the reversals of the Supreme Court," he stated; such decisions "contributed to the number of murders in the Indian Territory." He further complained that the appeal process allowed condemned convicts a "long breathing spell" before the high court heard their cases. And the justices in overturning convictions, Parker charged, "always" did so "upon the flimsiest of technicalities."[24]

Such anger was understandable. At fifty-six, his tawny hair and goatee now white, his once-trim frame grown paunchy, Isaac Parker perceived that his life's work was being undone by outsiders; therefore, characteristically, he attacked them. For twenty years he had labored ceaselessly to protect the innocent and to punish the guilty in the Indian Territory. But during the previous twelve years Congress had steadily reduced his powers over the region. In thirteen months, his jurisdiction would expire completely. Once the most powerful district judge in the United States, he now toiled under the seemingly capricious decisions of Supreme Court justices—some of whom never had tried a criminal case—and the edicts of unsympathetic administrators whose main concerns appeared to be cutting costs and maintaining control over their agencies. High court reversals damaged his judicial reputation and hurt his considerable pride. But Parker also believed sincerely that the appeal process impaired the administration of justice by undermining the "certainty of punishment" that he found so important to deterring crime. No one, he was convinced, understood the Indian country and its criminals as well as he did. If only the officials in Washington had listened to him and provided funding for additional guards, then, the judge reasoned, Larry Keating would not have died. And if Parker had not been required to delay Goldsby's execution pending a Supreme Court appeal, that miscreant would have hanged long before attempting to escape and murdering yet another "quiet, peaceful, law-abiding citizen."[25]

Disposing of Cherokee Bill consumed another eight months. On August 5, 1895, immediately upon returning to Fort Smith, Parker called the Western District Grand Jury into session; they indicted Goldsby within thirty minutes. The trial opened on Thursday, August 8, and concluded with a guilty verdict on the following Monday. On September 10, Judge Parker sentenced Cherokee Bill to death for the murder of Larry Keating. Defense attorneys postponed any action, however, by appealing the second murder conviction while their first petition was still pending. But on December 2, 1895, the Supreme Court affirmed the initial death sentence. Without waiting for resolution of the second appeal, Parker set a date for execution on the original offense. As a consequence, on March 17, 1896, Cherokee Bill died on the Fort Smith gallows.[26]

In 1895, while Judge Parker contended with the *Goldsby* cases, the high court reversed more sentences in appeals based on what had become the standard grounds: haphazard procedures, bias against defendants, and improper jury charges. In November 1893, during the murder trial of Thomas Thompson, a petit juror interrupted the proceedings to announce that he had served on the grand jury that indicted the defendant. Judge Parker, instead of declaring a mistrial at that point, dismissed the panel and ordered the bailiff to select new jurors from the bystanders in the courtroom, rather than choosing them from an official list. As a consequence, on February 13, 1895, the Supreme Court ordered a new trial. Again in 1894, the judge had interposed during testimony in the *John Allison* case when an inexperienced prosecutor forgot a crucial query. "What did [the witness] say about the old man having [fire]arms?" Parker inquired. "Oh, I didn't ask him about that," replied Assistant District Attorney James McDonough, who then quickly asked the question. Defense attorneys, however, did not receive any such coaching. And while instructing the jury in this case, the judge misstated the law on self-defense and made remarks impugning the defendant's alibi. Once again Parker's sentence was reversed.[27]

Because Judge Parker would not modify his methods, Solicitor General Edward B. Whitney continued to argue against appeals based on points of law that the Supreme Court considered to be settled. Early in 1896, he sought to ease these burdens. The high court had repeatedly castigated the lengthy jury charges in Parker trials, occasionally finding in the transcripts grounds for reversal not specifically mentioned in plaintiffs' Bills of Exceptions. Whitney therefore wrote to Parker, suggesting that those portions of the jury instructions "as are not assigned for error might with advantage be omitted" from the records forwarded to Washington. The solicitor general further decided not to pursue appeals in which Parker plainly had failed to correct procedures proscribed by previous Supreme Court rulings. On January 13, 1896, he filed Confessions of Error in two pending actions from the Western District Court, requesting that the justices remand both cases for new trials.[28]

Infuriated by Whitney's action, Parker once again criticized the Supreme Court, the Justice Department, and the entire appeal process; thus he initiated an unseemly public feud that lasted for weeks. On February 5, 1896, the *St. Louis Globe-Democrat* published an open letter from Parker to Attorney General Judson Harmon in which the judge defended himself while attacking his superiors. By his refusal to argue these two cases—an "unprecedented and unwarranted action," Parker declared—Solicitor General Whitney unwittingly provided "security to criminals and embolden[ed] the man of blood." The judge predicted that such Confessions of Error would "have the same effect on the criminal horde in the Indian Country as the numerous and unwarranted reversals of murder cases by the Supreme Court," which had "increased . . . murder 500 percent." But, Parker contended, "the blood of the innocent . . .

victims is not on my head" because "for twenty long, laborious years . . . I have sought to protect human life." He further censured the Supreme Court and its "mania for reversing murder cases." The high court repeatedly overruled his explanations of self-defense, yet, he contended, never "declared . . . what the law . . . is." Parker characterized three similar rulings in recent reversals as "special cases"—not general guidelines—and branded the opinion in *Hickory v. United States* "a philippic" demonstrating "vindictiveness against the trial court." Perhaps, he suggested, the justices, inexperienced as they were in criminal law, might understand and, therefore, uphold more murder convictions if the solicitor general argued such cases orally. Parker concluded by explaining his motives for publishing these charges, writing that he hoped to draw Attorney General Harmon's attention to "the true condition . . . of the criminal law of the United States" and to show "the country . . . the deplorable state" into which law enforcement "had fallen . . . in the hands of an appellate court."[29]

Although Harmon remained silent in public, Solicitor General Whitney and Judge Parker continued to clash in the press. On February 18, 1896, Whitney answered Parker in the pages of the *St. Louis Republic*. The Justice Department had "little difficulty in sustaining the judgment of other judges," he stated, but Parker refused to accept instruction. Whitney conceded that the judge meant well, but was "ignorant and careless" with the law, continuing to fill his jury charges "with gross errors," which were "more to be deplored because in most cases the prisoners [were] probably guilty, and would have been convicted" absent the objectional instructions. "On account of his great desire to secure convictions," Whitney concluded, Judge Parker had become "the best friend of the criminals, for he insures them reversals."[30]

Judge Parker responded harshly ten days later, denouncing the Whitney letter as a "bitter personal screed filled with the grossest misrepresentations, with manifest prevarications, and with lame attempts at the suppression of facts." The solicitor general's arguments were "outrageous" as well as "wholly untenable" and "radically wrong." Whitney himself was, Parker asserted, little more than a "legal imbecile" who knew "absolutely nothing of criminal law." Accordingly, Parker concluded, such "mental pygmies" as the solicitor general supported "the man of crime, the man of blood."[31]

On March 25, 1896, after this embarrassing public fracas between his officers had cooled somewhat, Attorney General Judson Harmon bluntly admonished Judge Parker both for his legal and his personal conduct. "I do not doubt your ability or devotion," Harmon wrote, "but it is quite apparent that you are . . . disposed to be insubordinate and not yield fully to . . . the Supreme Court." The attorney general also castigated Parker for jury charges "continually open to . . . criticism for being misleading and declaratory." In one case, he informed the judge, Supreme Court Justice Joseph Bradley had suggested that the very length of such an instruction might be grounds for reversal, in that "the ordinary mind would emerge from hearing it with no clear and definite conception of the law applicable to the case." Citing yet another appeal in which the Justice Department had recently filed a confession of error, Harmon argued that Parker's jury charge in *United States v. Cul Rowe* "slight[ed] and belittle[d] the presumption of innocence." If only the judge would abandon "the declamatory style" of his instructions, the attorney general assured him, "there certainly would be no trouble, for both the Court and this Department are as anxious as you . . . that justice be administered." He concluded, however, with this curt remonstrance: "I do not like the present state . . . when matters are discussed in the newspapers which have no business there."[32]

This communication only provoked Parker to another defense of his positions, albeit in a private letter to the attorney general, and not, thankfully, through the press. On April 2, 1896, he denied any insubordination, claiming once again that all the Supreme Court rulings based on his interpretation of self-defense were "special cases." As to the assertion that he had "belittled the presumption of innocence," Parker accused Harmon of "charging [him] with both duplicity and dishonesty." He then compared his instruction with the law as stated in *Coffin v. United States*, the preferred explication of the doctrine that a defendant was assumed to be innocent until proven guilty. The two explanations were "in exact harmony," according to Parker, "except I said 'We know this [the defendant's presumed innocence] is not true, but we take it to be true at the commencement of every trial.'" Parker asked how the attorney general could possibly find objectionable the statement that most defendants are not innocent, when it was "recognized by every one" to be correct. He also accused Justice Department officials of "prejudice" against him that arose from the statements of an unnamed individual "who claims to have full knowledge of the situation [at Fort Smith] when he knows nothing whatever of it, except what he has learned by slander and falsehood." Parker, recalcitrant and unbowed, then concluded with the familiar argument that Justice Department officials lacked sufficient experience in criminal law to assess his rulings, stating that "your judgment as to what are errors may be at fault" in the ongoing controversy.[33]

Parker continued to criticize reversals of his sentences for the brief remainder of his career, but he never again resorted to the public denunciations that characterized his battle with Whitney. The Supreme Court and the Justice Department clearly maintained the stronger arguments in the dispute. After 1889, the U.S. Supreme Court held the constitutional authority to reverse Parker decisions and, thereby, to redefine criminal law and procedure. Likewise, the officials of the U.S. Department of Justice legitimately oversaw the administrative affairs of his court. As challenges to his power mounted, Parker became insubordinate, just as Attorney General Harmon charged. At first he haughtily ignored high court decisions and supervisory orders, then unwisely vented his frustrations with the reversals in the press, misstating the law and blaming his superiors for everything from overturned sentences to increased crime. At the nadir of the controversy, he resorted to childish name-calling.

Still, Parker's position was not entirely indefensible; nor was he alone in his opinions. Although personal pride and consternation

over lost power, as well as a combative nature, certainly contributed to his responses, duty and principle also motivated him. Time
and again Parker expressed a sense of obligation to protect "the
innocent," and he repeatedly stated that judicial delays and reversals subverted that responsibility. Thus, he opposed the Court not
only out of hubris but also because he feared that increased crime
would result from its decisions. Moreover, not all of the Supreme
Court rulings overturning Parker sentences were unanimous; Justices
David J. Brewer and R. W. Peckham, in particular, often dissented
from majority opinions. Brewer, who once advocated abolition of
criminal appeals altogether, argued that the spirit of justice was
violated when criminals received new trials on technical grounds.
Punishment of the guilty and deterrence of crime—the administration of justice at its most basic—were more important to Brewer,
Peckham, and Parker than the evolving definition of fair criminal
procedure.[34]

And therein lay the problem. At the root of the controversy
between Judge Parker and the Supreme Court was his failure to
adapt to the development of federal criminal law, which had
lagged behind state practices during the nineteenth century. The
U.S. Supreme Court, by overruling Parker on procedural grounds,
mirrored the trend in state courts toward greater regulation of judicial behavior and more technical appellate procedure. In other
words, the high court brought the federal patchwork of statute and
common law up to contemporary state standards. Judge Parker,
on the other hand, continued in the common-law traditions under
which he had been trained nearly forty years before. His lengthy
jury charges and insistence on a "duty to retreat" in self-defense
rulings, for example, were throwbacks to medieval England. His
understanding of Supreme Court authority likewise reflected an
earlier age in American legal history. When Parker began practicing law in 1859, the high court had overturned only two federal
statutes in seventy years. In the decades following the Civil War,
the Court increased both its power and its prestige. By 1896 its
preeminence was virtually axiomatic, but not to Parker, especially

in the area of criminal law. The expanding powers of the Supreme Court and the evolution of criminal law between 1875 and 1889 somehow escaped Isaac Parker, who was isolated on the federal bench at Fort Smith. Because his decisions were not subject to appeal in those years, he overlooked such developments, being more concerned with the efficient trial of criminals under common law. By 1896, he was a judicial anachronism, a remnant of the time when familiarity with Blackstone's *Commentaries* and a brief apprenticeship were sufficient qualifications to join the bar. He was living now in an age of law schools and theorists like Oliver Wendell Holmes, Jr.[35]

As his tenure came to a close, Judge Parker offset continued Supreme Court reversals with a few crucial affirmations. In 1896 the Court overturned the convictions of Frank Carver (who killed his mistress, the daughter of former executioner George Maledon, during a drunken quarrel), Alexander Crain, Dennis Davis, Mollie King (by yet another Confession of Error), Eli Lucas, and Henry Starr. But the justices sustained the death sentences of Webber Isaacs, George and John Pearce, all five members of the so-called Buck Gang, and James Casharego. On April 30, 1896, Isaacs and the Pearce brothers were hanged. On July 1, Rufus Buck, Lucky and Lewis Davis, Sam Sampson, and Maoma July, all condemned for the rape of Mrs. Rosetta Hanson and the murder of Deputy Marshal John Garrett, were executed together. And less than a month later, on July 30, 1896, James Casharego became the last man to die on the Fort Smith gallows.[36]

By the time Casharego climbed the gibbet, however, Judge Parker was no longer presiding in court. Confined to bed by illness, he did not supervise the last days of Western District jurisdiction over the Indian Territory. In twenty-one years he had never missed a day due to sickness; now he was too weak to leave his room. The doctors diagnosed his malady as dropsy, an abnormal retention of fluid in body tissues that caused painful swelling, the result of long years of overwork. At first, Parker tried to conduct business from his sickbed, but the docket soon became backlogged. On August

24, 1896, Judge Henry Caldwell of the Eighth U.S. Circuit ordered
Oliver P. Shiras, federal judge for the Northern District of Iowa at
Dubuque, to preside over the Parker court long enough to deal
with pending cases. Shiras spent two days, August 27 and 28, in
Fort Smith, returning to Iowa before the official expiration of the
court's authority over the Indian country on September 1. Therefore, at the end of the session on August 28, 1896, court crier J. G.
Hammersly rose to announce, "Oyez! Oyez! The Honorable Circuit
and District Courts of the United States for the Western District of
Arkansas, having jurisdiction of the Indian Territory are now
adjourned, forever."[37]

On September 1, 1896, *St. Louis Republic* reporter Ada Patterson
arrived at Fort Smith to interview Judge Parker as his jurisdiction
over the Indian Territory officially expired. Propped up in bed by
pillows, the judge restated familiar themes in responding to her
questions, as wife Mary fanned him with a palm leaf. When
Patterson asked about his recent conflicts with the Supreme Court,
he replied predictably that "the justices are men from civil walks of
life; it is not then surprising that they are liable to err in criminal
cases." On his controversial courtroom conduct, he reiterated "I
have been accused of leading juries. I tell you a jury should be led
. . . if they are guided they will render justice." Parker asserted that
his critics "utterly forget the hardened character of the criminals I
have to deal with." He therefore chided the "good ladies"—such
as his wife—who had for years carried "flowers and jellies" to
condemned criminals. Seeing the convict in his cell, "they forget .
. . the family he has made fatherless." Such men deserved punishment, he argued, because definite retribution "halts crime." This
statement led to the obligatory question of how the "Hanging
Judge" viewed the death penalty. "I favor its abolition," he stated,
"provided there is a certainty of punishment." Shifting to the
subject of the Indian country, he praised American Indians as "reli-
giously inclined, law-abiding and authority-respecting," then criticized Congress for "depriving the Indian Country of the moral
force of a strong Federal Court." "I have ever had the single aim of

justice in view," he said, his weakened voice growing stronger as he summed up his long tenure. "'Do equal and exact justice' has been my motto, and I have often said to the grand juries, 'Permit no innocent man to suffer; let no guilty man escape.'"[38]

Critics surely contested most of these statements, but Parker was unable to respond with his usual force; in the weeks following this valedictory interview, his condition worsened rapidly. On October 9, he wrote his last letter to the Justice Department, defending his jury charge in the third trial of John Brown and complaining that "I have no health to go further into this question." Friends called to express their concern, as did most of the lawyers who had practiced in his court. The eldest of his two sons, Charles, returned to Fort Smith from St. Louis, where he had begun to practice law. The younger son, James, traveled home from the University of Michigan. By the middle of November, the judge had lapsed into a coma. But on the evening of November 16 he rallied enough to request a priest. Father Laurence Smyth, who had ministered to so many of the men that Parker had sentenced to death, baptized him as a Roman Catholic, then immediately administered the last rites. Early on the morning of November 17, 1896, at age fifty-eight, Isaac Parker died.[39]

The next day flags flew at half-staff as thousands of people from all walks of life paid their respects in the largest funeral that Fort Smith had ever witnessed. Every carriage, buggy, and wagon in town was pressed into service to transport mourners to the National Cemetery. Dignitaries joined the merely curious to push closer to the grave and hear Father Smyth conduct services. Representatives of the Loyal Order of Odd Fellows, the Grand Army of the Republic, and the Knights of Honor jostled with court employees, lawyers, and reporters to move within hearing range. Henry Dawes—a former congressional colleague who was in Fort Smith to arrange the final allotment of tribal lands in the Indian Territory—attended, along with members of the Presidential Commission that he headed and the representatives of the Five Civilized Tribes with whom they were negotiating. After the last prayer had been recited and holy water sprinkled on the grave, General Pleasant Porter, principal chief of the Creek Nation, stepped to the graveside for a final tribute. On behalf of all tribes in "the Nations," he placed a simple garland of wildflowers on the casket.[40]

CHAPTER TEN

"CRUEL THEY HAVE SAID I AM"

Reflections on a "Hanging Judge"

Isaac Parker died a tragic figure. After thirty years of dedicated governmental service, his personal flaws prevented him from bowing to public demands that he could not fully comprehend. Blinded by pride and ill temper, deceived by the conviction that he was indispensable, this once-powerful jurist concluded his life flailing impotently against the forces of judicial reform and national expansion. Such a long, dutiful career deserved a better end.

His achievements at Fort Smith were substantial. Parker salvaged the ruined reputation of his court and thereby established a foundation for legal order in the Indian Territory. In 1875, when he assumed his federal judicial duties, the Western District of Arkansas represented the worst in Reconstruction-era corruption, so scandal-ridden that Congress had seriously considered its abolition. Under Isaac Parker, the Western District Court attained a national reputation for the swift punishment of lawbreakers rather than the ethical malleability of its officials. Such a transformation enhanced law enforcement. Criminals in Parker's jurisdiction soon learned that, if captured, they faced a judge more concerned with meting out punishment than with lining his pockets.

Judge Parker, while expanding law enforcement in his bailiwick, certainly did not establish perfect order. Reported offenses outnumbered punished crime, but not for want of effort by the judge and his officers. The court disposed of over twelve thousand criminal cases during his tenure. But too many factors militated against efficient control in the Western District. From 1875 to 1883, the sheer size of the jurisdiction—74,000 square miles—deterred enforcement. Even if all of the two hundred deputies who "rode for Parker" during his tenure had served at the same time, policing such a vast expanse would have remained daunting. After 1883, when Congress first reduced the size of Parker's jurisdiction, growing population in the Indian country kept the Western District docket bulging. Unable to establish order permanently in the Indian Territory, Judge Parker at least laid a foundation, laboring for more than two decades, six days a week, from morning to night—as long as federal funding permitted—to enforce the law, to punish the guilty, and to protect the innocent.

Yet, ironically, this laudable dedication to do justice also led Parker to deny fair trials to many defendants. Sympathy for victims and a belief that swift, certain punishment deterred crime, as well as his early legal training and the judicial process itself, combined to influence Parker in favor of the prosecution. Only two years after completing the standard, rudimentary legal education of the time, young Isaac Parker had continued to learn the law while prosecuting criminal cases, first as Saint Joseph city attorney and then as Buchanan County prosecutor; much of his early practical experience taught him to think like a prosecutor. And, despite the vaunted presumption of innocence, the Western District criminal-justice process implied the guilt of the accused. U.S. commissioners issued writs only if they found sufficient evidence to justify the expenditure of time and resources that resulted from an arrest. Once the accused was in custody, further proceedings before a commissioner determined whether or not the testimony sufficed to support an indictment. If so, the case went to a grand jury. Only if that deliberative body found enough indication of guilt was the accused brought to trial. Thus, by the time a defendant faced the judge for arraignment, a U.S. commissioner, the district attorney, and the entire grand jury—all of whom held Parker's confidence and loyalty—had already determined that the individual was probably guilty. Little wonder, then, that Parker shared their presumptions and acted swiftly to mete out punishment in the hope of deterring similar offenses.

When the U.S. Supreme Court attempted to correct this bias, Parker interpreted the reversal of his sentences as personal attacks and responded in his usual manner—he struck back with invective. Whenever opponents had challenged him throughout his long career, whether on the floor of Congress or in his courtroom, Isaac Parker retaliated with rebuke that shifted the blame to his foes. Saint Joseph became "a hell-hole" when its politicians attacked his campaign for Congress, although Parker had, exactly as they charged, "bolted" the party. Fort Smith defense attorneys were "drunken lawyers" if they sought commutations for murderers whom Parker wanted executed, despite the fact that such applications were protected under the U.S. Constitution. Even the U.S. solicitor general became a "mental pigmy" after criticizing the judge for sloppy and outdated courtroom procedures that the Supreme Court had repeatedly overruled. Unable to distinguish criticism of his official conduct from personal reproach, Parker initiated a series of public tantrums against his superiors that marred his last years in office.

Judge Parker might have avoided such an unseemly episode, had he successfully pursued either of the judicial appointments available to him in 1889 and 1890, but he did not. After so many years of presiding over the Western District Court, Parker had become convinced that only he fully understood the complexities of his jurisdiction. The younger Isaac Parker, the politician who rose from frontier lawyer to U.S. congressman to federal district judge in a decade and a half, would have leapt at the opportunity for further advancement to U.S. circuit judge. But the consuming duties of the Fort Smith bench transformed the ego that drove such ambition into a brittle sense of rectitude and indispensability. Who else had as much experience with Indian Territory lawbreakers?

Who else had restored the reputation of the Western District Court? Who else had exerted such a "civilizing influence" over the Indian country and its inhabitants? To Parker, these questions were obviously rhetorical.

Surely no federal judge exercised as much power as Isaac Parker. Territorial judges dealt with similar offenders and offenses in vast, unsettled jurisdictions, but not with so little oversight. During his first seven years at Fort Smith, he exercised sole authority over the largest federal judicial district in the United States, checked only by the infrequent and inconsistent use of executive clemency. Although Congress reduced the size of his bailiwick after 1883, Parker became subject to the same appeals process as other federal jurists only during the last third of his tenure.

Infrequently challenged for fourteen years, Judge Parker grew accustomed to the unique powers of his office. That he rebelled when the Supreme Court finally began to review his judgments, or that so many of his decisions were reversed, was not surprising. Parker was a political appointee with enough legal background to satisfy the needs of the Grant administration in filling a judicial vacancy, not an insightful legal thinker or an honored jurist. At the time of his appointment, he possessed only a year and a half of judicial experience as a state circuit judge. He was a frontier attorney who had used the law as a means of political advancement. Better lawyers earned far more from their legal abilities than did Parker, who chose public service over private practice within the first two years of his career. In light of such professional limitations and the rapid transformation of American legal culture between 1865 and 1900, Parker's failure to keep abreast was understandable.

His long, successful career was all the more remarkable in light of such limited experience upon assuming the federal bench. After rising from frontier lawyer to U.S. district judge within fifteen years, Isaac Parker administered the busiest criminal court in the federal system effectively and honestly, if not always fairly and efficiently, for twenty-one years. True, he often denied defendants fair trials and frequently ruled against the American Indians he claimed to support; he rebelled against correction by his superiors and humiliated himself with public displays of temper. But Parker established a lasting reputation for himself and his court based on integrity and dedication to duty, and he fought lawlessness in his jurisdiction fiercely with all the resources available to him. The contradictions remained—an American Indian advocate who hastened the end of tribal sovereignty, an apostle of law who could not accept legal correction, a judge who handed down 161 capital sentences but claimed to oppose the death penalty—but ultimately Isaac Parker was a dedicated public servant, far more complex than suggested by the Hanging Judge image we remember.

NOTES

INTRODUCTION

1. Leigh Chalmers, Report on James C. Read, U.S. Attorney, W. Ark., February 17, 1896, Number 3410, File Number 4408, Letters Received, RG 60, 2–4, 6 (hereafter cited as "Chalmers Report").

2. *Saint Louis Globe-Democrat,* January 12, 1895, p. 4—July 27, 1895, p. 3—February 12, 1896, p. 3; Shirley, *Law West of Fort Smith,* 35–40, 187; Burton, *Indian Territory and the United States,* 226–28.

3. "Chalmers Report," Appendix B, 1; Shirley, *Law West of Fort Smith,* 9–10, 14–16, 192–193, and Harman, *Hell on the Border,* xvii–xx, 33–38, confirm Parker's chronology. Harman's count of eighty-eight hangings includes nine executions conducted before Parker took office. For the early legal history of Arkansas, see Arnold's *Colonial Arkansas, 1686–1804,* 125–70, 177–78, and his *Unequal Laws unto a Savage Race.* Ball, "Before the Hanging Judge": 199–213, details the early years of the Western District Court.

4. "Chalmers Report," Appendix B, 1–3.

5. Ibid., 4–5.

6. Ibid; Burton, *Indian Territory and the United States,* 215–16, 228.

7. Harman, however, was not the sole author. Fort Smith attorney J. Warren Reed contributed flattering accounts of his own exploits before the Parker court, while "compiler" C. P. Sterns probably performed most of the actual assemblage, amassing court records and

preparing biographical sketches. The book went out of print after the first edition; although occasionally reissued in severely edited form, the full volume only became widely available in a 1992 reprint. See Harman, *Hell on the Border*, xxi–xxii.

8. Croy, *He Hanged Them High*, 3–7; Harman, *Hell on the Border*, xxviii; Shirley, *Law West of Fort Smith*, vii–x; Emery, *Court of the Damned*. Croy repeated Harman's error in calculating the number of executions carried out under Judge Parker.

9. See, for example, Croy, *He Hanged Them High*, 3–15, 66–83, 101–18, 206–10; Shirley, *Law West of Fort Smith*, vii, 29–33, 99–109, 156, 159–74, 184–92; Emery, *Court of the Damned*, 37–45; 155–76.

10. Harrington, *Hanging Judge*; Shirley, *Law West of Fort Smith*, vii–x; Stolberg, "Politician, Populist, Reformer": 3–28; Stolberg, "The Evolution of Frontier Justice": 7–23.

11. "Chalmers Report," 1–5; Burton, *Indian Territory and the United States*, 230; Shirley, *Law West of Fort Smith*, 209–43; Croy, *He Hanged Them High*, 38. For a discussion of nineteenth-century criminal justice administration, see David J. Bodenhamer, *The Pursuit of Justice*, especially 9–116; see also Bodenhamer, *Fair Trial*, 48–91.

12. Shirley, *Law West of Fort Smith*, 17–24, 41–58; Burton, *Indian Territory and the United States*, 192–93, 206–8, 210–11. See also Shirley, *West of Hell's Fringe*, and Houts, *From Gun to Gavel*, for continued lawlessness in the Indian Territory after Parker's death.

13. "Crime Totals for All Years," Index to Criminal Case Files, n.d.; *United States v. Elias Jenkins, United States v. Thomas Triplett, United States v. Isham Seely, United States v. Gibson Ishtonubee, United States v. William Whittington*—all in Records of the District Courts of the United States, Arkansas, Western District, RG 21 (hereafter cited as District Court Records); *Coffeyville (Kansas) Journal*, August 5, 1879, p. 1; Burton, *Indian Territory and the United States*, pp. 192–211ff.

14. Roger Tuller, "'The Hanging Judge' and the Indians," master's thesis, 1993; Burton, *Indian Territory and the United States*, 106–22, 138–201.

15. Applications for Pardon, Jack Spaniard, Joe Marten, Records of the Department of Justice, Office of the Pardon Attorney, RG 36 (hereafter cited as Pardon Files); Stolberg, "Politician, Populist, Reformer": 13–14, 16; Burton, *Indian Territory and the United States*, 199; Shirley, *Law West of Fort Smith*, 33–35.

16. Stolberg, "Politician, Populist, Reformer": 11–12; Tuller, "'Hanging Judge' and the Indians," 18; Shirley, *Law West of Fort Smith*, 202–3; Croy, *He Hanged Them High*, 216.

CHAPTER 1

1. Croy, *He Hanged Them High*, 13; Shirley, *Law West of Fort Smith*, 25; Berry and Berry, *Early Ohio Settlers*, 23; Roseboom and Weisenburger, *A History of Ohio*, 206–9, 224–25; Wendell H. Stephenson, "Shannon, Wilson," in Dumas Malone, ed., *The Dictionary of American Biography*, 9:20–21.

2. Berry and Berry, *Early Ohio Settlers*, 7; Croy, *He Hanged Them High*, 11–12; Department of State, *Compendium of the Enumeration of the Inhabitants and Statistics of the United States*, 78–79, 276–82.

3. Shirley, *Law West of Fort Smith*, 25–26; Croy, *He Hanged Them High*, 12–13; Versteeg, *Methodism*, 95–102; Roseboom and Weisenburger, *History of Ohio*, 207.

4. Croy, *He Hanged Them High*, 12; Shirley, *Law West of Fort Smith*, 25–26. An exhibit at Fort Smith National Historic Site displays books recovered from Parker's home in Fort Smith following a cyclone in 1898, including the above-mentioned works. Author visit, August 1995.

5. Shirley, *Law West of Fort Smith*, 26.

6. Friedman, *A History of American Law*, 265–92, 525–46; Bakken, *Practicing Law in Frontier California*, 22–32; Walker, *Popular Justice*, 44–45; Croy, *He Hanged Them High*, 13.

7. Roseboom and Weisenburger, *History of Ohio*, 182; Friedman, *History of American Law*, 564–66; Bakken, *Practicing Law in Frontier California*, 20–21; Charles Francis Adams, *An Autobiography*, 41–42.

8. Croy, *He Hanged Them High*, 16–19; Shirley, *Law West of Fort Smith*, 26; *Saint Joseph City Directory, 1859*, 65.

9. *Saint Joseph City Directory, 1859*, 12; *Saint Joseph City Directory, 1859–1860*, 46, 65; Croy, *He Hanged Them High*, 26; Shirley, *Law West of Fort Smith*, 26; Berry and Berry, *Early Ohio Settlers*, 23, 27, 56. For Wilson Shannon's unsuccessful tenure as governor of Kansas Territory, see Jay Monaghan, *Civil War on the Western Border*, 29–66 ff., and Kenneth S. Davis, *Kansas: A Bicentennial History*, 51–52, 61, 67.

10. *Saint Joseph City Directory, 1860–61*, 82; *Buchanan County Missouri Order Book # 6* (October 1859–September 1862, hereafter cited as *County Order Book # 6*); *Recorder's Civil Court Minute Book, 1857–1865* (Saint Joseph, Missouri), 523, 633 (hereafter cited as *Minute Book*); Bakken, *Practicing Law in Frontier California*, 33–35.

11. *Revised Ordinances, 1857*, (Saint Joseph, Missouri), 20; *Minute Book*, 299; Croy, *He Hanged Them High*, 18–20; Shirley, *Law West of Fort Smith*, 27.

12. *Revised Ordinances, 1857*, 20–25.

13. *Minute Book*, 361, 365–67, 368, 371, 374–76, 378, 380.

14. Ibid., pp. 365, 375–76. Many residents of nineteenth-century frontier towns and cities kept pigs as a source of meat, allowing them to roam the streets and fatten themselves on garbage and other available forage. Municipal hog ordinances forbade the practice, responding to the perception that the animals posed a threat both to public safety and decency. On such ordinances, see Wade, *The Urban Frontier*, 72–100, 270–303; Hartog, *Public Property and Private Power*, 139–43.

15. *Record Book #2, July 12, 1858–May 16, 1862* (Saint Joseph, Missouri), April 8, 1861.

16. Ibid., April 8–May 2, 1861.

17. Monaghan, *Civil War on the Western Border*, 3–84, 286; Parrish, *A History of Missouri*, vol. 3, *1860–1875*, 36, 44–45, 52, 57, 64–70, 76–77; Michael Fellman, *Inside War*, 27–28, 33–34, 47, 56–57, 64, 88, 115, 152, 173. On the feud as a distinct form of Southern violence, see Ayers, *Vengeance and Justice*, 141–50, 263–64; Hindus, *Prison and Plantation*, 59, 63, 75, 78, 97; Montell, *Killings*, xxi, 1–22, 46, 105, 109, 116, 144–65; Wyatt-Brown, *Honor and Violence in the Old South*, 120,142–53.

18. *Saint Joseph Morning Herald*, February 9, 1861, p. 1; Croy, *He Hanged Them High*, 18, 22; Shirley, *Law West of Fort Smith*, 28.

19. Croy, *He Hanged Them High*, 21–22; Shirley, *Law West of Fort Smith*, 26. A review of Buchanan County marriage records failed to corroborate the date of the ceremony; either the records have been lost, or the couple married outside the county.

20. *Minute Book*, 377, 381; *Saint Joseph Morning Herald*, March 21, 1862, p. 2; Croy, *He Hanged Them High*, 19.

21. Croy, *He Hanged Them High*, 19–20; *Saint Joseph Morning Herald*, April 3, 1862, p. 1; *County Order Book # 6*, 608; *Buchanan County, Missouri, Order Book # 7* (September 1862–May 1865, hereafter cited as *County Order Book #7*), 84, 131, 295, 340, 387, 436, 444.

22. *Saint Joseph Morning Herald*, April 3, 1864, p. 1—June 2, 1864, p. 2—September 7, 1864, p. 3—December 3, 1864, p. 1; Croy, *He Hanged Them High*, 19–21; Shirley, *Law West of Fort Smith*, 27.

23. Siebert, *The Mysteries of Ohio's Underground Railroads*, 126–32; Foner, *Free Soil, Free Labor, and Free Men*, 301–8.

24. Croy, *He Hanged Them High*, 19–20; *Saint Joseph Morning Herald*, April 3, 1862, p. 1; *County Order Book # 6*, 608; *County Order Book # 7*, 84, 131, 295, 340, 387, 436, 444.

25. *County Order Book # 7*, 543–603; *Buchanan County, Missouri Order Book # 8* (September 1865–September 1867, hereafter cited as *County Order Book # 8*), 450, 483, 505, 516.

26. Swick, *Resident and Business Directory of Saint Joseph*, 10, 124–25; *Saint Joseph Morning Herald*, November 5, 1868, p. 1; Croy, *He Hanged Them High*, 242.

27. *Buchanan County, Missouri, Order Book # 10* (February 1, 1869–March 2, 1871, hereafter cited as *County Order Book # 10*), 162–319; Croy, *He Hanged Them High*, 22.

28. *County Order Book # 10*, 163–66, 168, 170; Croy, *He Hanged Them High*, 67; Shirley, *Law West of Fort Smith*, 79.

29. *County Order Book # 10*, 162–319, 504–641; *County Order Book # 8*, 450–516; *County Order Book # 7*, 340–444.

30. *Saint Joseph Daily Herald*, October 11, 1870, p. 2; Parrish, *History of Missouri*, 256–61; Parrish, *Missouri under Radical Rule*, 268–313.

31. *Saint Joseph Daily Herald*, September 13, 1870, p. 1; September 14, 1870, pp. 1, 2.

32. Ibid., September 14, 1870, p. 2.

33. Ibid., September 14, 1870, p. 1; September 20, 1870, p. 1.

34. Ibid., September 20, 1870, p. 1; September 21, 1870. p. 1; September 24, 1870, p. 1; October 1, 1870, p. 1; October 8, 1870, p. 1.

35. Ibid., October 8, 1870, p. 1; October 13, 1870, p. 1.

36. Ibid., October 26, 1870, p. 2; November 8, 1870, p. 1; November 12, 1870, pp. 1, 2.

37. C. Robert Haywood, *Cowtown Lawyers*, 104; Bakken, *Practicing Law in Frontier California*, 6, 9, 92, 104.

CHAPTER 2

1. *Congressional Globe*, 42d Cong., 1st sess., 5.

2. Ibid., 78, 177, 610; ibid., 2d sess., 197, 694, 1126, 1195, 1223, 1587, 1774; ibid., 3d sess., 10, 84, 220, 354; *Congressional Record*, 43d Cong., 1st sess., 66, 73, 87, 205, 210, 535, 763, 794, 1345, 1902, 1920, 2165, 2209, 2635, 2836, 2849, 4428, 4934, 5130, 5158; ibid., 2d sess., 19, 1301. For opposing views on Civil War veterans' pensions, see Gordon, *Pitied but Not Entitled*, 51; and Skocpol, *Protecting Soldiers and Mothers*, 102–52.

3. *Congressional Globe*, 42d Cong., 1st sess., 177; 2d sess., 2244–46, 2817; *Congressional Record*, 43d Cong., 1st sess., 66.

4. *Congressional Globe*, 42d Cong., 1st sess, 397–99, 801, 3298; ibid., 2d sess., 287–91, 4323.

5. Ibid., 3d sess., 1843; Foner, *Reconstruction*, 460–505; Stampp, *The Era of Reconstruction*, 187–201; Sproat, *"The Best Men,"* 3–89.

6. *Congressional Globe,* 42d Cong., 2d sess., 843, 1140, 1234; see also Beeton, *Women Vote in the West;* Bakken, *Rocky Mountain Constitution Making,* 85–100.

7. *Congressional Globe,* 42d Cong., 2d sess., 289–90, 830, 2954; ibid, 3d sess., 611–16, 648–55; *Congressional Record,* 43d Cong., 1st sess., 66; ibid., 2d sess., 72; Stolberg, "Politician, Populist, Reformer": 6–8. Homer Croy asserted that Parker's interest began with his first contacts with Native Americans in Saint Joseph, but offered no evidence in support; see *He Hanged Them High,* 23–24.

8. Burton, *Indian Territory and the United States,* 27–30, 33, 36, 134.

9. Stolberg, "Politician, Populist, Reformer": 6–8; *Congressional Globe,* 42d Cong., 2d sess., 2955; *Fort Smith Weekly Elevator,* January 18, 1895, p. 2; and January 25, 1895, p. 3.

10. *Saint Joseph Daily Herald,* August 7, 1872, p. 1; October 27, 1872, pp. 1, 2; November 5, 1872, p. 1; November 6, 1872, p. 1.

11. *Congressional Record,* 43d Cong., 1st sess., 5; ibid., 2d sess., 19, 72.

12. Ibid., 1st sess., 3471–76.

13. Ibid., 3475–76.

14. Ibid., 3546–47, 3730, 5218–19, 5318; *Saint Joseph Daily Herald,* May 8, 1874, pp. 1–2; *New York Times,* May 1, 1874, p. 4.

15. *Congressional Record,* 42d Cong., 1st sess., 2108.

16. Slotkin, *The Fatal Environment,* 62, 140–41, 222, 269, 316–21; Mardock, *The Reformers and the American Indian,* 1–8, 85–106; Fritz, *The Movement for Indian Assimilation,* 34–86. See also Dippie, *The Vanishing American.*

17. *Congressional Record,* 43d Cong., 1st sess., 4914, 4921, 5000–5003, 5007–5008, 5014, 5218; ibid., 2d sess., 593–94. In 1855 Congress created a Court of Claims to hear suits against the government, but an 1863 amendment excepted Indian cases from its jurisdiction. Thus tribes like the Choctaw and Chickasaw sought remedy directly from a Congress reluctant to satisfy their claims. In 1881 the Court of Claims renewed its jurisdiction over Indian claims, handling over two hundred such cases until Congress passed the Indian Claims Commission Act in 1946. Prucha, *American Indian Treaties,* 376–84. See also Green and Dickason, *The Law of Nations and the New World,* and Williams, *The American Indian in Western Legal Thought,* for the origins and evolution of American Indian legal status under colonial European and early U.S. law.

18. *Congressional Record,* 43d Cong., 2d sess., 19, 72, 440–42, 461–63, 466, 469, 594, 1085, 1086, 1988–90.

19. Shirley, *Law West of Fort Smith,* 28–29.

20. *Fort Smith Weekly New Era,* March 31, 1875, p. 2; Croy, *He Hanged Them High,* 24–25; Shirley, *Law West of Fort Smith,* 28–29.

21. Croy, *He Hanged Them High*, 24–25; U. S. Grant to United States Senate, March 16, 1875, *Journal of the Executive Proceedings of the Senate of the United States of America from March 5, 1875 to March 3, 1877, Inclusive*, 20: 31 (hereafter cited as *Senate Executive Journal*).

22. Stolberg, "Politician, Populist, Reformer": 5. In a pamphlet sold at Fort Smith National Historic Site, former National Park Service historians Guy Nichols, Leo Allison, and Thomas Crowson asserted that Grant asked Parker to take the Western District appointment. This version appears to stem from obituary accounts of Parker's career, based in turn on his last newspaper interview. The documentary evidence, however, confirms that Parker applied for the position a week before Grant submitted his name to the Senate for the Utah vacancy. See Nichols, Allison, and Crowson, "Judge Isaac Parker, Myths and Legends Aside," 1; *Arkansas Gazette*, November 17, 1896, p. 1; *Saint Louis Republic*, September 6, 1896, pp. 1–2.

23. *Congressional Record*, 43d Cong., 1st sess., 5316; ibid., 2d sess., 387–89; Croy, *He Hanged Them High*, 24–25. On relations between Mormons and the Utah Territorial Court, see Bakken, *The Development of Law on the Rocky Mountain Frontier*, 23, and "Constitutional Convention Debates in the West": 213–44; Firmage and Mangrum, *Zion in the Courts*, 129–278; Lamar, *The Far Southwest*, 305–402; Larson, *The "Americanization" of Utah for Statehood*, 8, 16, 19–20, 31–114, 247–51, 302; Lyman, *Political Deliverance*, 7–40.

CHAPTER 3

1. Shirley, *Law West of Fort Smith*, 17–24; Burton, *Indian Territory and the United States*, 3, 6–14; Harman, *Hell on the Border*, 33–35, 40–43; Croy, *He Hanged Them High*, 24; Stolberg, "Politician, Populist, Reformer": 8–11.

2. Harman, *Hell on the Border*, 33–43; Shirley, *Law West of Fort Smith*, 9–24.

3. Gillette, *Retreat from Reconstruction*, 136–37; Clayton, *The Aftermath of the Civil War*, 319–33.

4. Gillette, *Retreat from Reconstruction*, 137–38.

5. Ibid., 138–39.

6. Ibid., 139–43.

7. Stolberg, "Politician, Populist, and Reformer": 8–9; Harman, *Hell on the Border*, 129–30.

8. *House Executive Document 175* (1875), 43d Cong., 2d sess., 3–25ff. (hereafter cited as *Du Val Report*); *Congressional Record*, 43d Cong., 1st

sess., 4735–36; ibid., 2d sess., 387–89, 2118; Stolberg, "Politician, Populist, and Reformer": 10–11; Shirley, *Law West of Fort Smith*, 16–17; Burton, *Indian Territory and the United States*, 56–60; Harman, *Hell on the Border*, 40–43.

9. *Du Val Report*, 12, 31; Burton, *Indian Territory and the United States*, 52–53, 55–56. For a report that partially exonerates Judge Story, see Stephan, "The United States District Court for the Western District of Arkansas and Judge William H. Story, 1872–1874" (master's thesis, Arkansas State University, 1985).

10. Burton, *Indian Territory and the United States*, 57, 60; Harman, *Hell on the Border*, 42.

11. *DuVal Report*, 5–6, 8–11, 18.

12. Ibid., 8, 14–16.

13. Ibid., 2118. *Congressional Record*, 43d Cong., 2d sess., 387–89, 2118.

14. Ibid., 2118.

15. U. S. Grant to United States Senate, March 18, 1875, Resolution, *Senate Executive Journal*, 20: 40, 45.

16. *Fort Smith Weekly New Era*, March 17, 1875, p. 1; Stolberg, "Politician, Populist, Reformer": 10–11; Croy, *He Hanged Them High*, 23–26; Shirley, *Law West of Fort Smith*, 29–32.

17. *Fort Smith Weekly Herald*, May 8, 1875, p. 1; Stolberg, "Politician, Populist, Reformer": 12; Shirley, *Law West of Fort Smith*, 32–34. Parker's counterpart in U.S. District Court for the Western District of Missouri, Arnold Krekel, had faced a similar backlog ten years earlier resulting from wartime disruption of court proceedings. The U.S. District Court in Missouri—divided into separate Eastern and Western Districts in 1857—held jurisdiction of the Indian country immediately to the west of that state under the Indian Intercourse Act of 1834. When Congress created Kansas Territory from the Missouri jurisdiction in 1854, federal authority over the Indian country devolved on the U.S. District Court for the Western District of Arkansas. See Larsen, *Federal Justice in Western Missouri*, 1–74; Ball, "Federal Justice on the Santa Fe Trail."

18. Harman, *Hell on the Border*, 107–8, 117–18, 120–22, 127–30; Shirley, *Law West of Fort Smith*, 33–34; Stolberg, "Politician, Populist, Reformer": 12.

19. Isaac Parker to Attorney General Edwards Pierrepont, May 18, July 27, August 6, 1875, Source Chronological Letters Files, RG 60 (hereafter cited as Letters Received); Stolberg, "Politician, Populist, Reformer": 13–14.

20. *Fort Smith Western Independent*, April 6, 1876, p. 1, Stolberg, "Politician, Populist, Reformer": 13, 15. Parker's efforts were comparable to

those of William Higby in establishing legal institutions in the California gold fields during the 1850s; see Bakken, *Practicing Law in Frontier California*, 103–9.

CHAPTER 4

1. *Arkansas Gazette*, September 4, 1875, p. 1; *Saint Louis Republican*, September 4, 1875, p. 1; *Saint Joseph Morning Herald*, September 5, 1875, p. 1; Croy, *He Hanged Them High*, 50–51; Shirley, *Law West of Fort Smith*, 39.

2. Harrington, *Hanging Judge*, 30–31; Stolberg, "Politician Populist, Reformer": 12–13.

3. *Saint Joseph Morning Herald*, September 5, 1875, 1; Harman, *Hell on the Border*, 171, 200–205; Croy, *He Hanged Them High*, 33–38; Shirley, *Law West of Fort Smith*, 36.

4. Harman, *Hell on the Border*, 171, 207–8; Croy, *He Hanged Them High*, 44–45; Shirley, *Law West of Fort Smith*, 37.

5. *United States v. Frank Butler, Edmund Campbell, and Samuel Campbell*, Records of the District Courts of the United States, RG 21, Criminal Case Files (hereafter cited as District Court Records). "Judgment, Sentence, and Order," *United States v. Oscar Snow*, District Court Records; Duval and Cravens, attorneys at law to Edwards Pierrepont, Attorney General, July 6, 1875; William H. H. Clayton to Pierrepont, July 19, 1875—all in Application for Pardon, Oscar Snow, Record E 509, (hereafter cited as Pardon Records); Harman, *Hell on the Border*, 171, 205–11; Croy, *He Hanged Them High*, 40–46; Shirley, *Law West of Fort Smith*, 35–37.

6. Harman, *Hell on the Border*, 109; Croy, *He Hanged Them High*, 99; Application for Pardon, Oscar Snow, Pardon Records. For a more complete discussion of *Snow* and other pardon cases, see Chapter 5.

7. *Saint Louis Republican*, September 4, 1875, p. 1; Croy, *He Hanged Them High*, 50; Shirley, *Law West of Fort Smith*, 29, 35.

8. *Saint Louis Republican*, September 4, 1875, p. 1; *Arkansas Gazette*, September 4, 1875, p. 1; Croy, *He Hanged Them High*, 47, 49.

9. *Arkansas Gazette*, September 4, 1875, p. 1; *New York Times*, September 4, 1875, p. 1; *Saint Joseph Morning Herald*, September 5, 1875, p. 1; Harman, *Hell on the Border*, 209; Croy, *He Hanged Them High*, 50–52; Shirley, *Law West of Fort Smith*, 38–39.

10. *Saint Louis Republican*, September 4, 1875, p. 1; *New York Times*, September 4, 1875, p. 1; Shirley, *Law West of Fort Smith*, 39–40.

11. Harman, *Hell on the Border*, 93.

12. *Saint Louis Republican*, April 22, 1876, p. 1; Harman, *Hell on the Border*, 217–18; Shirley, *Law West of Fort Smith*, 211.

13. *Arkansas Gazette*, April 22, 1876, p. 1; Harman, *Hell on the Border*, 215–16; Shirley, *Law West of Fort Smith*, 210–11.

14. *United States v. William Leach*, District Court Records; *Arkansas Gazette*, April 22, 1876, p. 1; *Saint Joseph Morning Herald*, April 22, 1876, p. 1; Croy, *He Hanged Them High*, 62; Shirley, *Law West of Fort Smith*, 210.

15. *Saint Louis Republican*, April 22, 1876, p. 1; *Saint Joseph Morning Herald*, April 22, 1876, p. 1; *Arkansas Gazette*, April 21, 1876, p. 1—April 22, 1876, p. 2—April 23, 1876, p. 1.

16. *Arkansas Gazette*, April 22, 1876, p. 1; Croy, *He Hanged Them High*, 64.

17. *Saint Louis Republican*, April 22, 1876, p. 1; *Saint Joseph Morning Herald*, April 22, 1876, p. 1; *Arkansas Gazette*, April 21, 1876, p. 1—April 22, 1876, p. 2—April 23, 1876, p. 1; Croy, *He Hanged Them High*, 68.

18. *Arkansas Gazette*, April 22, 1876, p. 1; *New York Times*, April 22, 1876, p. 1.

19. Louis P. Masur, *Rites of Execution*, 25–49. For contemporary parallels, see Friedman and Percival, *Roots of Justice*, 303–7. For a cultural analysis of public executions, see Gatrell, *The Hanging Tree*. See also Foucault, *Discipline and Punish*, 3–72.

20. *Arkansas Gazette*, September 4, 1875, p. 1—April 22, 1876, p. 1; *Saint Joseph Morning Herald*, September 5, 1875, p. 1—April 22, 1876, p. 1; *Saint Louis Republican*, September 4, 1875, p. 1—April 22, 1876, p. 1; "Judgment, Sentence, and Order," *U.S. v. Frank Butler, Edmund Campbell, and Samuel Campbell*, District Court Records.

21. *Arkansas Gazette*, September 4, 1875, p. 1—April 22, 1876, p. 1; *Saint Joseph Morning Herald*, September 5, 1875, p.1—April 22, 1876, p. 1; *Saint Louis Republican*, September 4, 1875, p. 1—April 22, 1876, p. 1; Gatrell, *Hanging Tree*, 29–39.

22. *Arkansas Gazette*, September 4, 1875, p. 1—April 22, 1876, p. 1; *Saint Joseph Morning Herald*, September 5, 1875, p. 1—April 22, 1876, p. 1; *Saint Louis Republican*, September 4, 1875, p. 1—April 22, 1876, p. 1; Masur, *Rites of Execution*, 5–6, 26, 34–35, 39–45.

23. *Arkansas Gazette*, September 4, 1875, p. 1—April 22, 1876, p. 1; *Saint Joseph Morning Herald*, September 5, 1875, p. 1—April 22, 1876, p. 1; *Saint Louis Republican*, September 4, 1875, p. 1—April 22, 1876, p. 1; Croy, *He Hanged Them High*, p. 50; Masur, *Rites of Execution*, 6, 45–46, 96, 116.

24. Harman, *Hell on the Border*, 171, 219; Croy, *He Hanged Them High*, 5.

25. *New York Times*, December 21, 1878, p. 1—September 10, 1881, p. 1—April 14, 1883, p. 5—June 30, 1883, p. 5—January 15, 1887, p. 3—

March 18, 1896, p. 6; Shirley, *Law West of Fort Smith*, 212–31; Masur, *Rites of Execution*, 14, 31, 33–39, 103–5, 144; Gatrell, *Hanging Tree*, 156–57, 163–69, 168, 171–74, 284.

26. "Crime Totals for All Years," 1–2; *Statutes at Large of the United States of America*, 1:113; Croy, *He Hanged Them High*, 216; Shirley, *Law West of Fort Smith*, 209–31. For pardons and commutations, see Chapter 5.

27. Shirley, *Law West of Fort Smith*, 212–213; Harman, *Hell on the Border*, 220–21.

28. *New York Times*, December 21, 1878, p. 1—September 10, 1881, p. 1; Shirley, *Law West of Fort Smith*, 213–14; Harman, *Hell on the Border*, 220–26.

29. Attorney General Charles Devens to U.S. Marshal D. P. Upham, June 11, 1878, Records of the U.S. Department of Justice, Record Number B. 13. fr. 55, Letters Sent File, RG 60 (hereafter cited as "Letters Sent"); *New York Times*, September 10, 1881, p. 1; Shirley, *Law West of Fort Smith*, 82, 214.

30. Masur, *Rites of Execution*, 93–116; Shirley, *Law West of Fort Smith*, 216, 227.

CHAPTER 5

1. Shirley, *Law West of Fort Smith*, 41; Croy, *He Hanged Them High*, 3; Harrington, *Hanging Judge*, 179; Burton, *Indian Territory and the United States*, 197–98.

2. See Shirley, *Law West of Fort Smith*, 233–43, for an accurate listing of executions, pardons, and commutations.

3. "Judgment, Sentence, and Order," *United States v. Oscar Snow*, District Court Records; Duval and Cravens, attorneys at law to Edwards Pierrepont, Attorney General, July 6, 1875, and William H. H. Clayton to Edwards Pierrepont, July 19, 1875—both in Application for Pardon, Oscar Snow, Pardon Records; *Statutes at Large of the United States of America*, 1: 113; Burton, *Indian Territory and the United States*, 46–50.

4. Duval and Cravens to Pierrepont, July 6, 1875; Clayton to Pierrepont, July 19, 1875; Isaac Parker to Edwards Pierrepont, July 27, 1875; "Report"—all in Application for Pardon, Oscar Snow, Pardon Records.

5. Harman, *Hell on the Border*, pp. 221–22; Shirley, *Law West of Fort Smith*, pp. 233–34.

6. Petition for pardon, and letter from William H. H. Clayton to A. R. Dutton, chief pardon clerk—both in Application for Pardon, Irving Perkins (colored), Record F 413, Pardon Records.

7. Petition for pardon, ibid.

8. "Report, In Re Irving Perkins, W. Ark.," ibid.

9. Alexander F. Gray, "Report," April 19, 1877, and Charles Devens, "Report upon the Application for Pardon of Irving Perkins"—both in Pardon Records.

10. "In Re Charley Thomas, W. Ark—Report of Dist. Atty. and Judge, April 19, 1877," in Application for Pardon, Charley Thomas, Record F 414, Pardon Records.

11. Ibid.

12. A. S. Fowler to Rutherford B. Hayes, March 26, 1877, and Alexander F. Gray, "Report upon the Application for Pardon of Charley Thomas, Western Dist. of Arkansas, April 18, 1877," in Pardon Records; Richard Maxwell Brown, *No Duty to Retreat*, 3–5.

13. Valentine Dell to Rutherford B. Hayes, March 24, 1877; Fowler to Hayes, March 26, 1877; Gray, "Report upon the Application for Pardon of Charley Thomas"—all in Application for Pardon, Charley Thomas, Pardon Records.

14. Gray, "Report upon the Application for Pardon of Charley Thomas," and Charles Devens, "Report upon the Application for Pardon of Charley Thomas"—both in Pardon Records; Burton, *Indian Territory and the United States*, 50.

15. Isaac Parker to Charles Devens, April 23, 1877, and "Report of Dist. Att. and endorsement of Judge, April 9–16, 1877," in Application for Pardon, Charley Thomas, Record F 414, Pardon Records; Brown, *No Duty to Retreat*, 6–8.

16. Commutation Proclamation, *United States v. Joshua Wade*, District Court Records; Harman, *Hell on the Border*, 176, 221; Shirley, *Law West of Fort Smith*, 234.

17. William H. H. Clayton to Charles Devens, June 5, 1878, in Application for Pardon, Carolina Grayson, Peter W. Grayson, Man Lewis, and Robert Love, Record G 222, Pardon Records; Harman, *Hell on the Border*, 221; Burton, *Indian Territory and the United States*, 49–50.

18. Petition, Application for Pardon, Carolina Grayson, Peter W. Grayson, Man Lewis, and Robert Love, Record G 222, Pardon Records.

19. Letter from Clayton to Devens, June 5, 1876, and Charles Devens, "Report upon the Application for Pardon of Carolina Grayson, Peter Grayson, Man Lewis and Robert Love, W. D. Arkansas," June 15, 1878—both in Pardon Records.

20. Mifflin W. Gibbs to Rutherford B. Hayes, August 12, 1878; Thomas Marcum to Rutherford B. Hayes, August 12, 1878; Tillman Knox to the president of the U.S., August 16, 1878; Tillman Knox, "Statement to the

President," August 20, 1878—all in Pardon Records; Proclamation of Commutation, *United States v. Carolina Grayson*, District Court Records.

21. Isaac Parker to Charles Devens, August 21, 1878, and Application for Pardon, Carolina Grayson, Peter W. Grayson, Man Lewis, and Robert Love, Record G 222, Pardon Records.

22. Proclamation of Commutation, *United States v. Uriah M. Cooper*, District Court Records; Harman, *Hell on the Border*, 172, 176; Shirley, *Law West of Fort Smith*, 213–14, 234.

23. Indictment # 619, and Motion for a New Trial, January 23, 1880, both in *U.S. v. Uriah Cooper*, District Court Records; Harman, *Hell on the Border*, 224.

24. Application for Witnesses, May 5, 1879; Motion for a New Trial, January 23, 1880; Judgment, Sentence, and Order, March 29, 1880—all in *U.S. v. Uriah Cooper*, District Court Records; Harman, *Hell on the Border*, 225.

25. Motion for a New Trial, *U.S. v. Uriah Cooper*, District Court Records; Friedman, *Crime and Punishment in American History*, 244–47; Friedman and Percival, *Roots of Justice*, 186–89; Walker, *Popular Justice*, 69–78; Bodenhamer, *Fair Trial*, 61–63; Burton, *Indian Territory and the United States*, 48, 197; Harman, *Hell on the Border*, 90. For Supreme Court appeals, see Chapter 9. Ogden Hoffman, a contemporary federal district judge, was likewise prone to include his verdict preferences in jury instructions, but appears to have exercised somewhat more restraint over his biases in criminal cases than Parker. Hoffman also displayed more flexibility than Parker, reversing his opinions when necessary; see Christian G. Fritz, *Federal Justice in California*, 100–133.

26. Alexander F. Gray, "Report upon the Application for Pardon of Uriah M. Cooper, W. D. Ark.," June 7, 1880, in Application for Pardon, Uriah M. Cooper, Record H 300, Pardon Records; Proclamation of Commutation, *U.S. v. Uriah Cooper*, District Court Records.

27. Harman, *Hell on the Border*, 176, 225; Shirley, *Law West of Fort Smith*, 234.

28. "Re James N. Heaslet, W. D. Ark., Dist. Atty's Report, Rec'd June 1, 1880," Application for Pardon, James Heaslett, Record H 243, Pardon Records.

29. "Dist. Atty's Report," and "Re James N. Heaslett, W. D. Ark., Judge's opinion, Rec'd June 1, 1880," both in Pardon Records. Judge Parker did not fully explain his objections to the insanity defense, a controversial issue in the last half of the nineteenth century. The standard legal test was the "M'Naughten rule," requiring that the defendant not recognize the nature of his act, not understand whether it was right or wrong. Some states added an "irresistible impulse" test, allowing the

defendant to have understood the nature of the act, but, through mental illness, to have been overcome by an uncontrollable urge resulting in the crime. In New Hampshire, the question of insanity became a question of fact for juries alone to determine with Chief Justice Charles Doe's 1869 ruling in *State v. Pike*. Clearly Parker's conviction that juries needed to be led would have biased him against the New Hampshire rule. The nineteenth-century jurisprudential training that he received, emphazing criminal actions over motives, would have likewise reduced the viability of the insanity defense in his eyes. A year after Heaslett's pardon case was resolved, the insanity plea of President James Garfield's assassin, Charles Guiteau, focused national attention, but shed little light, on the insanity defense. See Friedman, *History of American Law*, 514–16; John Phillip Reid, *Chief Justice*, 94–109; Charles Rosenberg, *The Trial of the Assassin Guiteau*.

30. J. K. Pratt to L. M. Gunter, April 14, 1880; A. H. Garland, J. W. Adkin, W. H. Seemacy, and Jordan Branau to the President, April 22, 1880; William Brown to J. A. Garfield, March 9, 1880; Alexander F. Gray, "Report upon the App'n. for Pardon of James N. Heaslett," June 7, 1880—all in Application for Pardon, James Heaslett, Pardon Records.

31. Croy, *He Hanged Them High*, 3; Shirley, *Law West of Fort Smith*, 139–40; Harman, *Hell on the Border*, 171–72, 176.

32. Humbert, *The Pardoning Power of the President*, 124. On the history of the pardon power and its application in the nineteenth century, see also Moore, Pardons, 25–28, 49–54, and Friedman, *Crime and Punishment in American History*, 162.

CHAPTER 6

1. *U.S. Statutes at Large*, 1: 113; 4: 115; Burton, *Indian Territory and the United States*, 46–47; Shirley, *Law West of Fort Smith*, 23–24. Although federal statutes set the penalty for crimes such as murder, rape, and larceny, common law had defined such offenses and the district courts followed common-law procedures in their prosecution.

2. Common Law Record Book, vol. 5 (hereafter cited as Common Law Record Book), District Court Records, 39; Shirley, *Law West of Fort Smith*, 16–17.

3. Common Law Record Book, District Court Records, 39.

4. Ibid.

5. Complaint, Proceedings before Commissioner; Indictment 1806, *United States v. Thomas Triplett*, Common Law Record Book, District Court Records, 40.

6. Ibid.

7. Complaint, Proceedings before Commissioner, Indictment 1806, *United States v. Leonard Fulsome,* Common Law Record Book, District Court Records, 40.

8. Proceedings before Commissioner, *United States v. Frank Webster,* Common Law Record Book, District Court Records, 41.

9. Proceedings before Commissioner, Indictment 1808, Complaint, Mittimus, *U.S. v. Frank Webster,* District Court Records.

10. Indictment 190, Indictment 1804, Final Mittimus, *United States v. Isaac Morris,* Common Law Record Book, District Court Records, 41.

11. Common Law Record Book, District Court Records, 41.

12. Capias, Indictment, Writ of Arrest, Writ of Summons, Final Mittimus, *United States v. Frank Woods,* Common Law Record Book, District Court Records, 41–42.

13. Proceedings before Commissioner, *United States v. I. C. Miller,* Common Law Record Book, District Court Records, 42.

14. Capias, Proceedings before Commissioner, Request for Witnesses at Government Expense, Additional application of Defendant for Witnesses at U.S. Expense, Motion for Continuance, *U.S. v. I. C. Miller,* District Court Records.

15. Common Law Record Book, District Court Records, 43–44.

16. Proceedings before Commissioner, Indictment 1700, Final Mittimus, *United States v. Eastman Jones,* District Court Records.

17. Common Law Record Book, District Court Records, 42–43; *Fort Smith Weekly New Era,* August 6, 1881, p. 3.

18. *Fort Smith Weekly New Era,* August 6, 1881, p. 3; Martin, "Unsung Heroes": 22.

19. Mittimus, 1st sentence, August 6, 1881; Mittimus, 2d sentence, August 6, 1881; Mittimus, 3d sentence, August 6, 1881; Mittimus, 4th sentence, August 6, 1881; Mittimus, 5th sentence, August 6, 1881—all in *United States v. Frank Rocco,* District Court Records.

20. Bond for Defendant, *United States v. Green B. Parker;* Indictment 1718, Capias, *United States v. Tobias Ward;* Subpoena, Capias, Proceedings before Commissioner, Mittimus, *United States v. Joseph Davis;* Indictment 1794, *United States v. Thomas J. Ray;* Capias, Subpoena, Proceedings before Commissioner, *United States v. Charles Farley;* Common Law Record Book, 45–48—all in District Court Records.

21. Indictment 1616, Indictment 1617, Application of Defendant for Witnesses at U.S. Expense, Subpoena, *United States v. William Blue,* in Common Law Record Book, District Court Records, 49.

22. Proceedings before Commissioner, *United States v. Elias Jenkins,* in Common Law Record Book, District Court Records, 50.

23. Common Law Record Book, 50, Proceedings before Commissioner, Complaint, Indictment 1578, Subpoenas, *U.S. v. Elias Jenkins*, in Common Law Record Book, District Court Records, 50. For a full discussion of the common-law duty to retreat doctrine and its evolution, see Brown, *No Duty to Retreat*, 3–38.

24. Harrington, *Hanging Judge*, 56.

25. "Crime Totals for All Years," Index to Criminal Case Files, District Court Records.

26. Application of defendant for witnesses at U.S. Expense, November 12, 1881; Proceedings before Commissioner—both in *United States v. W. T. Sellars*, District Court Records.

27. "Crime Totals for All Years"; *United States v. Henry Bearpaw, United States v. Daniel Bearpaw, United States v. Union Bearhead, United States v. One Siller*—all in District Court Records; *Fort Smith Weekly New Era*, December 1, 1875, p. 3—December 8, 1875, p. 3—December 20, 1875, p. 3—May 14, 1880, p. 3; *Fort Smith Weekly Elevator*, July 4, 1891, p. 4.

28. *Fort Smith Weekly New Era*, September 11, 1881, p. 3; Prucha, *The Great Father*, 98–100; McGrath, *Gunfighters, Highwaymen, and Vigilantes*, 74–75, 184, 213–14, 255. Utley, *High Noon in Lincoln*, 172–74, 175–76, 233–34; Marks, *And Die in the West*, 20, 25, 36–38, 47–48, 130–31, 195–203, 300.

29. "Crime Totals for All Years," District Court Records; Croy, *He Hanged Them High*, 3–5, 7–8; 33–38, 161–66; Harman, *Hell on the Border*, 201–4, 495–511; Shirley, *Law West of Fort Smith*, 36, 159–70.

30. "Annual Crime Totals," Index to Criminal Case Files, 1625–53ff., District Court Records.

CHAPTER 7

1. Prucha, *The Great Father*, 89–114, 183–213; Harman, *Hell on the Border*, 33.

2. Burton, *Indian Territory and the United States*, 27–30, 33, 36, 134; Shirley, *Law West of Fort Smith*, 33–34. French and Spanish colonial authorities in Arkansas were more concerned with maintaining amicable trade relations with their Quawpaw neighbors than establishing legal protection of Indians and their lands; the military commander of the Arkansas Post garrison held civil law authority over relations with the local tribes for the first 120 years of European settlement. In the New England colonies, Puritan officials established numerous legal protections for American Indians and their lands, but such laws were frequently circumvented by

land-hungry squatters. Arnold, *Unequal Laws unto a Savage Race*, 66–77, 204–5, and *Colonial Arkansas*, 152–53, 156–57; Yasuhide Kawashima, *Puritan Justice*, 42–98, 198–93, 225–42. For U.S. legal status of American Indians, see Clark, *Lone Wolf v. Hitchcock*, and Sidney L. Harring, *Crow Dog's Case*.

3. *Fort Smith Weekly New Era*, May 12, 1875, p. 3; Harman, *Hell on the Border*, 33–35; Shirley, *Law West of Fort Smith*, 23–24.

4. *Fort Smith Weekly New Era*, May 12, 1875, p. 3.

5. Proceedings before Commissioner, *United States v. Matthew J. Flannigan*, District Court Records.

6. Mary Weaver to John Q. Tufts, August 28, 1886; L. P. Isabel to Tufts, n.d.; *U.S. v. Matthew J. Flannigan*—all in District Court Records.

7. Indictment 1624, Mittimus, *United States v. Matthew J. Flannigan*, District Court Records.

8. Capias (Complaint), Proceedings before Commissioner, *United States v. Ally Baily*, District Court Records.

9. Prucha, *The Great Father*, 98–104; *Sarlls v. United States*, 14 SC 721; Peter J. Hudson, "Temperance Meetings among the Choctaws," *Chronicles of Oklahoma*: 130–32; Foreman, "A Century of Prohibition," ibid.: 133–41; *Fort Smith Weekly New Era*, April 9, 1879, p. 2.

10. Harman, *Hell on the Border*, 44–45; Harrington, *Hanging Judge*, 164–178.

11. Proceedings before Commissioner, Complaint, Demurrer, *U.S. v. Ben Reese*, District Court Records.

12. Demurrer, *U.S. v. Ben Reese*, ibid.; Harrington, *Hanging Judge*, 175.

13. *Fort Smith Weekly New Era*, May 11, 1879, p. 1; Foreman, *History of Oklahoma*, 131–44, 210–14, 215–18; Rister, *Land Hunger*, 36–40.

14. *Fort Smith Weekly New Era*, May 11, 1879, p. 1; Rister, *Land Hunger*, 50–73; Foreman, *History of Oklahoma*, 215–18.

15. *Fort Smith Weekly New Era*, August 4, 1880, p. 1—August 11, 1880, p. 2—August 18, 1880, p. 3; Rister, *Land Hunger*, 65–73; Foreman, *History of Oklahoma*, 215–18.

16. Complaint, Summons, Deposition of Lieutenant Parder, Motion for Dismissal, Answer, Demurrer, Amended Answer, Demurrer to Amended Answer, *United States v. D. L. Payne*, Law Files, District Court Records.

17. Rister, *Land Hunger*, 94–96; Harrington, *Hanging Judge*, 175; Shirley, *Law West of Fort Smith*, 75–76.

18. Rister, *Land Hunger*, 99–129, 143–88; Foreman, *History of Oklahoma*, 216–19.

19. Common Law Record Book, District Court Records, vol. 81–2–12: 119–20; Harrington, *Hanging Judge*, 176. On grazing leases and the

relationship between the Cherokees, cattlemen, and the federal government, see Savage, *The Cherokee Strip Livestock Association.*

20. Common Law Record Book, District Court Records, vol. 81-2-12: 224, 534; Harrington, *Hanging Judge,* p. 176.

21. *Wheeler's Western Independent* (Fort Smith), January 2, 1878, p. 2; Shirley, *Law West of Fort Smith,* 73; Burton, *Indian Territory and the United States,* 67-68.

22. Petition for Writ of Habeas Corpus, Warrant, Requisition, *Ex Parte Morgan,* Habeas Corpus Case Files, District Court Records.

23. Petition for Writ of Habeas Corpus, *Ex Parte Morgan,* in District Court Records.

24. Writ of Habeas Corpus, Amended Answer to Writ of Habeas Corpus, Answer to Response, Petition for Writ of Habeas Corpus, *Ex Parte Morgan,* in ibid.

25. Opinion of the Supreme Court of California, Petition for Writ of Habeas Corpus, *Ex Parte Morgan,* in ibid.; Harrington, *Hanging Judge,* 172.

26. An act to grant the right of way through the Indian Territory to the Southern Kansas Railway Company and for other purposes, 23 *U.S. Stat.,* 73, Chap. 179.

27. Complaint, Transcript of Proceedings in the Office of Indian Affairs, *Cherokee Nation v. Southern Kansas Railway Company,* Equity Case Files, District Court Records.

28. Ibid.

29. Chancery Record Book, District Court Records, 3: 8, 17, 134-35.

30. Chancery Record Book, 3: 5, 168, and 4: 8-10; Mandate, *Cherokee Nation v. Southern Kansas Railway Company,* District Court Records.

31. Croy, *He Hanged Them High,* 4-5; Harman, *Hell on the Border,* 105-6; Harrington, *Hanging Judge,* 165-66, 168.

32. Burton, *Indian Territory and the United States,* pp. 67-69, 123-171ff.; Mardock, *The Reformers and the American Indian,* 221-23; Harrington, *Hanging Judge,* 166, 168; Shirley, *Law West of Fort Smith,* 76.

33. Burton, *Indian Territory and the United States,* 3-25ff., 68; Shirley, *Law West of Fort Smith,* 76; Harman, *Hell on the Border,* 143.

CHAPTER 8

1. I. C. Parker to Hiram Price, August 1, 1882, Record 14279, Letters Received; Croy, *He Hanged Them High,* 259.

2. Stolberg, "Politician, Populist, Reformer": 11; Croy, *He Hanged Them High,* 147-48, 158-60; Harman, *Hell on the Border,* 95.

3. *Congressional Record*, 46th Cong., 2d sess., 1298; ibid., 47th Cong., 2d. sess, 13, 102, 1449, 1607, 1634, 2725, 4511–12; Burton, *Indian Territory and the United States*, 71.

4. *U.S. Statutes at Large*, 22: 400; Burton, *Indian Territory and the United States*, 71, 121.

5. "Annual Crime Totals," Index to Criminal Case Files, District Court Records, 1639–53; Burton, *Indian Territory and the United States*, 71.

6. Common Law Record Book, District Court Records, vol. 81–2–12, pp. 119–20, 224, 534; Burton, *Indian Territory and the United States*, 134–35, 156–57. For more information on *Ex Parte Rogers*, see author's discussion in Chapter 7.

7. Stolberg, "The Evolution of Frontier Justice": 11; Stolberg, "Politician, Populist, Reformer": 24; Burton, *Indian Territory and the United States*, 172, 177–78, 196.

8. Charles Devens to I. C. Parker, October 5, 1878, and A. H. Garland to I. C. Parker, December 27, 1886, both in Letters Sent; Stolberg, "The Evolution of Frontier Justice": 10–11.

9. *Arkansas Gazette*, May 22, 1888, p. 1; Bearss, "Furnishing the New Federal Jail and the 1888 Report on Marshall Carroll's Activities": 33; Burton, *Indian Territory and the United States*, 172.

10. Shirley, *Law West of Fort Smith*, 64; Croy, *He Hanged Them High*, 84–85; Burton, *Indian Territory and the United States*, 69.

11. Shirley, *Law West of Fort Smith*, 64–65; Burton, *Indian Territory and the United States*, 69.

12. Bearss, "Furnishing the New Federal Jail": 29–30; Shirley, *Law West of Fort Smith*, 65–66.

13. W. H. H. Miller to Isaac C. Parker, March 25, 1889, Letters Sent; Jacob Yoes, U.S. Marshal, to Attorney General, November 16, 1889, Number 10,766, File 4779, in Source–Chronological Letters Files; Frank Strong and Howard Perry, "Report as to Jails," December 15, 1889, in ibid.; Shirley, *Law West of Fort Smith*, 66. For similar exchanges in the 1890s, see Yoes to Attorney General, February 13, 1891, Number 2136, File 4799; M. C. Johnson to Attorney General, October 26, 1891, Number 10,578, File 26; George J. Crump, U.S. Marshal, to Richard Olney, Attorney General, June 28, 1893, Number 6,513, File 5,485; W. D. McFadden to Olney, February 6, 1894, Number 1577; Willoughby Newton to Frank Strong, April 4, 1894, Number 3,857; Strong to Attorney General, September 15, 1894, Number 10,602; Perry to Attorney General, March 30, 1896, Number 5,475; Crump to Attorney General, April 11, 1896, Number 6,037. All of the foregoing are in Source–Chronological Letters Files.

14. Parker to Augustus Garland, May 27, 1885, Number 5,054, File 3,885; Parker to Garland, May 17, 1887, Number 3,632, File 9,513—both in Source–Chronological Letters Files; Garland to Parker, June 29, 1886, Letters Sent; Stolberg, "Politician, Populist, Reformer": 22–23; Walker, *Popular Justice,* 83–84, 86–87, 89, 91–92.

15. "Proceedings before Commissioner," *U.S. v. Fannie Echols,* District Court Records; "Report upon the Application for Commutation of Sentence of Fannie Echols: Western District of Arkansas," Application for Pardon, Fannie Echols, Record J 485, Pardon Records.

16. "Petition for Executive Clemency," Clayton to Attorney General, June 7, 1884; "Report upon the Application for Commutation of the Sentence of Fannie Echols: Western District of Arkansas"; Parker to the President, June 24, 1884—all in Application for Pardon, Fannie Echols, Record J 485, Pardon Records.

17. Parker to the President, June 24, 1884, Pardon Records.

18. Proceedings before Commissioner, Motion for New Trial, *U.S. v. Mat Music,* District Courts Records; "Report upon Application for Pardon of Matt [*sic*] Music," Application for Pardon, Mat Music, Record J 506, Pardon Records.

19. "Report upon Application for Pardon of Matt [*sic*] Music, W. District Arkansas," and Clayton to Attorney General, June 16, 1884—both in Application for Pardon, Mat Music, Record J 506, Pardon Records.

20. "Report upon application for pardon of Matt [*sic*] Music, W. District Arkansas," in Pardon Records.

21. "In the Matter of the Application for the Pardon of Jack Spaniard," "Sentence and Order," *U.S. v. Jack Spaniard*—all in Application for Pardon of Jack Spaniard, Record L 304, Pardon Records. Parker, like most federal district judges, held his deputies in high esteem, recognizing the dangers they encountered in fulfilling their duties and lauding their courage. For the dangers faced by western peace officers and the high regard in which judges held them, see Ball, *The United States Marshals of New Mexico and Arizona Territories,* and *Desert Lawmen.* For an alternative view that downplays the risks faced by western lawmen, see Prassel, *The Western Peace Officer.*

22. Parker to Miller, August 12, 1889, and Parker to President Benjamin Harrison, August 14, 1889, Pardon Records; Shirley, *Law West of Fort Smith,* 225–26.

23. *Congressional Record,* 50th Cong., 1st sess, 5611, 7551, 7636–37, 9098; ibid., 50th Cong., 2d sess., 566–67, 993–94; Harry P. Daily, "Judge Isaac C. Parker": 684–86; Burton, *Indian Territory and the United States,* 199; Stolberg, "The Evolution of Frontier Justice": 14; Shirley, *Law West of Fort Smith,* 145; Croy, *He Hanged Them High,* 208.

24. Congressional Record, 50th Cong., 2d sess., 566–67, 993–94; *U.S. Statutes at Large*, 25: 655–56; Burton, *Indian Territory and the United States*, 199.

CHAPTER 9

1. William H. H. Miller to Isaac Parker, December 9, 1889; Miller to Parker, January 21, 1890; Miller to Parker, March 10, 1890—all in Letters Sent; Parker to Benjamin Harrison, February 3, 1890, in *The Papers of Benjamin Harrison*, Reel 25; Parker to Harrison, February 8, 1890, ibid.; Parker to Harrison, July 23, 1890, ibid., Reel 72.

2. *Congressional Record*, 50th Cong., 2d sess., 2317–18, 2385–87, 2398–99, 2458–59, 2671; Burton, *Indian Territory and the United States*, 144–51.

3. Eugene Marshall to William H. H. Miller, March 6, 1891, Letters Received, File 2858–91; Jacob Yoes to Attorney General, March 17, 1891, ibid.; Parker to Miller, March 18, 1891, ibid.; Acting Attorney General to Parker, March 13, 1891, Letters Sent.

4. Parker to Richard Olney, November 21, 1893, Letters Received, Number 12,121, File 5,485; George Crump, U. S. Marshal, to Olney, October 1, 1894, ibid., Number 11,135; Crump to Olney, July 27, 1895, ibid, Number 10,930; William H. H. Miller to Parker, September 9, 1891, Letters Sent; Olney to Parker, November 27, 1893, ibid.; Olney to Parker, August 15, 1894, ibid.; Olney to Parker, November 24, 1894, ibid.

5. Indictment, *United States v. William Alexander*, District Court Records; Bill of Exceptions, *William Alexander v. United States*, Records of the Supreme Court of the United States, RG 267, Appellate Case Files (hereafter cited as Appellate Case Files), 6–10; Harman, *Hell on the Border*, 317–18; Shirley, *Law West of Fort Smith*, 148.

6. Bill of Exceptions, 6–10, and Judge's Charge, 1—both in *William Alexander v. U.S.*, Appellate Case Files; Shirley, *Law West of Fort Smith*, 147.

7. Judgment, Mandate, *William Alexander v. U.S.*, Appellate Case Files; Shirley, *Law West of Fort Smith*, 148–49. On December 24, 1892, after two subsequent trials ended in hung juries, District Attorney Clayton dropped the Alexander case; see Shirley, 149; Harman, *Hell on the Border*, 319.

8. *Congressional Record*, 51st. Cong., 1st sess., 8307, 10193–94, 10217–32, 10278–88, 10302–18, 10,363–65; ibid., 51st Cong., 2d sess., 3087, 3583–85, 3760; Frankfurter and Landis, *The Business of the Supreme Court*, 99–102; King, *Melville Weston Fuller*, 149–51.

9. *Sarlls v. United States*, 14 SC 721 (1895).

10. Ibid.

11. Mandates for *John Boyd and Eugene Standley v. United States, Lewis Alexander v. United States, John Brown v. United States, John Graves v. United States, Frank Collins v. United States, John Hicks v. United States, Sam Hickory v. United States, John Pointer v. United States, Lewis Holder v. United States*— all in Appellate Case Files; Shirley, *Law West of Fort Smith*, 239–40.

12. *Lewis v. United States*, 146 U.S. 370 (1892); *Hickory v. United States*, 151 U.S. 303 (1894); Brown, *No Duty to Retreat*, 24–29; Shirley, *Law West of Fort Smith*, 151–53.

13. *Hickory v. United States*, 160 U.S. 408 (1895).

14. Ibid. At the third trial, Western District prosecutor James Read reduced the charge to manslaughter; Hickory was convicted and sentenced to five years imprisonment. See Shirley, *Law West of Fort Smith*, 153.

15. Suggestion of Diminution of Record, and Motion for Certiorari, Bill of Exceptions, Mandate, *John Brown v. U.S.*, Appellate Case Files; *Lewis v. U.S.*, 146 U.S. 370 (1892). The late change in the record did not prevent a reversal of the Brown verdict.

16. Isaac Parker to Lawrence Maxwell, August 20, 1894, Letters Received, Number 740, File 15,624; James H. McKenney to Parker, September 5, 1894, ibid.; Parker to McKenney, September 10, 1894, ibid.

17. Motion for Leave to File Petition for Writ of Mandamus, *Ex Parte: In the Matter of Lafayette Hudson*, Records of the Supreme Court of the United States, RG 267, Original Jurisdiction Case Files (hereafter cited as Original Jurisdiction Case Files).

18. Parker to Maxwell, October 1, 1894, File 10,306–92, Number 11,370, Letters Received; Parker to Maxwell, November 2, 1894, Number 12,795, ibid.; Olney to Parker, November 16, 1894, Letters Sent; On the Matter of Taking Bail, *Ex Parte: In the Matter of Lafayette Hudson*, Original Jurisdiction Case Files.

19. *Hudson v. Parker*, 156 U.S. 277 (1895); James F. Read to Solicitor General, June 10, 1895, File 10,306, Number 8786, Letters Received; Parker to Attorney General Judson Harmon, October 10, 1895, Number 14760, ibid.; Burton, *Indian Territory and the United States*, 227; Stolberg, "The Evolution of Frontier Justice": 18.

20. *Congressional Record*, 53d Cong., 3d sess., 2842–43, 2871–72, 2961; *St. Louis Globe-Democrat*, January 12, 1895, p. 4; Burton, *Indian Territory and the United States*, 209, 215–16; Harman, *Hell on the Border*, 60–62.

21. Shirley, *Law West of Fort Smith*, 122–27; Harman, *Hell on the Border*, 399–400.

22. Assignment of Errors, *Crawford Goldsby v. United States*, Appellate Case Files; Shirley, *Law West of Fort Smith*, 128, 317.

23. Shirley, *Law West of Fort Smith*, 128–31; Harman, *Hell on the Border*, 402–7.

24. *St. Louis Globe-Democrat*, July 30, 1895, p. 9.

25. Ibid.

26. *New York Times*, March 18, 1896, p. 6; *St Louis Globe-Democrat*, March 18, 1896, p. 2; Shirley, *Law West of Fort Smith*, 132–37; Harman, *Hell on the Border*, 413–44ff.

27. Assignment of Errors, Mandate, *Thomas Thompson v. United States*, Appellate Case Files; Assignment of Errors, Mandate, *John Allison v. United States*, ibid.

28. Edward B. Whitney to Parker, January 29, 1896, Letters Sent; Confession of Error, *Thomas B. Thornton v. United States*, Appellate Case Files; Confession of Error, *Buz Lucky v. United States*, ibid.; Harrington, *Hanging Judge*, 188.

29. *St. Louis Globe-Democrat*, February 5, 1896, p. 3.

30. *St Louis Republic*, February 18, 1896, p. 3.

31. *Fort Smith Weekly Elevator*, February 28, 1896, p. 1.

32. Harmon to Parker, March 25, 1896, Letters Sent.

33. Parker to Harmon, April 2, 1896, File 600, Number 5716, Letters Received.

34. See, for example, dissents in *John Hicks v. United States, John Graves v. United States, Alexander Crain v. United States*, and *Alexander Allen v. United States*, all in Appellate Case Files; *St. Louis Globe-Democrat*, February 5, 1896, p. 3.

35. Friedman, *History of American Law*, 327–29, 340–58; Frankfurter and Landis, *Business of the Supreme Court*, 65–69; Ely, *The Chief Justiceship of Mellville W. Fuller*, 160–71; Brown, *No Duty to Retreat*, 28–30; Kutler, *Judicial Power and Reconstruction Politics*, 14–160ff.; Warren, *The Supreme Court in United States History*, 2: 663–89ff.; Burton, *Indian Territory and the United States*, 46–49. See also Fairman, *Reconstruction and Reunion*; Fiss, *Troubled Beginnings of the Modern State*; Gillman, *The Constitution Beseiged*; White, *Justice Oliver Wendell Holmes*.

36. Mandates in Appellate Case Files: *Frank Carver v. United States, Alexander Crain v. U.S., Dennis Davis v. United States, Eli Lucas v. United States, Henry Starr v. United States, Webber Issacs v. United States*; Confession of Error, *Mollie King v. United States*, Appellate Case Files; Shirley, *Law West of Fort Smith*, 230–31.

37. Harman, *Hell on the Border*, 97, 99; Shirley, *Law West of Fort Smith*, 202, 204.

38. *St. Louis Republic,* September 6, 1896, 6.

39. Parker to J. M. Dickinson, October 9, 1896; Croy, *He Hanged Them High,* 220–21; Harman, *Hell on the Border,* 99–100.

40. *Fort Smith Weekly Elevator,* November 20, 1896, p. 3; Croy, *He Hanged Them High,* 221–23; Shirley, *Law West of Fort Smith,* 204–6.

BIBLIOGRAPHY

PRIMARY SOURCES

Government Documents

FEDERAL DOCUMENTS

The Congressional Globe. 42d Cong. 1st, 2d, and 3d sessions.
The Congressional Record. 43d Cong. 1st, 2d, and 3d sessions.
——. 46th Cong. 2d sess.
——. 50th Cong. 1st and 2d sessions.
——. 51st Cong. 1st and 2d sessions.
——. 53d Cong. 3d sess.
The Papers of Benjamin Harrison. Washington, D.C.: Library of Congress, 1960.
Hickory v. United States, 151 U.S. 303 (1894).
Hickory v. United States, 160 U.S. 408 (1895).
House Executive Document 175. 43d Cong. 2d sess.
Hudson v. Parker, 156 U.S. 277 (1895).
Lewis v. United States, 146 U.S. 370 (1892).
Nichols, Guy, Leo Allison, and Thomas Crowson. "Judge Isaac C. Parker, Myths and Legends Aside." Washington, D.C.: National Park Service, n.d.
Sarlis v. United States, 14 SC 721 (1895).
Statutes at Large of the United States of America. Vols. 1, 22, 25.

U.S. Department of State. *Compendium of the Enumeration of the Inhabitants and Statistics of the United States as Obtained at the Department of State from the Returns of the Sixth Census.* Washington, D. C.: Thomas Allen, 1841.

U.S. Senate. *Journal of the Executive Proceedings of the Senate of the United States of America from March 5, 1875 to March 3, 1877, Inclusive.* Washington, D.C.: n.p., 1877.

LOCAL DOCUMENTS

Minute Book, 1857–1865. Office of the City Clerk, Saint Joseph, Missouri.
Revised Ordinances, 1857. Office of the City Clerk, Saint Joseph, Missouri.

FEDERAL COURT RECORDS

From Records of the Supreme Court of the United States. RG 267. National Archives and Records Administration, Washington, D.C.:
Alexander Allen v. United States
William Alexander v. United States
John Allison v. United States
John Boyd and Eugene Standley v. United States
John Brown v. United States
Frank Carver v. United States
Frank Collins v. United States
Alexander Crain v. United States
Dennis Davis v. United States
Ex Parte: In the Matter of Lafayette Hudson. Original Juisdiction Files
Crawford Goldsby v. United States
John Graves v. United States
John Hicks v. United States
Sam Hickory v. United States
Louis Holder v. United States
Webber Isaacs v. United States
Mollie King v. United States
Alexander Lewis v. United States
Eli Lucas v. United States
Buz Lucky v. United States
John Pointer v. United States
Henry Starr v. United States
Thomas Thompson v. United States
Thomas B. Thornton v. United States

From Records of the District Courts of the United States. RG 21. Arkansas, Western District. National Archives and Records Administration. Southwest Region. Fort Worth, Texas:

"Annual Crime Totals." Index to Criminal Case Files.

Chancery Record Book, Volume 3.

Cherokee Nation v. Southern Kansas Railway Company. Equity Case Files.

Common Law Record Book, Volume 5.

Common Law Record Book, Volume 81–2–12.

"Crime Totals for All Years." Index to Criminal Case Files.

Ex Parte Morgan. Habeas Corpus Case Files.

United States v. William Alexander.

United States v. Ally Baily.

United States v. Union Bearhead.

United States v. Daniel Bearpaw.

United States v. Henry Bearpaw.

United States v. William Blue.

United States v. Frank Butler, Edmund Campbell, and Samuel Campbell.

United States v. Uriah M. Cooper.

United States v. Joseph Davis.

United States v. Fannie Echols.

United States v. Charles Farley.

United States v. Matthew J. Flannigan.

United States v. Leonard Fulsome.

United States v. Gibson Ishtonubee.

United States v. Elias Jenkins.

United States v. Eastman Jones.

United States v. William Leach.

United States v. I. C. Miller.

United States v. Isaac Morris.

United States v. Matt [sic] Music.

United States v. Green B. Parker.

United States v. Thomas J. Ray.

United States v. Ben Reese.

United States v. Frank Rocco.

United States v. Isham Seely.

United States v. One Siller.

United States v. Oscar Snow.

United States v. Jack Spaniard.

United States v. Thomas Triplett.

United States v. Joshua Wade.

United States v. Tobias Ward.

United States v. Frank Webster.
United States v. William Whittington.
United States v. Frank Woods.

STATE AND LOCAL COURT RECORDS

Buchanan County (Missouri) Order Book. Northwest Missouri Genealogical Society, Saint Joseph, Missouri:
6 (October 1859–September 1862)
7 (September 1862–May 1865)
8 (September 1865–September 1867)
9 (September 1867–February 1869)
10 (February 1869–March 1871)
Record Book #2. July 12, 1858–May 16, 1862. Office of the City Clerk, Saint
Joseph, Missouri.

OFFICIAL CORRESPONDENCE

From Records of the Department of Justice. RG 60. National Archives and
Records Administration. Archives II. College Park, Maryland.
Acting Attorney General to Isaac C. Parker. Letters Sent Books.
Chalmers, Leigh. Report on James C. Read, U.S. Attorney, W. Ark.
February 17, 1896. Source–Chronological Letters Files.
Crump, George J., to Attorney General, April 11, 1896. Source–
Chronological Letters Files.
——— to Richard Olney, June 28, 1893. Source–Chronological Letters
Files.
——— to Richard Olney, October 1, 1894. Source–Chronological Letters
Files.
——— to Richard Olney, July 27, 1895. Source–Chronological Letters
Files.
Devens, Charles, to D. P. Upham, June 11, 1878. Letters Sent Books.
——— to I. C. Parker, October 5, 1878. Letters Sent Books.
Garland, Augustus H., to I. C. Parker, December 27, 1886. Letters Sent
Books.
Harmon, Judson, to Isaac C. Parker, March 25, 1896. Letters Sent Books.
Johnson, M. C., to Attorney General, October 26, 1891. Source–Chrono-
logical Letters Files.
Marshall, Eugene, to William H. H. Miller, March 6, 1891. Source–
Chronological Letters Files.

McFadden, W. D., to Richard Olney, February 6, 1894. Source–Chronological Letters Files.

McKenney, James, to Isaac C. Parker, September 5, 1894. Source–Chronological Letters Files.

Miller, William H. H., to Isaac C. Parker, March 25, 1889. Letters Sent Books.

——— to Isaac Parker, December 9, 1889. Letters Sent Books.

——— to Isaac Parker, January 21, 1890. Letters Sent Books.

——— to Isaac Parker, March 10, 1890. Letters Sent Books.

——— to Isaac Parker, September 9, 1891. Letters Sent Books.

Newton, Willoughby, to Frank Strong, April 4, 1894. Source–Chronological Letters Files.

Olney, Richard, to Isaac Parker, November 27, 1893. Source–Chronological Letters Files.

——— to Isaac Parker, August 15, 1894. Source–Chronological Letters Files.

——— to Isaac Parker, November 16, 1894. Source–Chronological Letters Files.

——— to Isaac Parker, November 24, 1894. Source–Chronological Letters Files.

Parker, Isaac C., to J. M. Dickinson, October, 9 1896. Source–Chronological Letters Files.

——— to Augustus Garland, May 27, 1885. Source–Chronological Letters Files.

——— to Augustus Garland, May 17, 1887. Source–Chronological Letters Files.

——— to Judson Harmon, October 10, 1895. Source–Chronological Letters Files.

——— to Judson Harmon, April 2, 1896. Source–Chronological Letters Files.

——— to Lawrence Maxwell, August 20, 1894. Source–Chronological Letters Files.

——— to Lawrence Maxwell, October 1, 1894. Source–Chronological Letters Files.

——— to Lawrence Maxwell, November 2, 1894. Source–Chronological Letters Files.

——— to James McKenney, September 10, 1894. Source–Chronological Letters Files.

——— to William H. H. Miller, March 18, 1891. Source–Chronological Letters Files.

———— to Richard Olney, November 21, 1893. Source–Chronological Letters Files.

———— to Edwards Pierrepont, May 18, 1875. Source–Chronological Letters Files.

———— to Edwards Pierrepont, July 27, 1875. Source–Chronological Letters Files.

———— to Edwards Pierrepont, August 6, 1875. Source–Chronological Letters Files.

Perry, Howard, to Attorney General, March 30, 1896. Source–Chronological Letters Files.

Read, James F., to Solicitor General, June 10, 1895. Source–Chronological Letters Files.

Strong, Frank, to Attorney General, September 15, 1894. Source–Chronological Letters Files.

———— and Howard Perry, "Report as to Jails." December 15, 1889. Source–Chronological Letters Files.

Whitney, Edward B., to Isaac C. Parker, January 29, 1896. Letters Sent Books.

Yoes, Jacob, to Attorney General, November 16, 1889. Source–Chronological Letters Files.

———— to Attorney General, February 13, 1891. Source–Chronological Letters Files.

———— to Attorney General, March 17, 1891. Source–Chronological Letters Files.

From Records of the Bureau of Indian Affairs. RG 75. National Archives and Records Administration, Washington, D.C.:

Parker, Isaac C., to Hiram Price, August 1, 1882. Letters Received.

PARDON RECORDS

W. Dist. Arkansas. Records of the Department of Justice. Files of the Pardon Attorney. RG 36. National Archives and Records Administration. College Park, Maryland.

Pardon Applications
  Uriah M. Cooper
  Fannie Echols
  Carolina Grayson, Peter W. Grayson, Man Lewis, & Robert Love
  James Heaslett
  Joe Marten
  Mat Music

Irving Perkins (colored)
Oscar Snow
Jack Spaniard
Charley Thomas

SECONDARY SOURCES

Books

Adams, Charles Francis. *An Autobiography*. New York: Russell and Russell, 1916.

Arnold, Morris S. *Unequal Laws unto a Savage Race: European Legal Traditions in Arkansas,1686–1836*. Fayetteville: University of Arkansas Press, 1985.

———. *Colonial Arkansas, 1686–1804: A Social and Cultural History*. Fayetteville: University of Arkansas Press, 1991.

Ayers, Edward L. *Vengeance and Justice: Crime and Punishment in the Nineteenth-Century American South*. New York: Oxford University Press, 1984.

Bakken, Gordon Morris. *The Development of Law on the Rocky Mountain Frontier: Civil Law and Society, 1850–1912*. Westport, Conn.: Greenwood Press, 1983.

———. *Rocky Mountain Constitution Making, 1850–1912*. New York: Greenwood Press, 1987.

———. *Practicing Law in Frontier California*. Lincoln: University of Nebraska Press, 1991.

Ball, Larry D. *The United States Marshals of Arizona and New Mexico Territories, 1846–1912*. Albuquerque: University of New Mexico Press, 1978.

———. *Desert Lawmen: The High Sheriffs of New Mexico and Arizona, 1846–1912*. Albuquerque: University of New Mexico Press, 1992.

Beeton, Beverly. *Women Vote in the West: The Woman Suffrage Movement, 1869–1896*. New York: Garland Publishing, Inc., 1986.

Berry, Ellen T., and David A. Berry, comps. *Early Ohio Settlers: Purchasers of Land in Southeastern Ohio, 1800–1840*. Baltimore: Genealogical Publishing Co., Inc., 1988.

Bodenhamer, David J. *The Pursuit of Justice: Crime and Law in Antebellum Indiana*. New York: Garland Publishing, Inc., 1986.

———. *Fair Trial: The Rights of the Accused in American History*. New York: Oxford University Press, 1992.

Brown, Jeffrey P., and Andrew R. L. Clayton, eds. *The Pursuit of Public Power: Political Culture in Ohio, 1787–1861.* Kent, Ohio: Kent State University Press, 1994.

Brown, Richard Maxwell. *No Duty to Retreat: Violence and Values in American History and Society.* New York: Oxford University Press, 1991.

Burton, Jeffrey. *Indian Territory and the United States, 1866–1906: Courts, Government, and the Movement for Oklahoma Statehood.* Norman: University of Oklahoma Press, 1995.

Clark, Blue. *Lone Wolf v. Hitchcock: Treaty Rights and Indian Law at the End of the Nineteenth Century.* Lincoln: University of Nebraska Press, 1994.

Clayton, Powell. *The Aftermath of the Civil War, in Arkansas.* New York: Neal Publishing Company, 1915.

Croy, Homer. *He Hanged Them High: An Authentic Account of the Fanatical Judge Who Hanged Eighty-Eight Men.* New York: Duell, Sloan, and Pearce, 1952.

Davis, Kenneth S. *Kansas: A Bicentennial History.* New York: Norton, 1976.

Dippie, Brian W. *The Vanishing American: White Attitudes and U.S. Indian Policy.* Middletown, Conn.: Wesleyan University Press, 1982.

Ely, James W., Jr. *The Chief Justiceship of Mellville W. Fuller.* Columbia: University of South Carolina Press, 1995.

Emery, J. Gladstone. *Court of the Damned: Being a Factual Account of the Court of Judge Isaac C. Parker and the Life and Times of the Indian Territory and Old Fort Smith.* New York: Comet Press Books, 1959.

Fairman, Charles. *Reconstruction and Reunion, 1864–1888. The Oliver Wendell Holmes Devise History of the Supreme Court of the United States.* Volume 7. New York: Macmillan, 1987.

Fellman, Michael. *Inside War: The Guerilla Conflict in Missouri during the American Civil War.* New York: Oxford University Press, 1989.

Firmage, Edwin B., and Richard C. Mangrum. *Zion in the Courts: A Legal History of the Church of Jesus Christ of Latter-day Saints, 1830–1900.* Urbana: University of Illinois Press, 1988.

Fiss, Owen M. *Troubled Beginnings of the Modern State, 1888–1910. The Oliver Wendell Holmes Devise History of the Supreme Court of the United States.* Vol. 8. New York: Macmillan, 1993.

Foner, Eric. *Free Soil, Free Labor, and Free Men: The Ideology of the Republican Party before the Civil War.* New York: Oxford University Press, 1970.

―――. *Reconstruction: America's Unfinished Revolution.* New York: Harper and Row, 1988.

Foreman, Grant. *History of Oklahoma.* Norman: University of Oklahoma Press, 1942.

Foucault, Michel. *Discipline and Punish: The Birth of the Prison*. New York: Vintage Books, 1979.

Frankfurter, Felix, and James M. Landis. *The Work of the Supreme Court: A Study in the Federal Judicial System*. New York: Macmillan, 1928.

Friedman, Lawrence M. *A History of American Law*. New York: Simon and Schuster, 1980.

———. *Crime and Punishment in American History*. New York: Basic Books, 1993.

——— and Robert V. Percival. *The Roots of Justice: Crime and Punishment in Alameda County, California 1870–1910*. Chapel Hill: University of North Carolina Press, 1981.

Fritz, Christian G. *Federal Justice in California: The Court of Ogden Hoffman, 1851–1891*. Lincoln: University of Nebraska Press, 1991.

Fritz, Henry E. *The Movement for Indian Assimilation, 1860–1890*. Philadelphia: University of Pennsylvania Press, 1963.

Gatrell, V. A. C. *The Hanging Tree: Execution and the English People*. Oxford: Oxford University Press.

Gillette, William. *Retreat from Reconstruction, 1869–1875*. Baton Rouge: University of Louisiana Press, 1979.

Gillman, Howard. *The Constitution Besieged: The Rise and Demise of Lochner Era Police Powers Jurisprudence*. Durham, N.C.: Duke University Press, 1993.

Gordon, Linda. *Pitied but not Entitled: Single Mothers and the History of Welfare, 1890–1935*. New York: Free Press, 1992.

Green, L. C., and Olive P. Dickason. *The Law of Nations and the New World*. Edmonton, Alberta, Canada: University of Alberta Press, 1989.

Harman, S. W. *Hell on the Border: He Hanged Eighty-Eight Men*. 1898. Reprint, Lincoln: University of Nebraska Press, 1992.

Harring, Sidney L. *Crow Dog's Case: American Indian Sovereignty, Tribal Law, and United States Law in the Nineteenth Century*. New York: Cambridge University Press, 1994.

Harrington, Fred Harvey. *Hanging Judge*. Caldwell, Idaho: Caxton Printers, Ltd., 1951.

Hartog, Hendrik. *Public Property and Private Power: The Corporation of the City of New York in American Law, 1730–1870*. Chapel Hill: University of North Carolina Press, 1983.

Haywood, C. Robert. *Cowtown Lawyers: Dodge City and Its Attorneys, 1876–1886*. Norman: University of Oklahoma Press, 1988.

Hindus, Michael Stephen. *Prison and Plantation: Crime, Justice, and Authority in Massachusetts and South Carolina, 1767–1878*. Chapel Hill: University of North Carolina Press, 1980.

Houts, Marshall. *From Gun to Gavel: The Courtroom Recollections of James Mathers of Oklahoma*. New York: William Morrow, 1954.

Humbert, W. H. *The Pardoning Power of the President*. Washington: American Council on Public Affairs, 1941.

Kawashima, Yasuhide. *Puritan Justice and the Indian: White Man's Law in Massachusetts, 1630–1763*. Middletown, Conn.: Wesleyan University Press, 1986.

King, Willard L. *Melville Weston Fuller: Chief Justice of the United States, 1888–1910*. New York: Macmillan, 1950.

Kutler, Stanley. *Judicial Power and Reconstruction Politics*. Chicago: University of Chicago Press, 1968.

Lamar, Howard R. *The Far Southwest: A Territorial History*. New Haven: Yale University Press, 1966.

Larson, Gustive. O. *The "Americanization" of Utah for Statehood*. San Marino, Calif.: Huntington Library, 1971.

Larsen, Lawrence H. *Federal Justice in Western Missouri: The Judges, the Cases, the Times*. Columbia: University of Missouri Press, 1994.

Lyman, Edward Leo. *Political Deliverance: The Mormon Quest for Utah Statehood*. Urbana: University of Illinois Press, 1986.

McGrath, Roger D. *Gunfighters, Highwaymen, and Vigilantes: Violence on the Frontier*. Berkeley: University of California Press, 1984.

Mardock, Robert Winston. *The Reformers and the American Indian*. Columbia: University of Missouri Press, 1971.

Marks, Paula Mitchell. *And Die in the West: The Story of the O. K. Corral Gunfight*. New York: Touchstone, 1989.

Masur, Louis P. *Rites of Execution: Capital Punishment and the Transformation of American Culture, 1776–1865*. New York: Oxford University Press, 1989.

Mohr, James C. *Doctors and the Law: Medical Jurisprudence in Nineteenth-Century America*. New York: Oxford University Press, 1993.

Monaghan, Jay. *Civil War on the Western Border, 1854–1865*. Boston: Little, Brown and Company, 1955.

Montell, William Lynwood. *Killings: Folk Justice in the Upper South*. Lexington: University of Kentucky Press, 1986.

Moore, Kathleen Dean. *Pardons: Justice, Mercy, and the Public Interest*. New York: Oxford University Press, 1989.

Parrish, William E. *A History of Missouri*. Vol. 3: *1860 to 1875*. Columbia: University of Missouri Press, 1973.

———. *Missouri under Radical Rule, 1865–1870*. Columbia: University of Missouri Press, 1965.

Prassel, Frank Richard. *The Western Peace Officer: A Legacy of Law and Order*. Norman: University of Oklahoma Press, 1972.

Prucha, Francis Paul. *The Great Father: The United States Government and the American Indians*. Lincoln: University of Nebraska Press, 1984.

———. *American Indian Treaties: The History of a Political Anomaly*. Berkeley: University of California Press, 1994.

Reid, John Phillip. *Chief Justice: The Judicial World of Charles Doe*. Cambridge: Harvard University Press, 1967.

Rister, Carl Coke. *Land Hunger: David L. Payne and the Oklahoma Boomers*. Norman: University of Oklahoma Press, 1942.

Roseboom, Eugene Holloway, and Francis Phelps Weisenburger. *A History of Ohio*. New York: Prentice-Hall, 1934.

Rosenberg, Charles. *The Trial of the Assassin Guiteau: Psychiatry and Law in the Gilded Age*. Chicago: University of Chicago Press, 1968.

Saint Joseph City Directory, 1859–1860; 1860–61. Saint Joseph, Missouri: H. Fotheringham & Co., Publishers, 1859, 1860.

Savage, William W. *The Cherokee Strip Livestock Association: Federal Regulation and the Cattleman's Last Frontier*. Norman: University of Oklahoma Press, 1990.

Shirley, Glenn. *Law West of Fort Smith: A History of Frontier Justice in the Indian Territory, 1834–1896*. Lincoln: University of Nebraska Press, 1968.

———. *West of Hell's Fringe*. Norman: University of Oklahoma Press, 1978.

Siebert, Wilbur Henry. *The Mysteries of Ohio's Underground Railroads*. Columbus, Ohio: Long's College Book Company, 1951.

Slotkin, Richard. *The Fatal Environment: The Myth of the Froniter in the Age of Industrialization, 1800–1890*. New York: Atheneum, 1985.

Skocpol, Theda. *Protecting Soldiers and Mothers: The Political Origins of Social Policy in the United States*. Cambridge: Belknap Press of Harvard University Press, 1992.

Sproat, John G. *The Best Men: Liberal Reformers in the Gilded Age*. New York: Oxford University Press, 1968.

Stampp, Kenneth M. *The Era of Reconstruction, 1865–1877*. New York: Vintage Books, 1965.

Swick, Frank, comp. *Resident and Business Directory of Saint Joseph*. Saint Joseph, Mo.: Frank Swick, 1868.

Utley, Robert M. *High Noon in Lincoln: Violence on the Western Frontier*. Albuquerque: University of New Mexico Press, 1987.

Versteeg, John M., ed. *Methodism: Ohio Area (1812–1962)*. N.p.: Ohio Area Sesquicentennial Committee, 1962.

Wade, Richard C. *The Urban Frontier: Pioneer Life in Early Pittsburgh, Cincinnati, Lexington, Louisville, and St. Louis*. Cambridge: Harvard University Press, 1959.

Walker, Samuel. *Popular Justice: A History of American Criminal Justice*. 2d ed. New York: Oxford University Press, 1998.

Warren, Charles. *The Supreme Court in United States History*. Vol. 2. Boston: Little, Brown, and Company, 1926.

White, G. Edward. *Justice Oliver Wendell Holmes: Law and the Inner Self*. New York: Oxford University Press, 1993.

Williams, Robert A., Jr. *The American Indian in Western Legal Thought: The Discourses of Conquest*. New York: Oxford University Press, 1990.

Wyatt-Brown, Bertram. *Honor and Violence in the Old South*. New York: Oxford University Press, 1986.

Journal Articles

Bakken, Gordon Morris. "Constitutional Convention Debates in the West: Racism, Religion, and Gender." *Western Legal History*, 3 (Summer-Fall, 1990): 213–44.

Ball, Larry D. "Federal Justice on the Santa Fe Trail: The Murder of Antonio José Chavez." *Missouri Historical Review*, 81 (October 1986): 1–17.

———. "Before the Hanging Judge: The Origins of the United States District Court for the Western District of Arkansas." *Arkansas Historical Quarterly* 69 (Autumn 1990): 199–213.

Bearss, Edwin C. "Furnishing the New Federal Jail and the 1888 Report on Marshal Carroll's Activities." *The Journal* (Fort Smith Historical Society), 3 (April 1979): 29–33.

Daily, Harry P. "Judge Isaac C. Parker." *Chronicles of Oklahoma*, 11 (March 1933): 673–90.

Foreman, Grant. "A Century of Prohibition." *Chronicles of Oklahoma*, 12 (June 1934): 133–44.

Hudson, Peter J. "Temperance Meetings among the Choctaws." *Chronicles of Oklahoma*, 12 (June 1934): 124–32.

Martin, Amelia. "Unsung Heroes: Deputy Marshals of the Federal Court for the Western District of Arkansas, 1875–1896." *The Journal* (Fort Smith Historical Society), 3 (April 1979): 19–26.

Stolberg, Mary M. "Politician, Populist, Reformer: A Reexamination of 'Hanging Judge' Isaac C. Parker." *Arkansas Historical Quarterly*, 47 (Spring 1988): 3–28.

———. "The Evolution of Frontier Justice: The Case of Judge Isaac C. Parker." *Prologue*, 20 (Spring 1988): 7–23.

Newspapers

Arkansas Gazette (Little Rock). September 4, 1875; April 22, 1876; April 23, 1876; May 22, 1888; November 17, 1896.

Coffeyville (Kansas) Journal. August 5, 1879.

Fort Smith (Arkansas) Weekly Herald. May 8, 1875.

New York Times. May 1, 1874; September 4, 1875; April 22, 1876; December 21, 1876; December 21, 1878; September 10, 1881; April 14, 1883; June 30, 1883; January 15, 1887; March 18, 1896.

Saint Joseph (Missouri) Daily Herald. September 13, 1870–November 12, 1870.

Saint Joseph (Missouri) Morning Herald. February 9, 1861; April 3, 1861–December 3, 1864; November 5, 1868; August 7, 1872; October 27, 1872; November 5, 1872; November 6, 1872; September 5, 1875; April 22, 1876.

St. Louis Globe-Democrat. January 12, 1895; July 27, 1895; July 30, 1895; February 5, 1896; February 12, 1876; March 18, 1896.

St. Louis Republic. February 18, 1896; September 6, 1896.

St. Louis Republican. September 4, 1875; April 22, 1876.

Times (Fort Smith, Arkansas). August 1, 9, 1889.

Weekly Elevator (Fort Smith, Arkansas). July 4, 1891; January 18, 1895; January 25, 1895; February 28, 1896; November 20, 1896.

Weekly New Era (Fort Smith, Arkansas). March 17, 1875; May 12, 1875; December 1, 1875; December 8, 1875; December 20, 1875; April 9, 1879; May 11, 1879; May 14, 1880; August 4, 1880; August 11, 1880; August 6, 1881; September 11, 1881.

Wheeler's Western Independent (Fort Smith, Arkansas). April 6, 1876; January 2, 1878.

Unpublished Manuscripts

Murphy, James. "The Work of Judge Parker in the United States District Court for the Western District of Arkansas." Master's thesis, University of Oklahoma, Norman, Oklahoma, 1939.

Stephan, Charles. "The United States District Court for the Western District of Arkansas and Judge William H. Story, 1871–1874." Master's thesis, Arkansas State University, State University, Arkansas, 1875.

Tuller, Roger. "'The Hanging Judge' and the Indians: Isaac C. Parker and U.S. Indian Policy, 1871–1896." Master's thesis, Texas Christian University, Fort Worth, Texas, 1993.

INDEX

CPSIA information can be obtained
at www.ICGtesting.com
Printed in the USA
LVHW071521230623
750604LV00002B/160